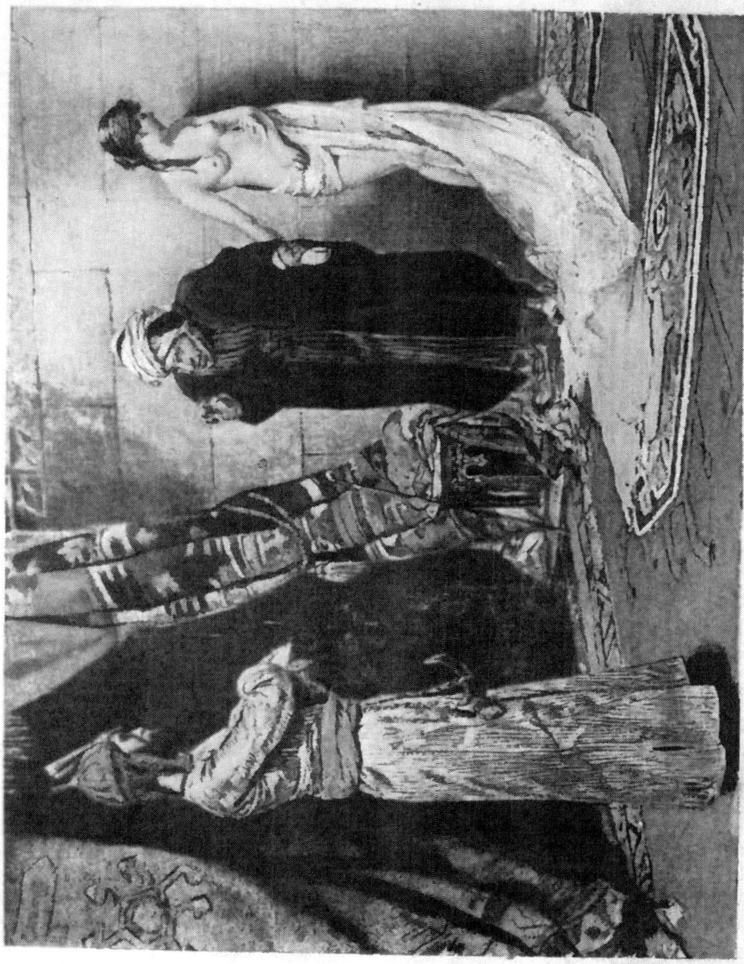

OTTOMAN LITERATURE

OTTOMAN LITERATURE

THE POETS AND POETRY OF TURKEY

TRANSLATED FROM THE ARABIC WITH
INTRODUCTION AND BIOGRAPHICAL NOTES

By
E. J. W. GIBB
Member of the Royal Asiatic Society

WITH
ARABIAN. PERSIAN. AND HEBREW POEMS,
AND A SPECIAL INTRODUCTION

By
THEODORE P. ION, J.D.
National University, Washington, D. C.

GYAN

Published by

Gyan Publishing House
5, Ansari Road
Daryaganj, New Delhi-110002
Phone: 011-47034999, 9811692060
E-mail: books@gyanbooks.com

Distribution Network
gyanbooks.com
India, USA, Canada, UK, Australia, France

ISBN : 978-81-212-6252-1 (PB)
First Published, 1901

2nd Impression 2022

Printed at: Gyan Press, Delhi.

OTTOMAN LITERATURE
Author: E. J. W. GIBB

A FAIR BARGAIN

Hand-painted photogravure after the original painting.

OTTOMAN LITERATURE

THE POETS AND POETRY OF TURKEY

TRANSLATED FROM THE ARABIC WITH INTRODUCTION AND BIOGRAPHICAL NOTES

BY

E. J. W. GIBB

Member of the Royal Asiatic Society

WITH

ARABIAN, PERSIAN, AND HEBREW POEMS, AND A SPECIAL INTRODUCTION

BY

THEODORE P. ION, J.D.

National University, Washington, D.C.

ILLUSTRATIONS

SPECIAL INTRODUCTION

OF LATE years explorers of human thought have taken a bolder step in their researches for the discovery of the progress achieved by the human intellect, not only of people akin to us, but also of races with whom we differ in more than one respect. The Turks or Ottomans, though known as a body politic, are still unknown, as far as their intellectual development is concerned. The attempt made recently to bring to light some specimens of their best thoughts, will no doubt help us to examine them from a different point of view than that to which we have been hitherto accustomed. They in their turn, on account of some peculiar prejudices of their own, be they the outgrowth of their education or the result of the erroneous interpretation of some tenets of their religion, shunned, ever since their early days, everything alien to and inconsistent with the trend of their thoughts and tendencies. Their eyes being constantly fixed, not toward the West, the seat of modern, but toward the East, the shrine of ancient civilization, and the country of their birth, it was natural for them to look for aid to the country of « the Great Kings,» whenever they felt the necessity of engrafting upon their intellectual culture new or better ideas. It was from Persia that their poets drew their inspiration; it was from the literature of these « barbarians » that they shaped numerous words and expressions of their poor Tartaric tongue. It is therefore through Persian, a language akin to Greek and Latin, on account of their Sanskrit origin, that Turkish is in some way connected with the Western languages.

On the other hand, their conversion to the teachings of Mohammed drew all their attention to the study of the captivating language of the « holy book.» The Koran has always been and still is the first and last book of the «faithful.» The study of Arabic has therefore been, ever since that time, the corner stone of the education of every Osmanli. The influence of that language was so great that even the moods and tenses of the Turkish grammar had to be remodeled according to those of the tongue of the «Prophet,» much to the advantage of the former. To use Arabic words and expressions, intermingled with Persian, was considered a high attainment of proficiency by Turks aspiring to literary fame. Thus the original Tartaric dialect of the Ottomans, blended with the refined and melodious language of the Arabs, and the sweet and harmonious tongue of the former followers of Zoroaster, formed what might be called the literary Turkish. Hence the variety in the expressions and the richness of the words of the literature of the Ottomans. The works of famous Persian poets, such as those of the witty Saadi, the lyrical Hafiz, and the mystic Dzelaleddin, were the constant companions, both of the Sultans of Stamboul and their high dignitaries of State, while Ibn Haldun, the Arabian Herodotus, Beizavi, the great commentator of the Koran, and Hairi, the popular poet of the Arabs, were only read by the cultured.

It is therefore no wonder that under such influences, the Turks by their writings gave a new lustre to Oriental literature. Nor has this emulation been slackened in any way during our days, notwithstanding the difficulties under which the Turkish writers are now laboring.

Turkish, as every other language, has had its evolution. The old ponderous style has been simplified and rendered more accessible to the masses. The knowledge therefore of literary Turkish, is not as formerly the privilege of a select class. It is to Shinassi that is attributed the first attempt of simplification. He is with justice regarded as the father of the modern school. Many followed his example, and among them Kemal Bey was the shining star of the Turkish literary world. His vigorous language imparted new life to Turkish. No author in his country seems as yet to have equaled him, either in imagination or in the descriptions of nature and people. His verses on « patriotism »— possibly the first ever written in that language — had aroused at the time the enthusiasm of the «indolent Ottomans.» On the other hand, his historical novel *Tzesmi*, the romance running through it of a young Turkish warrior gifted with poetical talent, and a Persian Princess, and some other writings, made him the most famous Turkish author of his century. Saadullah Pacha's style and Said Bey's judicious observations on the language, were also held in high esteem.

Among contemporary prose writers foremost of all is Midhat Effendi, the able editor of the *Hakikat*, the «Truth.» No Turk has ever written so much as this author. His influence on the language has been most beneficial on account of its further simplification by reducing it to shorter instead of the former long and endless sentences. Besides translating most successfully a great number of French works, he wrote some original novels depicting modern Turkish life and customs, which placed him in the first rank among the writers of Turkey. His defense of Mohammedanism, on the other hand, carried his fame beyond the confines of the Ottoman Empire.

The late State historian Dzevdet Pacha occupies also a most conspicuous place in Turkish literature. His history of the Ottoman Empire is admired for its style, while his works on the principles of Arabic philosophy, and the leading part he took in the codification of the civil law, proved him not only an excellent writer, but also a distinguished jurist, though he is not unfettered from the prejudices of his time and environment. In his daughter Fatime Alie, Turkish women found a determined champion of their actual condition. The authoress in her book on women, defends even «domestic slavery,» considering it not a very unsatisfactory condition of men and women, compared to that of the poor class of the Western people.

Abdul Hak Hamid's theatrical works, on the other hand, gave an impetus to Turkish authors in that line, which had been hitherto unknown, although some feeble attempts had been formerly made. In fact, tragedy or drama does not seem to agree with the genius of the Turkish people and did not, therefore, prove successful. The novels of this author describing the life of the Moors and their ancient splendor were, however, welcomed by the Ottomans, not only on account of their intrinsic value, but also because they saw in them the glorification of Mohammedan civilization.

The Turks, as other Oriental people, displayed a remarkable talent for versification. Being rather disciples of the Persians than the Arabs, in poetry they were entirely carried away by the thoughts of the authors of Ispahan and Shiraz, as being more adapted to their idiosyncrasy and genius. These were their guiding spirits, whether they indulged in witty versification, lyrical poetry, or in the description of the charms of contemplative life. Satirical poetry also proved to be an excellent weapon in the hands of Turkish Effendis. The late Zia Pacha was a clever satirist, and his caustic verses were relished by his friends and admirers. Nor was the talent of this author confined to the exposure of the weaknesses of his enemies. His poetry in general made him one of the most prominent Turkish writers of modern times. His eulogies of the late Sultan Aziz, though tinged with that Oriental obsequiousness customary to Eastern writers, are nevertheless appreciated for their excellent versification. But above all, his lyrical poetry and his verses devoted to the sufferings of a lover on being separated from his beloved, and generally his love songs, have with justice acquired for him a well-deserved fame.

In Ottoman and generally in Oriental poetry we may in vain look for anything capable of arousing the spirits or exalting the imagination. The Eastern poet seeks simply to express his sorrow and affliction. It is his grievance, and not his joy, that he strives to show in the most pathetic manner possible. It is by these dismal effusions of his saddened heart, that he seeks to take us into his confidence, looking for consolation and relief. Turkish poetry, besides, should be appreciated on its own merits, and not be judged by our standard; not by our own conception as to its value, but according to the effect it produces upon the people for whom it is written. If these relish it; if it goes to their very heart, then it should be conceded that such poetry responds to the genius of the people, and that they are the best judges as to its merit and value. It may sometimes be difficult for an alien to grasp the real meaning of the poet's thought, when these are shaped into another tongue. It may even be sometimes impossible to give in a foreign idiom certain ideas of the poet, which may be so interwoven with Oriental mysticism, that any attempt to discover their true meaning might be considered by the « pious dervish » as a sacrilege. It is with that spirit that we should judge Turkish or Oriental poetry, if we wish to render justice to its writers.

Theodore P. Ion.

CONTENTS

INTRODUCTION

I.—GENERAL CHARACTER OF OTTOMAN POETRY

Arabian and Persian literature have for a considerable period received the attention of Western scholars, and translations and editions of several of the most esteemed works in these two languages have from time to time appeared in Europe; but the literature, and especially the poetical literature, of the Ottoman Turks, the most illustrious family of the third great race of Islam, has been, with a few exceptions, notably that of Von Hammer, almost entirely neglected by European Orientalists.

The cause of this is hard to ascertain. It might have been thought that the facts of the Ottoman Turks being in Europe and having, for upward of five centuries, been in close contact with various European peoples, would have had for a result a more intimate acquaintance on the part of the latter with the studies and pursuits of their Muslim neighbors, than with those of the remoter nations of Asia. But it may be that these very circumstances of proximity and intercourse, which might have been conceived as furthering a European interest in the inner life and modes of thought of that wondrous and gifted shepherd clan which has played so brilliant a part in the world's history, have acted in an exactly contrary manner. It may well be that affrighted Europe, when she saw the Crescent gleaming over Constantinople, and heard the legions of Islam thundering at the gates of Vienna, wished rather to shield herself from their dreaded scimitar than to inquire whence that race of nomad warriors, before whom she trembled, were inspired with the dauntless valor, and the matchless devotion, which bore them so bravely on. But the Ottomans have long ceased to be aggressive, and such influences must have died out many years ago: terror gave place to hatred, not unnatural at first, but wholly unjust now; unless, indeed, we are to hold a people guilty of the crimes of their ancestors —if so, who can escape condemnation?

Antipathy of race and religious bigotry are virulent and hard to kill (unhappily, they exist to this day, scarcely less unjust and cruel than in bygone times), and it is difficult not to think that these are in some measure responsible for the gross ignorance that almost universally prevails, in England at any rate, regarding Turkey and all things Turkish.

To select one striking example: but recently did the writer of these pages read in a popular religious magazine that, « in Mohammedan countries (meaning Turkey), Woman is treated as having no soul.» This mediæval delusion of Isl*a*m's denying a soul to Woman has been clearly and decisively refuted by Mr. Redhouse,* who quotes passage after passage of the Qur*a*n, showing how utterly false it is —how Isl*a*m in reality no more denies Woman a soul than does Christianity itself. Possibly enough, this calumny may have arisen in error; but to proclaim it to-day shows, on the part of the traducer, either almost criminal ignorance, for it is, very wrong to condemn where one does not understand, or vile dishonesty, for it is vilely dishonest knowingly to propagate a lie. Yet the writer of the article in question was a missionary in Turkey! Either he had, as we hope and believe, not taken the trouble to learn anything of the truth about the faith of the people among whom he lived, never hesitating all the same to pass adverse judgment thereon; or he stood greatly in need of some one to expound to him the Ninth Commandment.†

* On the « History, System and Varieties of Turkish Poetry,» etc., pp. 7–10.

† For an exhaustive and *correct* account of Isl*a*m and its Founder, the reader is referred to Seyyid Ameer Ali's « Critical Examination of the Life and Teachings of Mohammed » (London: Williams and Norgate). This is by far the best English work on the Prophet and his Creed that I have read, and I would strongly recommend its careful perusal to all who desire to *understand* the teaching of the great Arabian Lawgiver.

It is not unfrequently said by the class of persons to which our missionary belongs, *i. e.*, those who pass judgment on what they know nothing about — and it may tend to discourage the study of Turkish — that the Turks are a barbarous people, possessed of no literature. To such an assertion as this, no better answer can be given than that Von Hammer-Purgstall, in his great work, *Die Geschichte der Osmanischen Dichtkunst*, gives translated extracts from *two thousand two hundred* Ottoman poets. Although perhaps poetry has been cultivated in Turkey with greater assiduity than any other branch of literature, yet the bare mention of the names and works of her most brilliant historians and romancers, and most gifted philosophic and scientific authors, would fill a goodly volume. There exist in Turkish many works famous throughout the East, on Astronomy, Astrology, Mathematics, Rhetoric, Ethics, Theology, Jurisprudence, Exegesis, Medicine, Chemistry, Geography, History, Chronology, Biography, and all the other sciences of the Muslims; but writers of no class are more frequently to be met with in the pages of the Ottoman biographers than poets, that class of writers whose very existence bears witness to the presence of national culture and refinement. Of the two thousand two hundred authors whose names are enshrined in Von Hammer's volumes, many indeed scarcely deserve the name of poets, and owe their place there merely to some little *gazel*, or, it may be, only to a stray *beyt*, or distich, preserved in the pages of some friendly biographer; for the distinguished Orientalist of Vienna, being at great pains to give a complete picture of the history of Ottoman Poetry, has inserted in his work almost all that can be gleaned from the Turkish *Tezkeras*, or biographies. As is the case in the literary history of every people, but comparatively few of these Ottoman versifiers can be regarded as really great poets; yet perhaps '*A*shiq Pasha is not very far behind his great prototype, the immortal Mevl*a*n*a* Jel*a*lu-'d-D*i*n, the author of the *Mesnevi*; the *gazels* of B*a*q*i*, in elegance of diction and depth of feeling, rival those of H*a*fiz; and the romances of L*a*mi'*i* yield not one whit in loveliness to the works of J*a*m*i* or Niz*a*m*i*. Yet these four Persian authors stand in the forefront of the ranks of the poets of *Iran*, and in the whole history of the literature of her nations, earth can show few names more illustrious than theirs. It will thus be seen that whatever be the cause of the neglect in this country of the study of Ottoman Poetry, it is not due to the absence of poets or to the quality of their effusions.

The difficulty of the language in which it is written, and the scarcity, till within recent years, of trustworthy grammars and dictionaries, have, no doubt, helped to discourage the study of Ottoman literature; while those scholars who have surmounted these preliminary obstacles have probably been deterred by the absence of originality which characterizes the poetry of the 'Osm*a*nlis from presenting many specimens to the European public, preferring to go direct to Persia, the fountain-head, where springs the stream that fructifies the garden of Turkish verse.

Now look we a little more closely at this Ottoman Poetry, its character, and the circumstances which tended to form the same.

As the poetry of the Ottomans is altogether founded upon that of the Persians, just as the literature of the European nation is the offspring of the writings of Rome and Greece, it will be well in the first place to cast a glance toward *Iran*. The poetry, then, of the Persians, and, therefore, that of their imitators, Turks, Muslim Indians, Afgh*a*ns, etc., is essentially an art. There is a limited (considerable enough, it is true, but yet limited) number of metres and variations of metres, each of which is divided into a definite number of feet, which, in their turn, are divided into a determined number of long and short (or, as the Orientals call them, *heavy* and *light*) syllables, following one another in a particular order, which may not be altered; and in one or other of these metres, or variations of metres, the author is bound to write his poem. Some of these metres are appropriated to one style of composition, one form of poem, and certain others to another form. Again, there is a definite number of verse-forms, some of Arabian, some of Persian origin (such as the *quasida*, *gazel*, etc., which will be explained afterward), in one of which the poet must write: he is no more permitted to link lines together in any way he chooses, than he may compose those lines of any number of syllables in any order he pleases; he is bound to observe the rules of the art.

It is almost a rule that the subjects of *gazels* (the form of verse in which a great portion of Persian and Ottoman Poetry is composed) be the beauty of a lady, the sufferings of her lover, the charms of spring, and the delights of wine; the natural result of which is very frequently a certain monotony and sameness among the various *gazels* of an author, indeed, of many authors. It requires a poet of exceptional originality to compose three or four hundred of these little odes, usually of from five to twelve couplets each, on the same subjects, without repetition of expression or sentiment, and without borrowing from the works of previous writers. The great number and variety of curious conceits that enter into the *belles lettres* of the East, and are so highly prized by scholarly Orientals, show very clearly the artificial character of Persian, and consequently of Ottoman, poetry. But apart from the necessity of composing in the recognized forms, and the advisableness — almost amounting to a necessity — of writing, in *gazels*, on certain set subjects, the poet is allowed the freest possible scope for the display of his individual talent, and of the bent of his genius. Such is the general external character of the poetry of the Persians, a character which, in all its details, has been adopted by the Ottomans.

The poetry of Muhammedan Persia, though based upon the Arabian system, comprises much, in sentiment, expression, form, and subject, that is not Arabian, but pure, native Persian. It is not so with that of Turkey, where nothing is native, nothing T*a*t*a*r, saving the language in which it is written. On every page of a Persian author we see allusions to the old religion and the ancient heroes of *Ira*n; but vainly do we look, from end to end, through the works of an Ottoman poet for any reference, however slight, to the religion and traditions of those Central Asian deserts whence his nation came. Religion and traditions, and not unromantic either, we know they had; but while we are continually encountering the Persians, Rustem and Jemsh*i*d Key-Khusrev and Fer*i*d*u*n, nowhere in the writings of their descendants can we catch a glimpse of Uguz or of Guk Khan, "Prince of the Sky." These old semi-legendary kings and champions of ancient Persia stand in precisely the same relation to Ottoman literature as do the gods and heroes of classic Greece and Rome to that of Western Europe; the Ottomans finding them frequently referred to by their Persian models, have introduced them no less frequently, and in exactly the same relations, into their own writings; just as the Frankish nations have preserved in their poetry many an old pagan fancy which they found in the authors of Greece and Rome, such as the Graces and the Fates, Diana's bow, and Phœbus' rays. But there is another series of ancient stories, another group of stately figures, scarcely less frequently to be met with than those, common, this time, to both Christian and Muslim lands; these are the traditions and heroes of the Jews. Poems describing or bearing allusion to the Creation of the Universe, the Fall of Man, and the Deluge, are as common among the followers of the Qur'*a*n, as among those of the Gospel. The virtue and loveliness of Joseph, the sweet singing of David, and the glories of Solomon, who like N*u*sh*i*r-v*a*n, the Persian, is the model of an Eastern sovereign, are darling themes with the poets of Isl*a*m. These Prophets — along with many others whose histories are detailed in the Qur'*a*n, and the Prophet Muhammed himself and the most distinguished of his contemporaries and immediate successors, especially his son-in-law 'Al*i* and his uncle Hemza; together with a few, a very few, of the pre-Isl*a*mitic champions of Arabia, of whom H*a*tim T*a*'*i* is the most frequently mentioned — these form the Semitic contribution to what may be called the *dramatis personæ* of Ottoman Poetry.

In the Persians we have already seen the Aryan contingent, in which also appear a few of the Grecian philosophers, notably Plato and Aristotle. From the *Shah-Nama* of Firdevs*i*, in which are recounted in noble strains the adventures and exploits of the kings and heroes of four mighty dynasties, the P*i*shd*a*d*i*, the Key*a*n*i*, the Ashek*a*n*i* and the S*a*s*a*n*i* (or the Achaemenian, the Median, the Parthian, and the Sassanian) have subsequent authors, well nigh numberless,—Persian, Turkish, and Indian,—drawn the materials for many beautiful poems. Often are sung the splendor and subsequent fall of Jemsh*i*d; famed are the glories of Khusrev Perv*i*z and his love for the enchanting Sh*i*r*i*n, whose very name means «sweet»; but of all the kings and heroes whose feats Firdevs*i* records in his famous epic, none is held so high, none has furnished the subject for so many romances, as the king and hero, the conqueror of the world, Iskender-i R*u*m*i*, Alexander the «Roman.» So enamored are the Persians of Alexander the Great, though he conquered their country and overthrew their splendid Key*a*n*i* dynasty, that they claim him as a member of their own race, declaring him to be the offspring of a Persian prince and a Grecian, or rather Roman, princess. So much for the characters, historical or legendary, which figure in the Poetry of the Ottomans: Semitic and Aryan we see them to be; of Turanian we can find no sign. The absence of all trace of T*a*t*a*r mythology may perhaps be thus accounted for. A mere tribe of rude and unlettered nomads was the little Turkish clan which, in the thirteenth century of our era, flying from the murderous hordes of Jeng*i*z Kh*a*n, left their home in the meadows of the lower Oxus and followed Suleym*a*n Sh*a*h into Asia Minor, and there under 'Osm*a*n, grandson of that Prince, formed the nucleus of that mighty Empire which still holds sway, direct or indirect, over some of the fairest portions of the three continents of the Old World. On their arrival in Asia Minor they found established there another Turkish race, the Selj*u*q*i*, whose empire, then near its fall, had lasted long enough and been sufficiently prosperous to extend to literature that encouragement which Muslim states, possessed of the necessary stability and tranquillity have never failed to accord. The literary education of these Selj*u*q*i*s had been entirely conducted by Persians, and judging from the extreme scarcity of Turkish works written by Selj*u*q*i* authors, it would seem that, like the Jagat*a*y* Turks, who in after years ruled so magnificently at Delhi, they adopted in their literature not only the tone and style, but even the very

* *Chagatay* is the true Central Asian form of this word; but the Ottomans write and pronounce it *Jagatay*.

language, of their *Irani* instructors. Hardly were 'Osman and his followers settled in their new home before the Seljuqi Empire went to pieces. Overthrown by fierce Mogul conquerors, strong enough to destroy but too weak to restore, the Empire split up into a number of provinces, each under a Turkish chieftain, by whose name the province was known so long as it enjoyed a separate existence. These provinces were gradually merged in the growing empire of Orkhan and his successors, when the inhabitants—Turks themselves, like the Ottomans—readily amalgamated with the latter, so that by far the greater portion of the people now and for long called Ottoman Turks are in reality renovated Seljuqis.

To these Seljuqis it is that the Ottomans owe their literary education: this fact at once explains the extremely Persian tone that runs through their whole literature; without any records of their own, they seem to have lost any lingering recollection of the traditions of their ancestors when brought face to face with the dazzling genius of Persia. Still, unlike many Turks brought under the Persian spell, the Ottomans did not adopt the *Irani* tongue as the language of their court and literature; on the contrary, they retained as such their native Tatar dialect, but embellished with every beauty that the Persian speech could lend.

A peculiarity of Persian and Ottoman Poetry is, that it almost always possesses, beneath its literal meaning, a subtle, esoteric, spiritual signification. Many poems, of which the *Mesnevi* of Jelalu-'d-Din and the *Diwan* of 'Ashiq Pasha are examples, are confessedly religious, moral, or mystic works; but a much larger number are allegorical. To this latter class belong almost all the long romantic *mesnevis* of the Persian and Ottoman poets; in the stories of the loves of Leyli and Mejnun, Yusuf and Zuleykha, Khusrev and Shirin, Selaman and Ebsal, and a hundred of like kind, we can see pictured, if we look beneath the surface, the longing of the soul of man for God, or the yearning of the human heart after heavenly light and wisdom. There is not a character introduced into those romances but represents some passion, not an incident but has some spiritual meaning. In the history of Iskender, or Alexander, we watch the noble human soul in its struggles against the powers of this world, and, when aided by God and guided by the heavenly wisdom of righteous teachers, its ultimate victory over every earthly passion, and its attainment of that point of divine serenity whence it can look calmly down on all sublunary things.

Of a similar character are the odes called *gazels;* these little poems, though outwardly mere voluptuous or bacchanalian songs, are in reality the outpouring of hearts overwhelmed, or as they themselves express it, drunken, with their love of God: He is that Fair One whom they so eagerly entreat to come to them, to throw off the veil that conceals His perfect beauty from the sight of their comprehension. Every word in these effusions has its spiritual or mystic signification, well known to the initiated: thus, the *mistress* is God; the *lover*, man; the *tresses*, the mystery of the Godhead, or Its impenetrable attributes; the *waist*, that state when nought remains to veil the lover from the Divine glories; the *ruby lip*, the unheard but understood words of God; the *embrace*, the discovery of the mysteries of the Godhead; *absence* or *separation* is the non-recognition of the Unity of God; *union*, His Unity, or the seeing of Him face to face; *wine* means the Divine love; the *cup-bearer*, the spiritual instructor, the giver of the goblet of celestial aspiration and love; the *libertine*, the saint who thinks no more of human conventionalities; the *tavern*, a place where one mortifies sensuality, and relinquishes his "name and fame"; the *zephyr*, the breathing of the spirit; the *taper*, the Divine light kindling the *torch*, the heart of the *lover*, man. And so on, through every detail is the allegory maintained.

Such is the true and original purport of the *gazel*, and the spirit in which most of the great poets of Persia and Turkey intended their compositions to be understood; but many writers (especially in Persia, where morals are lax) did no doubt mean literally all they said. Among the Ottoman *gazel*-writers there is a great number of men who cannot be regarded either as mystics or voluptuaries. All the sultans, princes, and vezirs, as well as the immense crowd of officials of all ranks, who wrote these odes, were men who had not the leisure, even if they had the wish, to be mystic devotees; neither would they have dared, no matter what they may have thought, to give expression in strict, orthodox Stamboul to such sentiments as are set forth in their songs, intending them to be literally understood. Moreover, we know from history that many of the royal poets could not possibly have intended a literal interpretation of their verses; for they were sincere and zealous Muslims, and visited with condign punishment the use of the forbidden wine. How then, it may be asked, did they write these poems, if they meant them neither literally nor figuratively? The answer seems to be: Fashion. Looking over the works of their Persian models, they would see that the great majority of the smaller poems (men of action would rarely have time to write long *mesnevis*) were in this strain, that the ideas and expressions were pretty, and so they would copy them without intending their words to be taken either in a literal or a metaphorical sense. But while this may be the case with regard to some writers, there are very many Ottoman poets, the earnestness of whose words proclaims the intensity and depth of the feeling that gave them birth, whose verses are free from that almost insensate enthusiasm which stamps too many *gazels* with insincerity. Some of these, too, held high offices of state; such was 'Izzet Molla, one of Sultan Mahm*u*d the Second's vice-chancellors, in many of whose *gazels* are traces of a profound philosophy. Every page also of the poet L*a*mi'*i* bears witness that he at least possessed an ardent and sincere love of nature.

A few words regarding the doctrine of the *Sufis* or Mystics, which is the creed of most of the Dervish Orders, and to which the *gazels*, when written in the proper spirit, *mesnevis* too, give expression, will not here be out of place. As no one has described this religion of Mysticism more accurately than Sir William Jones, I cannot do better than reproduce the following passage, from his "Essay on the Philosophy of the Asiatics":—

"The *Sufis* concur in believing that the souls of men differ infinitely in *degree*, but not at all in *kind*, from the Divine Spirit, of which they are *particles*, and in which they will ultimately be re-absorbed; that the spirit of God pervades the universe, always immediately present to His work, and, consequently, always in substance; that He alone is perfect benevolence, perfect truth, perfect beauty; that the love of Him alone is *real* and genuine love, while that of all other objects is *absurd* and illusory; that the beauties of nature are faint resemblances, like images in a mirror, of the Divine charms; that, from eternity without beginning to eternity without end, the Supreme Benevolence is occupied in bestowing happiness, or the means of attaining it; that men can only attain it by performing their part of the *primal covenant* between them and the Creator; that nothing has a pure, absolute existence but *mind* or *spirit;* that *material substances*, as the ignorant call them, are no more than gay *pictures*, presented continually to our minds by the spiritual artist; that we must be aware of attachment to such *phantoms*, and attach ourselves, exclusively, to God, who truly exists in us, as we exist solely in Him; that we retain, even in this forlorn state of separation from our beloved, the *idea of heavenly beauty* and the *remembrance* of our *primeval vows;* that sweet music, gentle breezes, fragrant flowers perpetually renew the primary *idea*, refresh our fading memory, and melt us with tender affections; that we must cherish these affections, and, by abstracting our souls from *vanity*, that is, from all but God, approximate to His essence, in our final *union* with which will consist our supreme beatitude." To what extent the spirit of this philosophy pervades the Poetry of the Ottomans, the following pages will amply show.

But there is much Ottoman Poetry, altogether unaffected by the Aryan Mysticism of Persia, tinged with a stately melancholy and breathing a sincere and simple religion which no one can possibly misunderstand. That is the spirit of Semitic Isl*a*m, a spirit sad and grave, but full of divine calm and inward joy and ineffable hope, a spirit that can incite those in whom it dwells to deeds of the highest daring, and sustain them unshaken in the bitterest anguish. Here, then, we see the influences of the genius of the two great races, Semitic and Aryan, uniting to form the soul of Ottoman Poetry; and here again we fail to discern any trace of a third and Turanian element. M. Servan de Sugny says, indeed, in his work called *La Muse Ottomane:* "The Turks have something distinct from the other two nations (Arabs and Persians); contemplative by nature, they love to fathom the mysteries of existence, to plunge in thought into the darkness of the other world, to ask the purpose and the end of all things here. Thus they are moralists *par excellence;* they have ever present in their mind the hour of death and the eternal destiny which awaits each man beyond the tomb. In even the most trivial works of their writers, there is almost always some religious or philosophic thought attached to the principal subject, to form its crown, or, if need be, its corrective. In a word, the Turks regard themselves as only camped in life, just as it has been said that their nation is only camped in Europe. One can imagine with what a solemnity such a manner of viewing things must impress their customs, and, in consequence, the creations of their genius." All that the French writer says here about the Ottomans and their mode of thought is absolutely true; but the spirit which brought about that mode of thought is that of Islam, working on the Turkish mind, no doubt, but still in itself Qur'anic, and therefore Semitic — not Turkish and Turanian. The proof of this is, that the same spirit can be seen in thousands of Arabic poems written after the mission of Muhammed and before the rise of Turkish literature.

Thus, as we have several times seen, one of the most noticeable characteristics of Ottoman Poetry is its lack of originality; saving that it differs in what may be called its local coloring, for it is the growth of another clime: it reflects as in a mirror every trait and feature of the poetic art of Persia. Persian it is in form, Persian in tone, and, generally, Persian in subject; even the Arabian ray, which we have noticed, comes to it through a Persian medium. The cause of this we have attempted to trace in the early history of the Empire of the Ottomans, and in the circumstances of their literary education.

While such is indeed the case with regard to the classic poetry of the Ottomans (which alone we are considering here), it is more than probable that in the popular songs

Shargis, or ballads, and such like, a distinct and national spirit will be found. In his «Popular Poetry of Persia,» M. Chodzko gives translations of some songs of the Persian Turks, made from the *Azerbayjani patois*, which forms the connecting link between the Eastern and Western — Jagatay and Ottoman — dialects of the great Turkish language, which extends, like an immense unbroken chain, from the Wall of China to the shores of the Adriatic; but these can hardly be expected to bear much resemblance to the every-day songs of Brusa and Stamboul. So far as I know, no collection of Ottoman popular songs has been published in Europe, either in original or translation.

Although the want of originality undoubtedly renders Ottoman Poetry less interesting than it would be were the case otherwise, that cannot be considered a sufficient reason for its neglect; if the poetry of Persia is beautiful and deserving of careful study (and few who are acquainted with it will deny that it is both), that of Turkey must be the same, seeing how close is the relationship between them. Roman science and literature stand in very much the same relation to Grecian as Ottoman do to Persian. Professor Max Müller even says, in his «Science of Language,»* «the Romans, in all scientific matters, were merely the parrots of the Greeks»; yet no one is deterred on that account from the study of the Latin poets, and why should a similar circumstance interfere with that of the Ottoman?

But it must not be thought that, because the Turkish race has shown a singular backwardness in the invention of poetic fancies and forms, it in any way lacks those qualities of character and individuality whereby nations raise themselves from obscurity to fame. Were it not a race endowed with great and special gifts, so many of its families would never have distinguished themselves in the world's history. The kingdoms of the Selj*u*q*i* Turks were once the most powerful in Western Asia; for two centuries the Qaram*a*n*i* Turks were the most formidable rivals of the 'Osm*a*nl*i*s; and those splendid Emperors known as the «Great Moguls,» who, down to the middle of the present century, ruled in India, were in reality Jagat*a*ys — Turks, pure as the Otto-

* Ed. 1873, Vol. I., p. 139.

mans themselves. Of these latter it is needless to speak; they were once the mightiest people on the earth; and, even now, after centuries of decline, it has taxed to its uttermost the whole military force of the greatest empire in Europe, backed up by rebel hordes from every province between the Euxine and the Adriatic, to worst their armies in the field.

II.—OTTOMAN VERSE-FORMS AND METRES

We shall now proceed to take a brief survey of the construction of Ottoman Poetry—of the various verse-forms and metres in which it is composed.

For their rhyming system, as for all else pertaining to the construction of their poetry, the Ottomans are indebted to the Persians, who are themselves beholden for the elements of their poetic art to the Arabs, to whose primitive system, however, they have added many new features of their own invention. Some, at least, of these features are, it is true, to be found in several later Arabic poetical works, but these must be regarded as copied from Persian or Turkish models. The rhyming system of the Ottomans (and Persians) divides itself naturally into two great branches: one, the primitive Arabian form; the other, an invention of the Persians.

The root of the first of these is the *qasida*, the form in which the famous *Mu'allaqat* and other old Arabic poems are written. It were well to state here that the invariable base, upon which Musulman poetry is built, is the *Beyt*, usually translated «distich» or «couplet,» which consists of two hemistichs (*misra'*) of equal length. The feature of the first, or Arabian, branch is, that throughout the entire poem, no matter how long it be—*i. e.*, of how many *beyts* it consist—the second hemistichs of all the *beyts* must rhyme together, thus carrying one and the same rhyme through the whole poem, while the first hemistichs do not rhyme at all. Usually, though not always, the first hemistich of the first *beyt*—*i. e.*, the first line of the poem—rhymes with its own second hemistich, and, consequently, with that of every succeeding *beyt*. Examples of this will be seen in every *gazel* in this collection

In the second, or Persian, branch, the two hemistichs of each *beyt* rhyme with one another, altogether independently of the rhymes of other *beyts*, whether preceding or following; this is called *mesnevi* rhyme. It is to be found in a vast number of English poems — those of Dryden and Sir Walter Scott, for example. This Persian style is chiefly used for very long poems, each of which is a complete book in itself; while the Arabian system is principally employed in shorter productions.

The two great branches of the rhyming system having been explained, the principal verse-forms require to be noticed. The *Qasida*, *Gazel*, and *Qit'a* are the most important of these in the Arabian style.

The *Qasida*: This is the old Arab form. The two hemistichs of the opening *beyt* rhyme with one another. The subject of poems written in this form is generally the praise of great personages, either living or deceased; occasional satire, and sometimes moral or religious reflections. As a rule, toward the end of the poem the name of the person praised is introduced. The *Qasida* is usually a poem of considerable length, and ought to be finished and elegant in point of style. An example of this form will be found among the selections from Baqi's poems.

The *Gazel* is in form precisely the same as the *qasida*, but much shorter, consisting of not less than five and not more than eighteen *beyts*, in the last, or second last, of which the poet almost always introduces his own *takhallus*, or poetic *nom de plume*. The matters of which it usually treats are the beauty of a mistress, and the woes of her absent, and generally despairing, lover; or the delights of wine; or the charms of spring and flowers, and the sweet notes of the nightingale; or it may be that a single *gazel* will touch on each and all of these varied subjects, devoting a *beyt* or two to each. Often, too, in the course of the poem, one comes across an allusion to the brevity of human life and the vanity of the things of earth; concerning the true meaning of these seemingly bacchanalian songs we have already spoken. A few *gazels* treat consecutively throughout of a given subject, as, for example, that of Baq*i* on Autumn, and that of Bel*i*g on a Dancing-Girl; but these are rare exceptions. In regard to style, the *gazel* must be highly finished; all imperfect rhymes, obsolete words, and vulgar expressions ought to be avoided. Each *beyt* must in itself contain a complete thought. There need be, and there usually is, no connection between the various *beyts*, which have been well compared to pearls upon a thread. "The thread will make them one necklace; but the value of the necklace lies in each pearl, not in the thread." The *gazel* is by far the favorite verse-form of the Ottoman and Persian poets. A point which calls for remark here is that some Ottoman *gazels* are addressed to boys, not to girls, the explanation of which is this: the old Arabian poets speak of women, frequently imaginary; but the Persians, considering this very immodest, usually assume a boy, also imaginary, to be the beloved object in their poems; and the Ottomans, according to their invariable custom, have simply copied the *Iranis*. This practice holds, too, in *modern* Arabic poetry.

The *Qit'a* differs in form from the *qasida* and *gazel* only in that the first hemistich of the first *beyt* does not rhyme with the second of the same and succeeding couplets. A *Qit'a* may contain as few as two *beyts*. If the first *beyt* of a *qasida* or *gazel* be taken away, the remainder is a *Qit'a;* or if a poet compose a *qasida* or *gazel* without rhyming the first line, the result is a *Qit'a*. The word *Qit'a* means "fragment."

As already mentioned, the *Qasida*, *Gazel*, and *Qit'a* are the principal verse-forms in which the Arabian system of rhyme prevails; the Persian style holds in one only, which now remains to be noticed.

The *Mesnevi*: In the Persian rhyme-system, as has been said, each hemistich rhymes with its fellow; but the same rhyme is not carried throughout the entire poem, as in *qasidas*, *gazels*, and *qit'as*. The name *mesnevi* is given alike to this style of rhyme and to a poem composed in it. The subject of a *mesnevi* is usually a romance or an epic. The stories of the loves of Leyl*i* and Mejn*u*n, W*a*miq and 'Azr*a*, Khusrev and Sh*i*r*i*n, and Y*u*suf and Zuleykh*a*, and the adventures of Iskender (Alexander the Great), and of the ancient princes of the East, are favorite themes with the writers of these poems. They not unfrequently treat of mystic or religious subjects; and the most famous work of this kind in any Muslim language is the great Persian mystic poem of Mevl*a*n*a* Jel*a*lu-'d-D*i*n er-R*u*m*i*, which is styled simply the *Mesnevi*, being the *mesnevi* of all *mesnevis*. The first Book of this master-work of Persian poetry — this text-book of the mystics of the East — has been recently translated into English verse by Mr. Redhouse. Historical poems are usually written in this form; they bear most frequently the name, *Nama*, *i. e.*, « Book, » as the *Shah-Nama*, *Iskender-Nama*, *Timur-Nama*, « The Book of Kings, » of « Alexander, » of « T*i*m*u*r. » Little descriptive poems included in *Diwans* (though not always in *mesnevi* rhyme) also often bear this name; such are the *Saqi-Nama Firaq-Nama*, *Pend-Nama*, « The Book of the Cup-bearer, » of « Separation, » of « Counsel. » Finally, to this form belongs that peculiar class of descriptive poems which bears the special title *Shehr-engiz*, « City-disturbing. » These are descriptions either of places or of people; they detail the beauties of the site and buildings of a city, or the charms of the youths and maidens who dwell there, and whose loveliness sets the whole town in an uproar. It will thus be seen that the Persian, or *mesnevi*, rhyme is chiefly used in descriptive poetry.

These are the most important verse-forms to be found in the works of Ottoman poets; but there are many minor varieties, some of which, as they frequently occur, require to be mentioned here. Amongst the most common of these is the class called *Musemmat*, which comprises poems consisting of a succession of four, five, or six-line strophes, and named accordingly, *Murebba'*, *Mukhammess*, and *Mueddes*, or « tetrastich, » « pentastich, » and « hexastich. »

Each of the strophes has a different rhyme, and the lines in each rhyme together. Often, however, the last line (sometimes the last two lines) of each strophe is the same throughout, thus forming a sort of refrain. Frequently again the last lines are different, but rhyme with each other and the first strophe. Several examples of these forms, which are really only varieties of the *Terji*'-*Bend* (which will be described further on), are included in the present collection. The subjects of the *musemmats* are usually the same as those of *gazels*.

Another very important form is the *Ruba*'i, or « quatrain.» This, as its name shows, is a short composition of four lines. The first, second, and fourth lines must rhyme with one another, the third may or may not, at the option of the poet. This form, which is in high favor with Oriental poets, may treat of any subject. The last line, or sometimes the last two lines, of a good *Ruba*'i must be either witty or epigrammatical, the preceding lines serve merely to introduce the *bon mot* of the last. Here is a celebrated *Ruba*'i, by the Ottoman poet 'I*zari*: *

> Struggling here fiercely my love for the fair;
> There, the flame, dread of rivals, cruel glare;
> Which to combat, in which I must burn, know not I:
> *Yonder torment of fire, O Lord, us spare!*

The last line here is a citation from the Qur'*an*, ch. ii., v. 197, which 'Ig*ari* quotes in the original Arabic.

Another great favorite with Ottoman writers is the *Tarikh*, or « Chronogram »; that is, a piece of verse which expresses at once an occurrence and the date of the same. All the letters of the Turkish alphabet have a numerical value, just as with us C represents 100, V, 5, and so on. If the numerical values of the letters occurring in a verse, a sentence, or even a word, on being added together, give the date of the event to which the words allude, that verse, sentence, or word is called a *Tarikh*. In poetical *Tarikhs* it is usually only the last line that contains the date, sometimes only certain of the letters in that line. The translation of a *Tarikh* on the death of a princess will be found among the selections from Leyl*a* Kh*a*nim's *Diwan*.

A *Nazira* is a poem written in imitation of, or in answer to, one writer by another. (See Note 54.)

A *Mustezad* is a *gazel* with an addition of some words to each line. This addition must have the same rhyme and the same metre as the last half of the line to which it is

* Quoted by Qin*ali*-Z*a*da and Mr. Redhouse.

attached. These short lines, or additions, may be either read or omitted without spoiling the sense of the poem; indeed there are compositions which occur in some MSS. as simple *gazels* that in others appear as *Mustezads*.

The *Terkib-Bend* is a poem consisting of a series of strophes in the form of *gazels*, each of the same metre, but with different rhymes, and connected with one another by *beyts* of the same metre as themselves, but differing from them in rhyme. Sometimes the *bend*, that is the «bond,» the connecting *beyt*, is the same throughout; sometimes it varies between each strophe. The poet does not introduce his *takhallus* into each of the *gazel*-like strophes, but only once toward the end of the poem. B*a*q*i*'s Elegy on Sultan Suleym*a*n affords an example of the *Terkib-Bend*.

The *Terji*'-*Bend* consists likewise of several strophes, all the hemistichs of each of which, however, rhyme together, thus differing from the strophes of the *Terkib-Bend*, which rhyme in the *gazel* style; but like those of the *Terkib*, each strophe of the *Terji*' takes a new rhyme. As in the *Terkib*, again the strophes here are connected by a *beyt* (the *Bend*), which may or may not be variable, and which may or may not rhyme with the first stanza. An example of the *Terji*'-*Bend* will be found in W*a*sif's Eulogy on Huseyn Pasha.

The *Takhm*is is often met with in the later writers. Here the poet takes a *gazel* of another author, and proceeds to build a *mukhammes* upon it in the following manner. He takes the first, or non-rhyming, lines of the couplets which make up the *gazel*, and prefixes to each of them three lines of his own composition having the same metre and rhyme as those to which they are joined. The second, or rhyming, lines of the *gazel* are then added in regular order to these four-line strophes, and thus form the fifth, or odd, lines of the *mukhammes*. An example which will make this clear will be found in this volume among the specimens of Leyl*a* Kh*a*nim's poetry, where that lady has made a *Takhm*is upon one of B*a*q*i*'s *gazels*: to render the process quite distinct I have printed B*a*q*i*'s lines in italics. The word *Takhm*is means «the making (of anything) five»; here, it is the building of a «cinquain» upon a couplet. A *mukhammes* may also be built upon a single line, and a *museddes* upon a single couplet by the poet composing all the four lines of the prefixed strophes. Of course, in this case, the poem may be of any length; whereas, in the former the number of its strophes is necessarily that of the couplets of the *gazel*. A *museddes* built upon a couplet of Mahmud Nedim Pasha is given among Ziya Beg's poems. In the case of a *museddes*, the poem and process are called *Tesdis*, "a making six."

The *Takhallus* is the literary *nom de plume* given to, or assumed by, persons on becoming writers, and by which, except in the cases of the Sultan, his sons, and certain of his ministers, they are ever afterward commonly known. A variety of circumstances may affect an author in the choice of his *Takhallus*; sometimes he forms it from his own name; thus, the name of Baqi, the greatest of the Ottoman lyric poets, was Mahmud 'Abdu-'l-Baqi; sometimes from his birthplace, from his own or his father's occupation, or from some incident in his life. In the *Tezkeras*, as the Biographies of the Poets are called, the authors are arranged under their *Takhalluses* in alphabetical order.

A book in which are collected the various works of a poet (except *Mesnevis*, which, from their great length, usually form books of themselves) is named a *Diwan*. The order in which the various forms of poetry are arranged in these collections is generally as follows: *Qasidas*, *Tarikhs*, *Gazels*, *Terji'*- and *Terkib-Bends* and *Musemmats*; *Ruba'is*, *Qit'as*, and, finally, a chapter of Logogriphs and Enigmas, named respectively, *Mu'amma* and *Lugaz*. The difference between these is, that in the *Mu'amma* the *letters* of a word form the subject of the riddle, while in the *Lugaz* it is the *meaning* of the word — the thing itself — that forms the puzzle: a specimen of the latter, by Sultan Murad IV., will be found among the translations; the former are untranslatable. Before the section of *Qasidas*, a *Diwan* always contains some religious poems; first, the *Hamd*, or "Praise of God"; then the *Na't*, or "Praise of the Prophet"; and, thirdly, the *Munajat*, or the poet's prayer for himself.

A remarkable feature in Ottoman Poetry is the *Redif*; that is, one or more words, always the same, added to the end of every rhyming line in a poem, which word or words, though counting in the scansion, are not regarded as the rhyme; the true rhyme must in every case be looked for immediately before them. The lines,—

> «There shone such a truth about thee,
> I did not dare to doubt thee,»

afford an English example of this; here the word «thee» is a *Redif*, «about» and «doubt» forming the true rhyme. In translating, I have generally, but not invariably, preserved the *Redif*. It chiefly occurs in *gazels*.

The *Gazel*, the *Ruba*'i, the *Takhallus*, and the *Redif* are, like the *Mesnevi*, inventions of the Persians.

It may here be stated that in Musulman poetry there is no such thing as blank verse. In books written in mingled prose and verse, a style in which Orientals greatly delight, and of which the *Gulistan* of the Persian Sa'd*i* and the «Thousand and One Nights» form beautiful and well-known examples, one frequently comes across *beyts*, the two hemistichs of which do not rhyme together. These are usually either the opening distich of some *qit'a*, or quotations from the middle of a *gazel* or *qasida;* writers of such works, however, not unfrequently compose *beyts* of this sort in one of the metres, to express in elegant and forcible language some sentiment they wish to convey; but compositions of this nature never exceed a single *beyt;* four lines of poetry containing no rhyme is a thing unknown.

The Prosody of the Ottomans is, needless to say, identical with that of the Persians, which is founded upon the Arabian system. There is a considerable number of metres, each of which has many variations; some, of course, are much more frequently employed than others. The following are very much used for *gazels* and *musemmats*:—

Hezej-i Musemmen-i Salim

⏑ — — — | ⏑ — — — | ⏑ — — — ‖ ⏑ — — — | ⏑ — — — | ⏑ — — —

Remel-i Musemmen-i Maqsur

— ⏑ — — | — ⏑ — — | — ⏑ — ‖ — ⏑ — — | — ⏑ — — | — ⏑ —

Muzari'-i Musemmen-i Akhreb-i Mekfuf-i Maqsur

— — ⏑ | — ⏑ — ⏑ | ⏑ — — ⏑ | — ⏑ — ‖ — — ⏑ | — ⏑ — ⏑ | — ⏑ —

A great number of others are constantly used, but these three are the commonest.

For *mesnevis* the following three are favorites:—

Hezej-i Museddes-i Maqsur

— — — | ⏑ — — — | ⏑ — — ‖ ⏑ — — — | ⏑ — — — | ⏑ — —

Remel-i Museddes-i Maq*sur*

— ⏑ — — | — ⏑ — — | — ⏑ — ‖ — ⏑ — — | — ⏑ — — | — ⏑ —

Mutaqarib-i Musemmen-i Maq*sur*

⏑ — — | ⏑ — — | ⏑ — — | ⏑ — ‖ ⏑ — — | ⏑ — — | ⏑ — — | ⏑ —

All the metres detailed here show the scansion of a *beyt*, the double line indicating the division between the two hemistichs. The great majority of the poems translated in this work are written in one or other of these six metres.

The reader will observe the great excess of long over short syllables in these measures, a feature which gives to Eastern poetry a peculiarly grave and stately dignity; but at the same time renders the reproduction into English of the rhythm, syllable for syllable, a matter of impossibility. The number of little words, such as articles, prepositions, etc., which are usually required in English to make up even a short sentence, as well as the unaccented syllables in words of more than monosyllabic length, none of which can become, as they all can in Turkish «long by position," form, I think, an insurmountable barrier to the exact and absolute reproduction of the Oriental metres; especially when, as must always be the case in translating, one is fettered with the necessity of having to say a certain thing, and nothing else. And so, in translating the following poems, although I have almost invariably preserved the number of syllables of the originals, I have been unable always to reproduce long syllable for long, and short for short; but in every case I have done my best to give a fair idea of the rhythm-movement of the Turkish verse. In the reproduction of the rhyme I have, I venture to think, been more successful; I have here in every instance followed the original absolutely; always making a rhyme in the translation where the Turkish showed one, never where it did not. The Orientals, as has been already remarked, do not «measure» lines, neither do they speak of «long» and «short» syllables; but they «weigh» them, and their syllables are «heavy» and «light.»

It may be interesting here to notice a few of the curious technical words used by the Muslims in connection with their prosody, as they clearly show the desert origin of that art, which, as we have seen, had its rise among the Arabs. The terms are all Arabic; but they are used by every Mus-ulman people. The word *beyt* means «a house,» or, as here, «a tent»; the feet of the metres are called *erkan*, or «supports»; these are made up of the *sebeb*, «the rope,» the *veted*, «the tent-peg,» and the *fasila*, «the tent-pole.» The two hemistichs are known as the «folds,» or «leaves,» of the double door of the tent. A metre they name *bahr*, which means «an ocean,» but by analogy, «the space inside a tent.» Some, however, say that it is called «an ocean,» because, as an ocean contains a vast variety of pearls, corals, etc., so does a metre comprise an infinite number of poems; others, again, explain it thus, that as an ocean is perplexing and confusing, so is a metre on account of the many changes which its feet undergo.

The *Hezej* metres are said to be properly employed for love-poetry, the *Remel* for philosophical poetry, the *Khafif* for festive poems, and the *Mutaqarib* for war epics and festive poems.

Of a great number of literary conceits and embellishments which continually occur in Eastern poetry, the commonest and most striking is that called *Tejnis*, which may be translated «*equivoque.*» It consists in bringing together two or more words of the same or similar sound and form, but of different meanings, and admits of many varieties. When the two words are in sound and form identical, the *tejnis* is perfect; thus — «Each of the *band* was secured by a *band*» (strap). When the vowels or the initials are different, it is defective, thus: «*Bound* by a *bond* like an iron *band*»; and, «*Bound* to forfeit a *pound*»; and so on, through a considerable number of varieties, each of which has its special technical name. Those which are defective — *i.e.*, in which the words are more or less different — are quite as much esteemed as those in which they are identical. An admirable example of the *tejnis* is afforded by Mr. Eastwick's exceedingly happy rendering of the Persian proverb, *Gurbat kurbat ast*, «Travel is travail.»

There are in Ottoman Poetry a number of what may be called stock metaphors and similes; thus, a fair woman is always *a moon;* a graceful figure, *a cypress;* the hair, *musk;* or a *dark cloud* about the *moon*-face, or the *hyacinth* fallen over the *rose*-cheek; and so on, with many others of like kind. It is not a point with the poet to invent new metaphors of this sort — those in existence are probably as apposite and beautiful as any he is likely to hit upon; a good writer rather tries to show his originality by presenting the stereotyped and time-honored similes in new combinations. Thus a poet says: —

> «A moon were she, were but the moon of cypress form;
> A cypress she, had but that tree the moon's fair breast.»

Although nothing is commoner that the comparison of a girl to the moon or the cypress, that couplet is quite original by reason of the condition so cleverly introduced.

Authors sometimes display their ingenuity by writing poems (which partake of the nature of acrostics) in the forms of wheels, trees, squares, etc., the initials of all the verses of which spring from a common centre. When round they are called *mudevver*, «circular»; when tree-shaped, *mushejjer*, «arboriform»; when square, *murebba'*. Of course, these forms cannot be reproduced in a translation; but the original of a *mudevver*, or circular, *gazel* is shown in the Frontispiece of the present work.

III.—THE RISE AND PROGRESS OF OTTOMAN POETRY

Von Hammer divides his « History of Ottoman Poetry » into five periods, corresponding to those of his « History of the Empire »; but as this division would be of little utility in a small volume like the present, I have not thought it advisable to observe it, and have simply arranged the authors (with a few exceptions) in chronological order.

We have already seen that when the Turkish clan, which, under the name of 'Osmanli, or Ottoman, was destined to become so prominent in after history, sought refuge in Asia Minor from the ferocious conqueror Jengiz Khan, it found ruling there the Turkish dynasty of the Seljuqis; and we have likewise noticed how great an influence was exercised by Persia over the education and literature of these Seljuqi Turks. Before this time (Sa'du-'d-Din gives the year 616 [1219] as the date of the passage of Suleyman Shah and his tribe into Armenia), Firdevsi and Nizami had come and gone, and, by the magic of their poetry, had given to Persian literature and Persian taste that position of pre-eminence in Western Asia which they have ever since retained. Sa'di and Jelalu-'d-Din, worthy successors of the two great poets just named, were contemporaries of Er Togrul, the son of Suleyman, and as the latter of these, the author of the *Mesnevi*, resided at Qonya, the Seljuqi capital, we cannot be surprised at the extent to which the spirit of Persian poetry and philosophy pervaded the literary life of Asia Minor about that time. For the *Mesnevi* of Jelalu-'d-Din is one of the grandest works, not only in Persian, but in all literature; a poem (or rather, series of poems) the beauty of the language and the depth of the philosophy of which have ever created a profound impression on the minds of those who have studied it. The almost entirely religious or mystic character of Ottoman Poetry from its birth till the capture of Constantinople in 1453 is directly traceable to the influence of the master-mind of the great Mevlana.

Some twelve years after his flight into Armenia, Suleyman Shah, having heard of the death of Jengiz Khan, determined to return with his tribe to his own country; but when crossing the Euphrates on the homeward journey, he was accidentally drowned. Two of his four sons, with the greater part of the clan, carried out their intention, returned to their native land, and there are lost from sight. But Er Togrul and Dundar remained behind; only four hundred families stayed with them, and these, settling a few years later in the northwest of Asia Minor, under 'Osman son of Er Togrul, became the ancestors of the glorious Ottoman nation. The reign of 'Osman (who is regarded as the first independent sovereign of the race, and from whom it takes its name 'Osmanli, corrupted into Othoman and Ottoman) was little else than one continuous battle for existence; but in the time of his son Orkhan, when the youthful state had grown stronger and better able to protect itself and secure periods of repose, appeared the first recorded singer of this people, who is known by no other name than 'Ashiq, « The Lover » — the herald of that long line of poets which has continued in unbroken succession from those days till now.

As has been hinted, '*A*shiq's poem (his *Diwan*, as it is termed, though the name seems strangely misapplied; perhaps it was then employed more loosely than it is now) is in subject theological, influenced, as was natural, by the spirit then so powerful in Asia Minor. Within a period of forty years had died Jelalu-'d-Din, his son Sultan Veled, the mystic poet Sheykh Sadru-'d-Din, and the immortal Sa'di — all Persian writers. The first three had been resident in Asia Minor. Thus, with the religio-mystic spirit and Persian taste so powerful in the very land where the Ottomans were receiving their literary education, and at the very time when that education was beginning, it would indeed have been strange had the result been any other than that which actually was the case. Ottoman Poetry was, in its earlier days, well-nigh altogether religious in tone and Persian in taste. It lost its almost exclusively theological character about the time of the fall of Constantinople — the *Muhammediyya* of Yaziji-Oglu may be considered as the last work of the first period — but it has retained its Persianism to this day. Of course, these statements must be taken in a general sense; there were a few poets, such as Ahmed Da'i, who were in nowise theologians, and although religion was indeed the dominating theme, it was not the sole one. Before the capture of Stamboul, the Ottomans had tried their strength in all the branches of Persian poetry — the heroic, the romantic, and the lyric: in the first of these, as early as the reign of Bayezid I., when Ahmedi wrote the *Iskender-Nama;* and in the second, when Sheykhi composed his beautiful poem on the legend of Khusrev and Shirin. These works cannot be considered exceptions to the religious literature of the period, for they are really allegories, not mere stories. Von Hammer thinks that Ahmedi and Sheykhi have never been surpassed by any heroic or romantic poet of their nation. Nesimi and Ahmed Da'i lead the van of the mighty host of lyric poets; the first of these was a sufi, whose heretical opinions on religious matters drew upon him the hatred of the orthodox party, by whom he was put to death. The second was a poet of a very different stamp, whose gay and flowery songs of love and wine found high favor at the joyous court which Prince Suleyman, son of Bayezid I., held at Adrianople, when the Empire was for a time rent in pieces — the result of that terrible day when the Ottoman flag went down before Timur on the plain of Angora. Unlike the first heroic and romantic writers, these two earliest lyric poets are very far from being the best that the nation has produced. Among the purely religious writers of this period, the first, 'Ashiq, surnamed Pasha, and the last, Muhammed Yaziji-Oglu, undoubtedly stand highest.

When Constantinople became the seat of the Empire, a change took place: lyric poetry (*gazels* and *qasidas*) began to receive the largest share of the attention of Ottoman poets, which, as we have seen, had till then been devoted to long religious poems, each an entire book in itself, sometimes more. As the Empire grew and prospered, and extended its boundaries far and wide on every side, literature and poetry grew and prospered with it. It is a curious fact that the tone and standard of Ottoman poetry have almost always kept pace with the political fortunes of the Empire, being high when these were brilliant, and sinking when they became obscured. In the bright days of Muhammed II. and his son Bayezid II., flourished some of the greatest lyric poets of the nation; Ahmed Pasha, Nejati, Zati, and Mesihi are famous names in the annals of Ottoman Poetry. Ahmed Pasha stood chief of the lyrists of his nation till his lustre sank before the star of Nejati, which for a whole century continued to be the brightest object in the sky of 'Osmanli Poetry, when, with all lesser lights, it paled before the radiance of the rising sun of Baqi, the most glorious luminary in the hemisphere of Turkish Literature.

A romantic poem, worthy to be placed alongside of Sheykhi's *Shirin*, on the oft-told story of Yusuf and Zuleykha, was at this time written by Hamdi, son of the famous Sheykh Aq Shemsu-'d-Din. The learned legist Ahmed Kemal Pasha-Zada, whom Sultan Selim I. took along with him to the conquest of Egypt, also composed a poem on the same very favorite subject. About this time, too, occurs the first mention of poetesses in the Ottoman Biographies: Zeyneb and Mihri are the names of the two ladies who, so far as we know, first cultivated the poetic art among their people.

At this period, as indeed at every period when the Empire has been in a flourishing condition, all possible encouragement was given to Poetry as well as to every other branch of literature. Not only did the Sultans, Princes, and Vezirs foster Poetry by rewarding and patronizing authors, but they wrote poems themselves. Murad II., father of the Conqueror of Constantinople, was the first of the Poet-Sultans of the Ottomans; a few distichs by him are embalmed in the pages of the biographers. The House of 'Osman has been gifted to a very remarkable degree with the poetic vein; among its members — Sultans, Princes, and Princesses — it can perhaps show a greater number of poets than any other royal line in the whole course of history. Muhammed II., the Conqueror, was himself a good poet, though he was surpassed by his son, the talented, but unfortunate Prince Jem, who vainly contested the throne with his elder brother Bayezid II., likewise a poet. Sultan Selim I., Bayezid's son, is said to be the best of all the imperial poets, but his writings are mostly in Persian.

Following their masters' example, many of the great officers of state devoted their leisure to the study and composition of poetry; among the most remarkable of these are the Vezirs Ahmed Pasha, the great lyrist, and Mahmud Pasha, who wrote under the name of 'Adeni.

Under Suleyman I. and Selim II. the Ottoman Empire reached the summit of its glory; throughout these two reigns it was the mightiest power on earth. Never did the Crescent shine so brightly as during the long reign of the wise and valiant Suleyman; north and south, east and west, went the Ottoman armies, «conquering and to conquer»; while the Ottoman fleets swept the Mediterranean from end to end. Before the walls of Vienna and on the shores of Malta alone did Fortune refuse to smile upon their arms. Many causes had tended to bring about this result, one of the chief of which was, that all the first ten Sultans were individually and innately great men—men who would have distinguished themselves no matter what their position or circumstances might have been. They were great administrators no less than great warriors; had they not been so—had they been mere barbarian Tatar conquerors like Jengiz or Timur—their empire would, like the empires of these two soldiers, at once have fallen to pieces.

The Poetry of the Ottomans, like their Empire, had now reached its zenith. Baqi, Lami'i, Fuzuli, Yahya Beg, Gazali, and Fazli are all great poets; the first two, the very greatest. Suleyman himself wrote *gazels* under the name of Muhibbi. Of his sons, his successor, Selim II., and the Princes Mustafa, Bayezid, Muhammed, and Jihangir composed verses, and were besides protectors of poets. Selim II., very different from his gallant predecessors, was a drunken profligate, with scarce a spark of the Ottoman in his breast; however, notwithstanding his faults, this Sultan wrote some very pretty *gazels*. under the *takhallus* of Selimi.

On the accession of Murad III. in 1574, the Empire began to decline, and, under a succession of effeminate sovereigns, continued on the downward path till arrested, half a century later, by the iron arm of Murad IV. Although this period was lit up with some bright flashes, such as the Battle of Kerestes (in some respects one of the most remarkable victories ever gained by the Ottomans over their Christian foes), it was by far the darkest through which the Empire had yet passed. Along with political glory, sank poetry; not that writers of verse were not numerous, but few of them deserved the name of poets. 'Ata'i, the Mufti Yahya, and (a little later) the satirist Nef'i are the only really great poets of this time. The five feeble Sultans Murad III., Muhammed III., Ahmed I., Mustafa I., and 'Osman II., who occupied the throne between Selim II. and Murad IV., all composed poems, some of which are not lacking in grace and tenderness.

Very different from these was Sultan Murad IV., brother of 'Osman II.; in his breast burned the strong fierce spirit of the First Selim: to such a state had corruption and anarchy reduced the Empire that probably nothing short of tyrant vigor could preserve it from dissolution; and of this Murad had ample store. He was successful; not only did he save the state from death, he inspired it with new life; and in the reign of his nephew Muhammed IV., for the second time, broke the wave of Turkish military might against the walls of Vienna. The stream of reviving vigor coursed through the whole frame and spirit of the Empire, and with national greatness rose once more literary excellence. The illustrious family of the Kuprulus, whose wise administration did so much to strengthen the tottering fabric of the state, did not neglect, among more pressing duties, to extend their protection to men of letters.

We may pause here to notice that from Murad II. to Murad IV., inclusive, we have an unbroken line of Poet-Sultans: verses by each of the twelve monarchs whose reigns fall within that period are preserved to this day. When regard is had to this and to the further fact that *gazels* have been composed by several other Sultans (notably, Selim III. and

Mahmud II.), as well as by many Princes who never ascended the throne, it must he conceded that the claim which, a page or two back, was advanced for the House of 'Osman is not unworthy of consideration. But although the Ottoman Sultans may perhaps have cultivated Poetry with greater assiduity and success than any other race of Kings, they are very far from being the only Oriental sovereigns who have practiced this graceful art; indeed the composition of verses seems to have been always a favorite pursuit of Muslim monarchs: and many poems, some of high merit, written by Arabian and Spanish Khalifas Tatar Sultans, Persian Shahs, Afghan Emirs, Crimean Khans, and Indian Emperors, remain to attest the learning and refinement that adorned those Asian sovereigns.

The fresh strength with which the energetic but fierce genius of Murad IV. had inspired the Empire lasted through the reigns of his brother the voluptuary Ibrahim and his nephew, the great huntsman, Muhammed IV., till the terrible disaster before Vienna thrust the Ottoman Power once more on to the steep incline of ruin. In spite of the noble efforts of the Kuprulus, which, though they did much to break the fall, could not avert it, the state sank rapidly till, in the days of Selim III., it reached the very verge of extinction. The history of Poetry shows during this period of decline one great name, Nabi, a poet whose works are unsurpassed by those of any subsequent author. 'Arif, Sami, the two Vehbis and, later, Galib are good poets; for the rest, though numerous, they have little merit.

Selim III. saw the woeful plight of his country; he perceived that sweeping changes were imperatively called for in every department of the state, especially in the army and navy, to enable the Ottoman Empire to hold out against her aggressive foes. The introduction of these reforms, which marks the beginning of a new and brighter era of Turkish history, cost this brave but unfortunate monarch his life. The Empire has never been so feeble as it was during this period of transition, when its ancient legions had ceased to exist, and its modern army was yet unformed. Sultan Selim III. wrote many poems which show how deeply he felt the sadness of his lot. Mahmud II.

(another poet) successfully continued his cousin's work; and his successors have done the same. Though the Empire has sustained many shocks during the reigns of these last Sultans, they have been almost always caused by foreign violence or treachery, and are not the results (as used to be the case) of internal weakness and anarchy. Even when such blows have taken the form of insurrections, they are still almost invariably to be traced, as in the instance of last revolts in Bulgaria and Servia, to the intrigues of foreign emissaries. The old race of rebellious Pashas, who, setting the Sultan's authority at defiance, and ofttimes making successful war upon his troops, used to carve out of his provinces ephemeral kingdoms for themselves, has long since passed away. Even in extent of territory, the Empire may be said not to have decreased, but increased; for, though many of its old European provinces have fallen away from the sway of Constantinople, Sultan 'Abdu-'l-Ham*i*d II. holds rule over vast territories in Africa, of which "even Suleym*a*n in all his glory" was ignorant of the very names.

Of the many illustrious poets who have flourished in the present century, none holds a higher position than 'Izzet Molla, the author of the *Mihnet-i Keshan;* and the talented Ziy*a* Pasha, who died but a few years ago, may also justly lay claim to a distinguished position among the poets of his nation.

OTTOMAN POEMS

NOTE ON ORIENTAL WORDS

The Ottoman vowel system is very intricate. To simplify it we have avoided the use of accents by using Roman type for accentuated vowels in the Italicized words, and Italics for the vowels in the Roman text-type.

a	may be	pronounced as	a in «father,» the latter rather longer than the former.
e	"	"	e in «when.»
i	"	"	i in «thin.»
ī	"	"	i in «ravine.»
o	"	"	o in «go.»
u	"	"	oo in «good,» the latter rather longer.
ay	"	"	the word «eye.»
ey	"	"	ey in «they.»
ch	is to	"	ch in «church.»
g	"	"	in «get»; never soft, as in «gem.»
kh	"	"	ch in the German word «Nacht.» Until the true pronunciation is acquired, it is better to pronounce this letter (it is a single letter in Turkish) as a single h than as a k; thus «han» is a better pronunciation for «*khan*» than «kan.»
q	"	"	k. It is used here to replace the Semitic *Qāf*, of which it is the lineal descendant, cf. *Qarashat* and Q R S T.
s	"	"	sharp, as in «set»; never soft like z, as in «reason.»
sh	"	"	in «shall.»

' represents the Arabic letter '*Ayn;* and ' the sign *Hemza*, or (in Arabic compound names) an elided *Elif*. These are not sounded in the language of Constantinople.

The other letters present no difficulty; they are to be pronounced as in English.

OTTOMAN POEMS

‘*A*SHIQ PASHA

733 [1332][1]

From the ‘*A*shiq Pasha D*i*w*a*ni[2]

Kulli ‘alem bir isharet dir heman

All the Universe, one mighty sign, is shown;
God hath myriads of creative acts unknown:
None hath seen them, of the races jinn[3] and men,
Nône hath news brought from that realm far off from ken.
Never shall thy mind or reason reach that strand,
Nor can tongue the King's name utter of that land.
Since 'tis His each nothingness with life to vest,
Trouble is there ne'er at all to His behest.
Eighteen thousand worlds, from end to end,[4]
Do not with Him one atom's worth transcend.

AHMED*I*

815 [1412]

I

From the Iskender-N*a*ma[5]

Suweylegil ey bulbul-i 'anqa-sifat!

Up and sing! O 'anq*a*-natured nightingale![6]
High in every business doth thy worth prevail:
Sing! for good the words are that from thee proceed;
Whatsoever thou dost say is prized indeed.
Then, since words to utter thee so well doth suit,
Pity were it surely if thy tongue were mute.
Blow a blast in utt'rance that the Trusted One,[7]
When he hears, ten thousand times may cry: « Well done! »
Up and sing! O bird most holy! up and sing!
Unto us a story fair and beauteous bring.
Let not opportunity slip by, silent there;
Unto us the beauty of each word declare.
Seldom opportunities like this with thee lie;
Sing then, for th' occasion now is thine, so hie!
Lose not opportunities that thy hand doth find,
For some day full suddenly Death thy tongue shall bind.
Of how many singers, eloquent of words,
Bound have Death and Doom the tongues fast in their cords!
Lose not, then, th' occasion, but to joy look now,
For one day thy station 'neath earth seek must thou.
Whilst the tongue yet floweth, now thy words collect;
Them as meaning's taper 'midst the feast erect,
That thy words, remaining long time after thee,
To the listeners hearing shall thy record be.
Thy mementoes lustrous biding here behind,
Through them they'll recall thee, O my soul, to mind.

Those who've left mementoes ne'er have died in truth;
Those who've left no traces ne'er have lived in sooth.
Surely with this object didst thou come to earth,
That to mind should ever be recalled thy worth.
"May I die not!" say'st thou, one of noble race?
Strive, then, that thou leavest here a name of grace.

II

From the Same [8]

Pes dedi bir gun Vezira Taj-ver

Once unto his Vezír quoth the Crownèd King:
"Thou, who in my world-realm knowest every thing!
With my sword I've conquered many and many a shore;
Still I sigh right sorely: 'Ah! to conquer more!'
Great desire is with me realms to overthrow;
Through this cause I comfort ne'er a moment know.
Is there yet a country whither we may wend,
Where as yet our mighty sway doth not extend,
That we may it conquer, conquer it outright?
Ours shall be the whole earth — ours it shall be quite."
Then when heard the Vezír what the King did say,
Quoth he: "Realm-o'erthrowing Monarch, live for aye!
May the Mighty Ruler set thy crown on high,
That thy throne may ever all assaults defy!
May thy life's rose garden never fade away!
May thy glory's orchard never see decay!
Thou'st the Peopled Quarter ta'en from end to end; [9]
All of its inhabitants slaves before thee bend.
There's on earth no city, neither any land,
That is not, O Monarch, under thy command.
In the Peopled Quarter Seven Climes are known,
And o'er all of these thy sway extends alone!"

SHEYKHI

830 [1426ca]

I

From Khusrev and Shirin[10]

Meger qondugu yer Perviz Shahin.

The spot at which did King Khusrev Perviz light
Was e'en the ruined dwelling of that moon bright.[11]
Whilst wand'ring on, he comes upon that parterre,
As on he strolls, it opes before his eyes fair.
Among the trees a night-hued courser stands bound
(On Heaven's charger's breast were envy's scars found).
As softly moved he, sudden on his sight gleamed
A moon that in the water shining bright beamed.
O what a moon! a sun o'er earth that light rains—
Triumphant, happy, blest he who her shade gains.
She'd made the pool a casket for her frame fair,
And all about that casket spread her dark hair.
Her hand did yonder curling serpents back throw—[12]
The dawn 'tis, and thereof we never tired grow.[13]
He saw the water round about her ear play;
In rings upon her shoulders her dark locks lay.
When yon heart-winning moon before the King beamed,
The King became the sun—in him Love's fire gleamed.
The tears e'en like to water from his eyes rolled;—
Was't strange, when did a Watery Sign the Moon hold?[14]
No power was left him, neither sport nor pleasure;
He bit his finger, wildered beyond measure.[15]
Unconscious of his gaze, the jasmine-breasted,—
The hyacinths o'er the narcissi rested.[16]
When shown her day-face, from that musky cloud bare[17]
Her eyes oped Shirin and beheld the King there.

Within that fountain, through dismay and shamed fright,
She trembled as on water doth the moonlight.
Than this no other refuge could yon moon find
That she should round about her her own locks bind.
The moon yet beameth through the hair, the dark night,[18]
With tresses how could be concealed the sun bright?
To hide her from him, round her she her hair flung,
And thus as veil her night before her day hung.

II

From the Same

Gunul bagladi chun Shirina Ferhad

When Ferhad bound to fair Shírín his heart's core,
From out his breast Love many a bitter wail tore.
On tablet of his life graved, shown was Shírín;
Of all else emptied, filled alone with Shírín.
As loathed he the companionship of mankind,
In wild beasts 'midst the hills did he his friends find.
His guide was Pain; his boon-companion, Grief's throe;
His comrade, Sorrow, and his closest friend, Woe.
Thus wand'ring on, he knew not day from dark night;
For many days he onward strayed in sad plight.
Although before his face a wall of stone rise,
Until he strikes against it, blind his two eyes.
Though yearning for his love he from the world fled;
From out his soul into his body Death sped.
Because he knew that when the earthly frame goes,
Eternal, Everlasting Being love shows,
He fervent longed to be from fleshly bonds free,
That then his life in very truth might Life see.
In sooth, till dies the body, Life is ne'er found,
Nor with the love of life the Loved One e'er found.[19]

YAZIJI-OGLU

853 [1449]

From the Muhammediyya [20]

The Creation of Paradise [21]

Gel beri ey talib-i Haqq isterisen ibtihaj

Hither come, O seeker after Truth!
if joy thou wouldest share,
Enter on the Mystic Pathway,
follow it, then joy thou'lt share.[22]
Hearken now what God (exalted high His name!)
from nought hath formed.
Eden's bower He hath created; Light,
its lamp, he did prepare;
Loftiest its sites, and best and
fairest are its blest abodes;
Midst of each a hall of pearls—
not ivory nor teak-wood rare.
Each pavilion He from seventy ruddy
rubies raised aloft,—
Dwellings these in which the dwellers sit
secure from fear or care.
Round within each courtyard seventy splendid
houses He hath ranged,
Formed of emeralds green, houses these
no fault of form that bear.
There, within each house, are seventy
pearl and gem-encrusted thrones;
He upon each throne hath stretched out
seventy couches broidered fair;
Sits on every couch a maiden of the
bourne of loveliness:

Moons their foreheads, days their faces, each
a jeweled crown doth wear;
Wine their rubies,[23] soft their eyes, their
eyebrows troublous, causing woe:
All-enchanting, Paradise pays tribute
to their witching air.
Sudden did they see the faces of those
damsels dark of eye,
Blinded sun and moon were, and Life's Stream
grew bitter then and there.
Thou wouldst deem that each was formed of
rubies, corals, and of pearls;
Question there is none, for God thus in
the Qur'*a*n doth declare.[24]
Tables seventy, fraught with bounties,
He in every house hath placed,
And on every tray hath spread out seventy
sorts of varied fare.

* * * * * * *

All these glories, all these honors,
all these blessings of delight,
All these wondrous mercies surely for
his sake He did prepare:
Through His love unto Muhammed,
He the universe hath framed;[25]
Happy, for his sake, the naked
and the hungry enter there.
O Thou Perfectness of Potence!
O Thou God of Awful Might!
O Thou Majesty of Glory!
O Thou King of Perfect Right!

Since He Eden's Heaven created,
all is there complete and whole,
So that nought is lacking; nothing
He created needs repair.
Yonder, for His righteous servants,
things so fair hath He devised,
That no eye hath e'er beheld them;
ope thy soul's eye, on them stare.

Never have His servants heard them,
neither can their hearts conceive;
Reach unto their comprehension
shall this understanding ne'er.[26]
There that God a station lofty,
of the loftiest, hath reared,
That unclouded station He the
name Vesíla caused to bear,
That to His Belovèd yonder station,
a dear home may be,[27]
Thence ordained is Heaven's order
free from every grief and care.
In its courtyard's riven center,
planted He the Tuba-Tree;
That a tree which hangeth downward,
high aloft its roots are there:
Thus its radiance all the Heavens
lighteth up from end to end,
Flooding every tent and palace,
every lane and every square.[28]
Such a tree the Tuba, that that Gracious One
hath in its sap
Hidden whatso'er there be of gifts and
presents good and fair;
Forth therefrom crowns, thrones, and jewels,
yea, and steeds and coursers come,
Golden leaves and clearest crystals,
wines most pure beyond compare.
For his sake there into being hath He
called the Tuba-Tree,
That from Ebu-Qasim's hand might
everyone receive his share.[29]

*   *   *   *   *   *   *

SULTAN MURAD II

855 [1451]

RUBA'I

Saqi, gutur, gutur yene dunki sherabimi

CUP-BEARER, bring, bring here again my
yestereven's wine; [30]
My harp and rebeck bring, them bid
address this heart of mine:
Whilst still I live, 'tis meet that I should mirth
and glee enjoy;
The day shall come when none may e'en my
resting-place divine.

‘AVNI

(SULTAN MUHAMMED II)

886 [1481]

I

Gazel

Zulfuna bad-i saba erdikja janler depreshir

Souls are fluttered when the morning breezes
through thy tresses stray;
Waving cypresses are wildered when thy
motions they survey.[32]
Since with witchcraft thou hast whetted
keen the lancet of thy glance,
All my veins are bleeding inward through
my longing and dismay.
« Why across thy cheek disordered float thy
tresses?» asked I her.
« It is Rum-Eyli; there high-starred heroes
gallop,» did she say.[33]
Thought I, though I spake not: « In thy quarter,
through thy tint and scent,[34]
Wretched and head-giddy, wand'ring, those who
hope not for stray.»
« Whence the anger in thy glances, O sweet love? »
I said; then she:
« Silence! surely if I shed blood, I the
ensigns should display.»
Even as thou sighest, ‘Avni, shower thine
eyes tears fast as rain,
Like as follow hard the thunder-roll the
floods in dread array.[35]

II

Fragment of Gazel

Jigerim paraladi khanjer-i jevr u sitemin

Torn and pierced my heart has been by thy scorn
and tyranny's blade;
Rent by the scissors of grief for thee is the robe
that my patience arrayed.
Like the mihrab of the Ka'ba, as shrine where
in worship to turn,[36]
Thy ward would an angel take, if thy foot-print
there he surveyed.
They are pearls, O mine eye! thou sheddest
her day-bright face before;
Not a tear is left — *these* all are dried by the beams
by her cheek displayed.

III

Gazel

Imtisal-i Jahidu' fi-'llah *olup dur niyyetim*

To obey *Fight hard for Allah*[37] is my aim
and my desire;
'Tis but zeal for Faith, for Islam,
that my ardor doth inspire.
Through the grace of Allah, and th' assistance
of the Band Unseen,[38]
Is my earnest hope the Infidels to crush
with ruin dire.
On the Saints[39] and on the Prophets surely
doth my trust repose;
Through the love of God, to triumph and to
conquest I aspire.
What if I with soul and gold strive here
to wage the Holy War?
Praise is God's! ten thousand sighs for battle
in my breast suspire.
O Muhammed! through the chosen Ahmed
Mukhtar's glorious aid,[40]
Hope I that my might may triumph over
Islam's foes acquire!

‘ADENÎ

(THE GRAND VEZÎR MAHMÛD PASHA)

879 [1474]

I

Gazel

Shad olmaq isteyen gam ila mubtela gerek

Who pleasure seeks must oftentimes experience
  sad pain, in sooth;
He must a beggar be who doth desire to
  win domain, in sooth.
Whene'er I sigh, up rise my tears, they, boiling,
  fast o'erflow my eyes;
Winds surely must full fiercely blow, with waves
  to fill the main, in sooth.
My heart's domain now thought of thee, now
  grief for thee, alternate rule;
This realm to wreck and waste to lay those two
  sublime Kings strain, in sooth.
Spite zeal and prayers, Truth sure is found within
  the cup that's filled with wine;
So acts of rakes are free from all hypocrisy's
  foul stain, in sooth.[41]
O ‘Adenî, rub thou thy face low 'midst the dust
  that lines her path;
For eyes with blood filled stand in need of *tutya*,
  health to gain, in sooth.[42]

II

Fragment of Gazel

Gurdugumja 'anberin zulfun rukh-i dildarda

When I saw my love's hair, ambergris-hued,
o'er her visage shake,[43]
«Strange,» I thought, «a moon, musk-shedding,
'midst the flowers its bed should make!»[44]
How thy locks, moon-face, are fallen o'er thy
cheek in many a curl!
As in day he lies reposing, so in strength
doth gain the snake.[45]
From thy cheek the rose and tulip tint and
scent have stol'n indeed;
Therefore through the *bazar* round they bear them,
bounden to the stake.[46]

*A*FIT*A*B*I*

880 [1475 *ca.*]

Gazel

Yene dish yarasi var sib-i zenakhdaninda

Again, then, doth this apple, thy chin, tooth-marks wear![47]
Again they've eaten peaches in thine orchard fair![48]
If strange hands have not reached thee, O rosebud-lipped one,
Doth thy rose-garden's pathway a foot-step print bear!
I cannot reach thee before rivals all throng thee round:
Less for true lover than vile dog dost thou care.
Witness that thou with my rivals the cup drain'dst last night,
Bears the sleepless and worn look thy languid eyes wear.
With whom didst thou last even carouse, that this day
Morn's zephyr about thee did so much news declare?
Beholding thy lips hurt,[49] *Afitabi* hath said:
« Again, then, doth this apple, thy chin, tooth-marks wear!»

ZEYNEB

886 [1481 *ca.*]

Gazel

Keshf et niqabini, yeri guku munevver et

Cast off thy veil, and heaven and earth in
dazzling light array!
As radiant Paradise, this poor demented
world display!
Move thou thy lips, make play the ripples light
of Kevser's pool! [50]
Let loose thy scented locks, and odors sweet
through earth convey!
A musky warrant by thy down was traced,
and zephyr charged :—[51]
"Speed, with this scent subdue the realms
of China and Cathay!"[52]
O heart! should not thy portion be the Water
bright of Life,
A thousand times mayst thou pursue Isken-
der's darksome way.[53]
O Zeyneb, woman's love of earthly show
leave thou behind;
Go manly forth, with single heart, forsake
adornment gay! [54]

THE MORNING BATH

Photogravure after the painting by Gérome.

PRINCE JEM

901 [1495]

I

Gazel

Dil helak eyler guzun, khancher cheker jan usiuna

Ah! thine eyes lay waste the heart, they 'gainst the
soul bare daggers dread;
See how sanguinary gleam they — blood aye upon
blood they shed.
Come, the picture of thy down bear unto this
my scorchèd breast,—
It is customary fresh greens over the broiled
flesh to spread.[55]
Said I: « O Life! since thy lip is life,
to me vouchsafe a kiss.»
Smiling rose-like, « Surely, surely, by my life,»
she answerèd.
As I weep sore, of my stainèd eyebrow
and my tears of blood,
« 'Tis the rainbow o'er the shower stretched,»
were by all beholders said.
Whilst within my heart thine eye's shaft,
send not to my breast despair;
Idol mine! guest after guest must not to one
same house be led.
Through its grieving for thy hyacinthine down,
thus feeble grown
Is the basil, that the gardeners nightly o'er
it water shed.[56]
Quoth I: « O Life! do not shun Jem,
he a pilgrim here hath come;»
« Though a pilgrim, yet his life doth on a
child's face hang,» she said.

II

Fragment

Tashiarl aukunup yurur ab-i rewani gur

Lo! THERE the torrent, dashing 'gainst the rocks, doth wildly roll;
The whole wide realm of Space and Being ruth hath on my soul.[57]
Through bitterness of grief and woe the morn hath rent its robe;
See! O in dawning's place, the sky weeps blood, without control!
Tears shedding, o'er the mountain-tops the clouds of heaven pass;
Hear, deep the bursting thunder sobs and moans through stress of dole.

AHMED PASHA

(GRAND VEZIR)

902 [1496]

GAZEL

Jana qalmaz buse'-i la'l-i leb-i yar isteyen

HE WHO longs for ruby lip's kiss may not
    calm of soul remain;
He his head must yield who hopes the
    dusky locks' sweet scent to gain.
Still in heart abides not longing's flame when
    one her ward beholds;
Him who seeks her face contents not even
    Heaven's flowery plain.
Yonder sugar-lip's surrounded by her cheek's
    down; — where art thou,
O thou seeker of the rose's company without
    thorn's pain?
Wouldest thou delight? Then plunge thou
    deep beneath Love's ocean surge;
He who would for regal pearls dive, surely
    should know well the main.[58]
Though the loved one mocks at Ahmed's faults
    and failings, what of that?
He who seeks a friend that's blameless must
    without a friend remain.

NEJATI

914 [1508]

I

From his Winter Qasida[59]

Oldu chunkim melakh berf hewaden nazil

LOCUST-LIKE down from the sky
the snowflakes wing their way;
From the green-plumaged bird, Delight,
O heart! hope not for lay.
Like drunken camels, spatter now the clouds
earth's winding-sheet;
Laded the caravan of mirth and glee,
and passed away.
With lighted lamps in daytime seek
the people for the sun;
Yet scarce, with trouble, a dim,
fitful spark discover they.

* * * * *

The Moon in Sign of Bounteousness!
the Shade of Allah's grace!
The King, star-armied! he in aspect fair
as Hermes' ray—
The Khan Muhammed! at the portal
of whose sphere of might
To wait as servants would Darius and
Key-Khusrev pray![60]
E'en should the sun till the Last Day
it measure with gold beam,
Nor shore nor depth could e'er it
find to th' ocean of his sway!

II

From his Spring Qasida

Khandan eder jihani yene fasl-i nev-bahar

The early springtide now hath made earth
smiling bright again,
E'en as doth union with his mistress
soothe the lover's pain.
They say: « 'Tis now the goblet's turn,
the time of mirth 'tis now »;
Beware that to the winds thou castest not
this hour in vain.
Theriaca within their ruby pots
the tulips lay:[61]
See in the mead the running streamlet's
glistening, snake-like train.
Onwards, beneath some cypress-tree's
loved foot its face to rub,
With turn and turn, and singing sweet,
the brook goes through the plain.
Lord! may this happy union of
felicity and earth,
Like turn of sun of Love, or Jesu's life,
standfast remain![62]
May glee and mirth, e'en as desired,
continuous abide,
Like to a mighty Key-Khusrev's, or Jemshid's,
glorious reign![63]

* * * * *

Sultan Muhammed! Murad's son!
the Pride of Princes all;
He, the Darius, who to all earth's Kings
doth crowns ordain!
Monarch of stars! whose flag's the sun,
whose stirrup is the moon!
Prince dread as Doom, and strong as Fate,
and bounteous as main!

III

From His Qasida on the Accession of Sultan Bayezid II.

Bir dun ki qilmishidi jemalina afitab

One eve, when had the Sun before her
radiant beauty bright
Let down the veil of ambergris,
the musky locks of night;
(Off had the royal hawk, the Sun,
flown from the Orient's hand,
And lighted in the West; flocked after
him the crows in flight;)
To catch the gloomy raven, Night, the fowler
skilled, the Sphere,
Had shaped the new-moon like the claw of
eagle, sharp to smite;
In pity at the doleful sight of sunset's
crimson blood,
Its veil across the Heaven's eye had drawn
the dusky Night.

* * * * *

Sultan of Rome![64] Khusrev of the
Horizons![65] Bayezid!
King of the Epoch! Sovereign!
and Centre of all Right!
The tablet of his heart doth all th' affairs
of earth disclose;
And eloquent as page of book the words
he doth indite.
O Shah! I'm he who, 'midst th' assembly
where thy praise is sung,
Will, rebeck-like, a thousand notes upon
one cord recite.[66]
'Tis meet perfection through thy name to my
poor words should come,
As to rosewater perfume sweet is brought
by sunbeam's light.

IV

Gazel

Haqqa bu dur ki sahn-i jihan kim qonaq digil

Truth this: a lasting home hath yielded
ne'er earth's spreading plain:
Scarce e'en an inn where may the caravan
for rest remain.
Though every leaf of every tree is verily
a book,
For those who understanding lack doth earth
no leaf contain.
E'en though the Loved One be from thee
as far as East from West,
« Bagdad to lovers is not far," O heart,
then strive and strain.
One moment opened were her ebriate,
strife-causing eyne,
By us as scimitars, not merely daggers,
were they ta'en.
Yearneth Nejati for the court of
thy fair Paradise,
Though this a wish which he whilst here
on earth can ne'er attain.

V

RUBA'IS [66]

Ey destmal gunderin ol nigara, chiq

O HANDKERCHIEF! I send thee — off to
yonder maid of grace;
Around thee I my eyelashes will make
the fringe of lace;
I will the black point of my eye rub up
to paint therewith; [67]
To yon coquettish beauty go — go look thou
in her face.

O Handkerchief! the loved one's hand take,
kiss her lip so sweet,
Her chin, which mocks at apple and at orange,
kissing greet;
If sudden any dust should light upon
her blessèd heart,
Fall down before her, kiss her sandal's sole,
beneath her feet.

A sample of my tears of blood thou,
Handkerchief, wilt show,
Through these within a moment would a
thousand crimson grow;
Thou'lt be in company with her,
while I am sad with grief;
To me no longer life may be,
if things continue so.

MES*I*H*I*

918 [1512]

I

From His Spring Qas*i*da[68]

Kh,ab-i gafletden uyanmaga 'uyun-i ezhar

Up from indolent sleep the eyes of the
flowers to awake,
Over their faces each dawn the cloudlets
of spring water shake.
Denizens all of the mead now with new
life are so filled,
That were its foot not secured, into dancing
the cypress would break.
Roses' fair cheeks to describe, all of their
beauty to tell,
Lines on the clear river's page rain-drops and
light ripples make.
Silvery rings, thou would'st say, they hung
in the bright water's ear,
When the fresh rain-drops of spring fall on the
stretch of the lake.
Since the ring-dove, who aloft sits on the
cypress, its praise
Sings, were it strange if he be sad and
love-sick for its sake?

* * * * *

Prince of the Climate of Speech,
noble Nish*a*nji Pasha,
To the mark of whose kindness the shaft
of thought can its way never make.
When poets into their hands the chaplet,
thy verses, have ta'en,
"*I pardon implore of the Lord*" for
litany ever they take.

II

Murebba'[69]

Dinle bulbul qissasin kim geldi eyyam-i bahar

Hark the bulbul's lay so joyous: « Now have
come the days of spring.»
Merry shows and crowds on every mead they spread,
a maze of spring;[70]
There the almond-tree its silvern blossoms scatters,
sprays of spring:
Drink, be gay, for soon will vanish, biding not,
the days of spring.

Once again with varied flow'rets decked themselves
have mead and plain;
Tents for pleasure have the blossoms raised in
every rosy lane.
Who can tell, when spring hath ended, who
and what may whole remain?
Drink, be gay, for soon will vanish, biding not,
the days of spring.

All the alleys of the parterre filled with
Ahmed's Light appear,[71]
Verdant herbs his Comrades, tulips like his
Family bright appear;
O ye People of Muhammed! times
now of delight appear:
Drink, be gay, for soon will vanish,
biding not, the days of spring.

Sparkling dew-drops stud the lily's leaf like
sabre broad and keen;
Bent on merry gipsy-party, crowd they
all the flow'ry green;[72]
List to me, if thou desirest, these beholding,
joy to glean:
Drink, be gay, for soon will vanish, biding not,
the days of spring.

Rose and tulip, like to lovely maidens' cheeks,
all beauteous show,
Whilst the dew-drops, like the jewels in their ears,
resplendent glow;
Do not think, thyself beguiling, things will
aye continue so:
Drink, be gay, for soon will vanish, biding not,
the days of spring.

Rose, anemone, and tulip — these, the garden's
fairest flowers—
'Midst the parterre is their blood shed 'neath the
lightning-darts and showers.[73]
Art thou wise? — then with thy comrades dear
enjoy the fleeting hours:
Drink, be gay, for soon will vanish, biding not
the days of spring.

Past the moments when with sickness were the
ailing herbs opprest,
When the garden's care, the rose-bud, hid its sad
head in its breast;[74]
Come is now the time when hill and rock with
tulips dense are drest:
Drink, be gay, for soon will vanish, biding not,
the days of spring.

Whilst each dawn the clouds are shedding
jewels o'er the rosy land,
And the breath of morning's zephyr fraught with
Tatar musk is bland;
Whilst the world's fair time is present, do not
thou unheeding stand:
Drink, be gay, for soon will vanish, biding not,
the days of spring.

With the fragrance of the garden, so
imbued the musky air,
Every dew-drop, ere it reaches earth,
is turned to attar rare;

O'er the parterre spread the incense-clouds
a canopy right fair;
Drink, be gay, for soon will vanish, biding not,
the days of spring.

Whatsoe'er the garden boasted smote the
black autumnal blast;
But, to each one justice bringing, back hath come
Earth's King at last;
In his reign joyed the cup-bearer, round the
call for wine is past:
Drink, be gay, for soon will vanish, biding not,
the days of spring.

Ah! I fondly hope, Mesíhí, fame may to
these quatrains cling;
May the worthy these four-eyebrowed beauties
oft to mem'ry bring;—[75]
Stray amongst the rosy faces, Bulbul,
who so sweet dost sing;[76]
Drink, be gay, for soon will vanish, biding not,
the days of spring.

HARIMI

(PRINCE QORQUD)

918 [1512]

Fragment

Taj u qabayi terk edip 'uryan olayin bir zemain

Both crown and robe forsake shall I, I'll roam
by these unprest, a while;
'Midst foreign lands, far off from here, I'll dwell a
wayworn guest, a while.
O minstrel fair, both harp and lute's sweet
music hushed must now remain;
Woe's feast is spread, ah! there the flute:—my
sighs by grief opprest, a while.
Sometimes I'll fall, sometimes I'll rise, sometimes
I'll laugh, sometimes I'll weep,
Blood drinking now,[77] woe tasting then,
distracted sore I'll rest a while.

MIHRÍ

920 [1514 *ca*]

I

Gazel

Kh,abden achdim guzum na-gah qaldirdim seri

Once from sleep I oped my eyes, I raised my head, when full in sight
There before me stood a moon-faced beauty, lovely, shining, bright.
Thought I: « In th' ascendant's now my star, or I my fate have reached,
For within my chamber sure is risen Jupiter this night.» [78]
Radiance from his beauty streaming saw I, though to outward view
(Whilst himself a Muslim) he in garb of infidel is dight.
Though I oped my eyes or closed them, still the form was ever there;
Thus I fancied to myself: « A fairy this or angel bright? »
Till the Resurrection ne'er shall Mihrí gain the Stream of Life;
Yet in Night's deep gloom Iskender gleamed before her wond'ring sight.[79]

II

Gazel

Ben umardim ki bana yar-i wefa-dar olasin

Faithful and kind a friend I hoped that
thou wouldst prove to me;
Who would have thought so cruel and fierce a
tyrant in thee to see?
Thou who the newly-oped rose art of the
Garden of Paradise,
That every thorn and thistle thou lov'st — how
can it fitting be?
I curse thee not, but of God Most High,
Our Lord, I make this prayer —
That thou may'st love a pitiless one in tyranny
like to thee.
In such a plight am I now, alack! that the
curser saith to his foe:
"Be thy fortune dark and thy portion black,
even as those of Mihri!"

SELIMI

(SULTAN SELIM I.)

926 [1520]

GAZEL[80]

Leshker ez takht-i Istanbol su-yi Iran takhtem

FROM Istambol's throne a mighty host
to Iran guided I;[81]
Sunken deep in blood of shame I made
the Golden Heads to lie.[82]
Glad the Slave, my resolution, lord of
Egypt's realm became:[83]
Thus I raised my royal banner e'en as the
Nine Heavens high.[84]
From the kingdom fair of 'Iraq to Hijaz
these tidings sped,[85]
When I played the harp of Heavenly Aid
at feast of victory.
Through my sabre Transoxania drowned
was in a sea of blood;
Emptied I of kuhl of Isfahan the
adversary's eye.[86]
Flowed adown a River *Amu*[87] from each
foeman's every hair—
Rolled the sweat of terror's fever—if
I happed him to espy.
Bishop-mated was the King of India by
my Queenly troops,[88]
When I played the Chess of empire
on the Board of sov'reignty.
O Selimi, in thy name was struck the
coinage of the world,
When in crucible of Love Divine,
like gold, that melted I.[89]

MUHIBBÍ

(SULTAN SULEYMÁN I.)

974 [1566]

I

Gazel

Senin derdin bana dermana benzer

My pain for thee balm in my sight resembles;
Thy face's beam the clear moonlight resembles.
Thy black hair spread across thy cheeks, the roses,
O Liege, the garden's basil quite resembles.
Beside thy lip oped wide its mouth, the rosebud;
For shame it blushed, it blood outright resembles.
Thy mouth, a casket fair of pearls and rubies,
Thy teeth, pearls, thy lip coral bright resembles:
Their diver I, each morning and each even;
My weeping, Liege, the ocean's might resembles.
Lest he seduce thee, this my dread and terror,
That rival who Iblís in spite resembles.[90]
Around the taper bright, thy cheek, Muhibbí
Turns, and the moth in his sad plight resembles.[91]

II

Gazel

Ikhtiyar-i jaqr eden dergah u eywan istemez

He who poverty electeth, hall and fane
desireth not;
Than the food of woe aught other bread
to gain desireth not.
He who, king-like, on the throne of blest
contentment sits aloft,
O'er the Seven Climes as Sultan high to
reign desireth not.
He, who in his bosom strikes his nails,
and opes the wound afresh,
On the garden looks not, sight of rosy lane
desireth not.[92]
He, who is of Love's true subjects,
bideth in the fair one's ward,
Wand'ring there distracted, mountain lone or
plain desireth not.
O Muhibbî, he who drinketh from the
Loved One's hand a glass,
E'en from Khizar's hand Life's Water bright
to drain desireth not.[93]

FIGANI

933 [1526]

GAZEL

(On a Damaskeened Sword)

Hiddet wuruna tigi nigarin zebane dir

A FLAME that Picture's[93] sabre in its
deadliness of blow;
Like sparks upon its face the marks of
damaskeening glow.
Is't strange that by thy side the bird, my heart,
should rest secure?
Thy sabre damaskeened to it doth grain
and water show!
The watered scimitar within thy grasp
an ocean is,
In which the lines and marks are scattered
pearls unique, I trow.
Thy sword a sky, its stars the marks of
damaskeening shine,
My heart's blood there upon its face like break
of dawn doth glow.
What though I call that Picture's brand a
branch of Judas-tree?[94]
For there the damask marks and grains like
flowers and blossoms blow.
Figani's verse on yonder King of Beauty's
empire's sword
Doth like unto a running stream of
limpid water flow.

LAMI'I

938 [1531]

I

From his Munazarat-i Shita u Bahar

On Autumn

Gel ey shuride dil sevda demi dir

O sad heart, come, distraction's hour is now high,
The air's cool, 'midst the fields to sit the time nigh.
The Sun hath to the Balance, Joseph-like past,
The year's Zuleykha hath her gold hoard wide cast. [95]
By winds bronzed, like the sun, the quince's face glows;
Its Pleiads-clusters, hanging forth, the vine shows.
In saffron flow'rets have the meads themselves dight;
The trees, all scorched, to gold have turned, and shine bright.
The gilded leaves in showers falling to earth gleam;
With gold-fish [96] filled doth glisten brightly each stream.
Ablaze each tree, and blent are all in one glare,
And therefore charged with glistening fire the still air.
Amidst the yellow foliage perched the black crows—
As tulip, saffron-hued, that spotted cup shows.
A yellow-plumaged bird, now every tree stands,
Which shakes itself, and feathers sheds on all hands.
Each vine-leaf paints its face, bride-like, with gold ink; [97]
The brook doth silver anklets round the vine link. [98]
The plane-tree hath its hands, [99] with hinna, red dyed, [100]
And stands there of the parterre's court the fair bride.
The erst green tree now like the starry sky shows,
And hurling meteors at the fiend, Earth, stones throws. [101]

II

From the Same

On Spring

Zevq u sevq u haletinden bu demin

From the pleasure, joy, and rapture of this hour,
In its frame to hold its soul earth scarce hath power.
Rent its collar, like the dawning, hath the rose;
From its heart the nightingale sighs forth its woes.
Dance the juniper and cypress like the sphere;
Filled with melody through joy all lands appear.
Gently sing the running brooks in murmurs soft;
While the birds with tuneful voices soar aloft.
Play the green and tender branches with delight,
And they shed with one accord gold, silver, bright.[102]
Like to couriers fleet, the zephyrs speed away,
Resting ne'er a moment either night or day.
In that raid the rosebud filled with gold its hoard,
And the tulip with fresh musk its casket stored.
There the moon a purse of silver coin did seize;
Filled with ambergris its skirt the morning breeze;
Won the sun a golden disc of ruby dye,
And with glistening pearls its pocket filled the sky:
Those who poor were fruit and foliage attained;
All the people of the land some trophy gained.

III

From the Same

Gel ey dil nale qil bulbuller ila

O HEART, come, wail, as nightingale thy woes show;
'Tis Pleasure's moment this, come, then, as rose blow.
In burning notes make thou thy tuneful song rise;
These iron hearts soft render with thy sad sighs.
Within thy soul place not, like tulip, dark brand;[61]
When opportunity doth come, then firm stand.
From earth take justice ere yet are these times left,
And ere yet from the soul's harp is breath's song reft.
They call thee — view the joys that sense would yield thee;
But, ere thou canst say "Hie!" the bird is flown, see.
Give ear, rose-like, because in truth the night-bird
From break of dawn its bitter wail hath made heard.
Their chorus all around the gleeful birds raise;
The streamlets sing, the nightingale the flute plays.
The jasmines with their fresh leaves tambourines ply;
The streams, hard prest, raise up their glistening foam high
Of junipers and cypresses two ranks 'tween,
The zephyr sports and dances o'er the flower-green.
The streamlets 'midst the vineyard hide-and-seek play
The flowerets with, among the verdant leaves gay.
Away the morning's breeze the Jasmine's crown tears,
As pearls most costly scatters it the plucked hairs.
The leader of the play's the breeze of swift pace;
Like children, each the other all the flowers chase.
With green leaves drest, the trees each other's hands take;
The flowers and nightingales each other's robes shake.
Like pigeon, there, before the gale that soft blows,
Doth turn in many a somersault the young rose.[103]
As blaze up with gay flowerets all the red plains,
The wind each passes, and the vineyard next gains.
The clouds, pearl-raining, from the meteors sparks seize;
And flowers are all around strewn by the dawn-breeze.

The waters, eddying, in circles bright play,
Like shining swords, the green leaves toss about they.[104]
With bated breath the Judas-trees there stand by;
And each for other running brook and breeze sigh.
The gales tig with the basil play in high glee;
To dance with cypress gives its hand the plane-tree.[9]
The soft winds have adorned the wanton bough fair,
The leader of the frolics[105] 'midst the parterre,
The narcisse toward the almond-tree its glance throws;
With vineyard-love the pink upbraids the dog-rose.
The water's mirror clear doth as the Sphere gleam;
Its stars, the flowers reflected, fair and bright beam.
The meads are skies; their stars, the drops of dew, glow;
The jasmine is the moon; the stream, the halo.
In short, each spot as Resurrection-plain seems;
None who beholds of everlasting pain dreams.
Those who it view, and ponder well with thought's eye,
Is't strange, if they be mazed and wildered thereby?
Up! breeze-like, Lami'i, thy hermitage leave!
The roses' days in sooth no time for fasts give!

KEMAL PASHA-ZADA

941 [1534]

From His Elegy on Sultan Selím I.[106]

'Azmda nev-juwan, hazmda pír

He, an old man in prudence, a youth in might;
His sword aye triumphant, his word ever right.
Like Asef in wisdom, the pride of his host;[107]
He needed no vezír, no mushír in fight.
His hand was a sabre; a dagger, his tongue;
His finger, an arrow; his arm, a spear bright.
In shortest of time many high deeds he wrought;
Encircle the world did the shade of his might.
The Sun of his Day, but the sun at day's close,
Throwing long shadow, but brief while in sight.[108]
Of throne and of diadem sovereigns boast,
But boasted of him throne and diadem bright.
Delight would his heart in that festival find,
Whither doth sabre's and fife's clang invite.
In feats with the sword, eke at feasts at the board,[109]
On his peer ne'er alight did the aged Sphere's sight;
Sped he to the board's feast — a Sun beaming bright!
Swept he to the sword's field — a Lion of fight!
Whenever the war-cries: Seize! Hold! echo far,
The sword, weeping blood, shall that Lion's fame cite.
Alas! Sultan Selím! alas! woe is me!
Let both Pen and Sabre in tears mourn for thee!

GAZALI

941 [1534]

I

Qit'a

From his Elegy on Iskender Chelebi

Mir Iskender i'tibari gurup

High honored once was the noble Iskender;
O heart, from his destiny warning obtain.
Ah! do thou see what at length hath befall'n him!
What all this glory and panoply gain!
Drinking the poison of doom, ne'er a remnant
Of sweetness's taste in his mouth did remain.
Retrograde, sank down his star, erst ascendant,
From perfect conjunction, alas, did it wane.[111]
Dust on the face of his honor aye stainless
Strewn hath the blast of betrayal profane.[112]
The Lofty Decree for his high exaltation
Did Equity's Court, all unlooked for, ordain;
Forthwith to the Regions of Eden they bore him,
They raised him from earth's abject baseness and stain.
Circling and soaring,[113] he went on his journey,
From the land of his exile to Home back again.
Neck-bounden he stood as a slave at the palace,
Freed is he now from affliction's hard chain.
Joyous he flew on his journey to Heaven,
Rescued for ever from earth gross and vain.
In life or in death from him never, ay, never
Was honor most lofty, most glorious ta'en!

II

Fragment

Erdi khizani 'umrumun veh ki dakhi qarari yoq

Come is the autumn of my life, alas, it thus
should pass away!
I have not reached the dawn of joy, to sorrow's
night there is no day.
Time after time the image of her cheek falls on
my tear-filled eye;
Ah! no pretension to esteem can shadows in the
water lay!
Oh! whither will these winds of Fate impel
the frail barque of the heart?
Nor bound nor shore confining girds Time's
dreary ocean of dismay! [114]

ISHAQ CHELEBI

944 [1537]

GAZEL

Gamdan uldum, ey meh-i na-mihrbanim, qanda sen?

DEAD am I of grief, my Moon no love who shows,
ah! where art thou?
Reach the skies, the plaints and wails born of
my woes, ah! where art thou?
Save within thy rosy bower rests not the
nightingale, the heart;
Figure fair as waving cypress, face as rose, ah!
where art thou?
Through thy lips the rose drops sugar at the
feast of heart and soul;
Where, my Parrot whose sweet voice doth love
disclose, ah! where art thou? 115
Though with longing dead were Ishaq, live should he,
did once she say:
"O my poor one, wildered, weary, torn by woes, ah!
where art thou?"

ZATI

953 [1546]

Gazel

On the Prophet Muhammed

Qametin ey bustan-i La-Mekan Pirayesi!

That thy form, O Beauty of His orchard who
doth all pervade!
Is a cypress, wrought of light, that casteth on
earth's face no shade.[116]
Though the gazers on the loveliness of Joseph cut
their hands,[117]
Cleft in twain the fair moon's palm, when in thy
day-bright face surveyed.[118]
To the mart of the Hereafter, when a man hath passed,
he gains
Through the money bright, thy love, which is of
joy the stock-in-trade.
This my hope, that yonder Cypress in the bowers
of Paradise
Shelter *Zati*, and all true believers, 'neath
his blissful shade.

LUTF*I*

(GRAND VEZ*I*R)

957 [1550]

GAZEL

Firqatindan chiqdi jan, ey verd-i khandanim, meded!

THROUGH thine absence, smiling Rosebud,
forth my soul doth go, alas!
Earth is flooded by the tears down from my
eyes that flow, alas!
Should'st thou ask about my days, without thee
they're black as thy hair;
'Midst of darkness, O my Stream of Life,
I'm lying low, alas![53]
With the stones of slander stone me all the
cruel rival throng;
O my Liege, my Queen, 'tis time now mercy
thou should'st show, alas!
When I die through longing for thee, and thou
passest o'er my breast,
From my dust thou'lt hear full many bitter
sighs of woe, alas!
In his loved one's cause will Lutf*i* surely die
the martyr's death;
Let her brigand eyes from mulct for blood
of mine free go, alas!

MUKHLISÍ

(PRINCE MUSTAFA)

960 [1552]

Gazel

Rif'at istersen eger mihr-i jihan-ara gibi

If 'tis state thou seekest like the world-adorning sun's array,
Lowly e'en as water rub thy face in earth's dust every day.
Fair to see, but short enduring is this picture bright, the world;
'Tis a proverb: Fleeting like the realm of dreams is earth's display.
Through the needle of its eyelash never hath the heart's thread past;
Like unto the Lord Messiah bide I half-road on the way.[119]
Athlete of the Universe through self-reliance grows the Heart,
With the ball, the Sphere — Time, Fortune — like an apple doth it play.
Mukhlisí, thy frame was formed from but one drop,[120] yet, wonder great!
When thou verses sing'st, thy spirit like the ocean swells, they say.

KHIYALI

964 [1556]

GAZEL

Bir ebed milkina janim hem-jiwar etmek, nije?

ONE with Realms Eternal this my soul to make;
what wouldest say?
All Creation's empire's fancies to forsake;
what wouldest say?
Wearing to a hair my frame with bitter
sighs and moans, in love,
Nestling in the Fair One's tresses, rest to take;
what wouldest say ?
Yonder gold-faced birds within the
quick silver-resplendent deep; [121]
Launching forth the hawk, my striving,
these to take; what wouldest say?
Yonder Nine Smaragdine Bowls [122] of Heaven [84]
to quaff at one deep draught,
Yet from all ebriety's fumes free to break;
what wouldest say?
To an autumn leaf the Sphere hath turned
Khiyali's countenance;
To the Spring of Beauty, that a gift to make;
what wouldest say?

SHAHI

(PRINCE BAYEZID)

969 [1561]

Gazel[123]

Ben nije zayi' edem tul-i emella nefesi?

With longing fond and vain, why should I make
my soul to mourn?
One trace of love of earth holds not my
heart — all is forsworn.
There ready stands the caravan, to Death's dim
realms addrest,
E'en now the tinkling of its bells down on my ears
is borne.[124]
Come then, O bird, my soul, be still, disquiet
leave far off;
See, how this cage, the body, is with years
and suffering worn.
But yet, to weary, wasted, sin-stained Shahi,
what of fear?
Since Thou'rt the God of Love, the helping
Friend of those forlorn!

FUZULI

970 [1562]

I

Gazel

Saba, lutf etdin, ehl-i derda dermanden khaber verdin

O BREEZE, thou'rt kind, of balm to those whom pangs
affright, thou news hast brought,
To wounded frame of life, to life of life's delight thou
news hast brought.
Thou'st seen the mourning nightingale's despair in
sorrow's autumn drear,
Like springtide days, of smiling roseleaf fresh and bright,
thou news hast brought.
If I should say thy words are heaven-inspired, in truth,
blaspheme I not;
Of Faith, whilst unbelief doth earth hold fast and tight,
thou news hast brought.
They say the loved one comes to soothe the hearts of
all her lovers true;
If that the case, to yon fair maid of lovers' plight
thou news hast brought.
Of rebel demon thou hast cut the hope Suleyman's
throne to gain;
That in the sea secure doth lie his Ring of might,
thou news hast brought.[125]
Fuzuli, through the parting night, alas, how
dark my fortune grew!
Like zephyr of the dawn, of shining sun's fair light
thou news hast brought.

II

Gazel

Ey wujud-i kamilin esrar-i hikmet masdari

O thou Perfect Being, Source whence wisdom's
mysteries arise;
Things, the issue of Thine essence, show wherein
Thy nature lies.
Manifester of all wisdom, Thou are He whose
pen of might
Hath with rays of stars illumined yonder gleaming
page, the skies.
That a happy star, indeed, the essence clear of
whose bright self
Truly knoweth how the blessings from Thy
word that flow to prize.
But a jewel flawed am faulty I: alas,
for ever stands
Blank the page of my heart's journal from thought
of Thy writing wise.
In the journal of my actions Evil's lines are
black indeed;
When I think of Day of Gathering's terrors,
blood flows from my eyes.
Gathering of my tears will form a torrent on
the Reckoning Day,
If the pearls, my tears, rejecting, He but
view them to despise:
Pearls my tears are, O Fuzuli, from the ocean
deep of love;
But they're pearls these, oh! most surely,
that the Love of Allah buys!

III

Gazel

Nola reshk-i rukhsarinla bagri khublerin qan dir?

Is't strange if beauties' hearts turn blood through
envy of thy cheek most fair?[126]
For that which stone to ruby turns is but the
radiant sunlight's glare.[127]
Or strange is't if thine eyelash conquer all the
stony-hearted ones?
For meet an ebon shaft like that a barb of
adamant should bear!
Thy cheek's sun-love[128] hath on the hard, hard hearts
of fairy beauties fall'n,
And many a steely-eyed one hath received thy
bright reflection fair.[129]
The casket, thy sweet mouth, doth hold spell-bound
the *huri*-faced ones all;
The virtue of Suleym*a*n's Ring was that fays
thereto fealty sware.[130]
Is't strange if, seeing thee, they rub their faces
lowly midst the dust?
That down to Adam bowed the angel throng doth
the Qur'*a*n declare![131]
On many and many a heart of stone have fall'n the
pangs of love for thee!
A fire that lies in stone concealed is thy heart-burning
love's dread glare!
Within her ward, with garments rent, on all sides
rosy-cheeked ones stray;
Fuz*u*l*i*, through those radiant hues, that
quarter beams a garden fair.

IV

Gazel

Ruzgarim buldu devran-i felekden inqilab

From the turning of the Sphere my luck hath seen
reverse and woe;[114]
Blood I've drunk,[77] for from my banquet wine arose
and forth did go.
With the flame, my burning sighs, I've lit the
wand'ring wildered heart;
I'm a fire, doth not all that which turns about
me roasted glow?
With thy rubies wine contended—oh! how it hath
lost its wits!
Need 'tis yon ill-mannered wretch's company
that we forego.
Yonder Moon saw not my burning's flame upon
the parting day—
How can e'er the sun about the taper all
night burning know?[132]
Every eye that all around tears scatters,
thinking of thy shaft,
Is an oyster-shell that causeth rain-drops
into pearls to grow.[133]
Forms my sighing's smoke[134] a cloud that veils
the bright cheek of the moon;
Ah! that yon fair Moon will ne'er the veil
from off her beauty throw!
Ne'er hath ceased the rival e'en within her
ward to vex me sore;
How say they, Fuzuli: "There's in Paradise
nor grief nor woe?"[135]

V

MUSEDDES [136]

Dun saye saldi bashima bir serv-i ser-bulend

A STATELY Cypress yesterday her shade
threw o'er my head;
Her form was heart-ensnaring, heart-delighting
her light tread;
When speaking, sudden opened she her smiling
rubies red,
There a pistachio I beheld that drops of
candy shed.[137]
"This casket[130] can it be a mouth? Ah! deign!"
I said: said she:
"Nay, nay, 'tis balm to cure thy hidden smart;
aye, truly thine!"

Down o'er her crescents she had pressed the
turban she did wear,[138]
By which, from many broken hearts,
sighs raised she of despair;
She loosed her tresses — hid within the cloud
her moon so fair,[139]
And o'er her visage I beheld the curls of her
black hair.
"Those curling locks, say, are they then a chain?"
I said; said she:
"That round my cheek, a noose to take thy heart;
aye, truly thine!"

The taper bright, her cheek, illumined day's
lamp in the sky;
The rose's branch was bent before her figure,
cypress-high;
She, cypress-like, her foot set down upon
the fount, my eye,
But many a thorn did pierce her foot,
she suffered pain thereby.[140]

« What thorn unto the roseleaf-foot gives pain? »
I said; said she:
« The lash of thy wet eye doth it impart;
aye, truly thine! »

Promenading, to the garden did that jasmine-cheeked
one go;
With many a bright adornment in the early
springtide's glow;
The hyacinths their musky locks did o'er the
roses throw;[141]
That Picture[98] had tattooed her lovely feet
rose-red to show.[142]
« The tulip's hue whence doth the dog-rose
gain? »[143] I said; said she:
« From blood of thine shed 'neath my glance's dart;
aye, truly thine! »

To earth within her ward my tears in torrents
rolled apace;
The accents of her ruby lip my soul crazed
by their grace;
My heart was taken in the snare her musky
locks did trace,
That very moment when my eyes fell on
her curls and face.
« Doth Scorpio the bright Moon's House
contain? »[144] I said; said she:
« Fear! threatening this Conjunction dread,
thy part; aye, truly thine! »

Her hair with ambergris perfumed was waving o'er
her cheek,
On many grieving, passioned souls it cruel
woe did wreak;
Her graceful form and many charms my wildered
heart made weak;
The eye beheld her figure fair, then heart and
soul did seek.

« Ah! what bright thing this cypress of the plain? »
I said; said she:
« 'Tis that which thy fixed gaze beholds apart;
aye, truly thine! »

When their veil her tulip and dog-rose had let
down yesterday,[145]
The morning breeze tore off that screen which o'er
these flow'rets lay;
Came forth that Envy of the sun in garden
fair to stray,
Like lustrous pearls the dew-drops shone,
a bright and glistening spray.
« Pearls, say, are these, aye pearls from 'Aden's
main? »[146] I said; said she:
« Tears, these, of poor Fuz*u*l*i*, sad of heart;
aye, truly thine! »

VI

Mukhammes

Ey harîr ichre tenin mutlaq bilûr ichre gul-ab

Attar within vase of crystal, such thy fair form
silken-gowned;
And thy breast is gleaming water, where the
bubbles clear abound;[147]
Thou so bright none who may gaze upon thee on the
earth is found;
Bold wert thou to cast the veil off, standing forth
with garland crowned:
Not a doubt but woe and ruin all the wide world
must confound!

Lures the heart thy gilded palace, points
it to thy lips the way;
Eagerly the ear doth listen for the words thy
rubies say;
Near thy hair the comb remaineth, I despairing
far away;
Bites the comb, each curling ringlet, when it
through thy locks doth stray:[148]
Jealous at its sight, my heart's thread agonized
goes curling round.

Ah! her face the rose, her shift rose-hued,
her trousers red their shade;
With its flame burns us the fiery garb in which
thou art arrayed.
Ne'er was born of Adam's children one like thee,
O cruel maid!
Moon and Sun, in beauty's circle, at thy
fairness stand dismayed:
Seems it thou the Sun for mother and the
Moon for sire hast owned.[149]

Captive bound in thy red fillet, grieve I through thy
musky hair;
Prone I 'neath those golden anklets which thy
silvern limbs do wear; [150]
Think not I am like thy fillet, empty of thy
grace, O fair!
Rather to the golden chain, which hangs thy
cheek round, me compare: [151]
In my sad heart pangs a thousand from thy glance's
shafts are found.

Eyes with antimony darkened, hands with hinna
crimson dyed; [152]
Through these beauties vain and wanton like to
thee was ne'er a bride.
Bows of poplar green, thy painted brows; thy
glances shafts provide.[153]
Poor Fuzuli for thine eyes and eyebrows
aye hath longing cried:
That the bird from bow and arrow flees
not, well may all astound.

VII

From his Leyl*i* and Mejn*u*n[154]

The Gazel of the Master

Jan verma gam-i 'ishqa ki 'ishq afet-i jan dir

Yield not the soul to pang of Love, for Love's the
soul's fierce glow;
That Love's the torment of the soul doth all
the wide world know.
Seek not for gain from fancy wild of pang of
Love at all;
For all that comes from fancy wild of Love's
pang is grief's throe.
Each curving eyebrow is a blood-stained
sabre thee to slay;
Each dusky curl, a deadly venomed snake to
work thee woe.
Lovely, indeed, the forms of moon-like
maidens are to see —
Lovely to see, but ah! the end doth bitter
anguish show.
From this I know full well that torment dire in
love abides,
That all who lovers are, engrossed with sighs,
rove to and fro.
Call not to mind the pupils of the black-eyed
damsels bright,
With thought: « I'm man,» be not deceived,
'tis blood they drink, I trow.[155]
E'en if Fuz*u*l*i* should declare: «In fair ones there
is troth;»
Be not deceived: « A poet's words are falsehoods
all men know.»[156]

VIII

From the Same

MEJNUN ADDRESSES NEVFIL

Mejnun dedi: «Ey yegane'-i 'ahd!»

QUOTH Mejnun: « O sole friend of true plight!
With counsel many have tried me to guide right;
Many with wisdom gifted have advice shown,
But yet this fiend hath been by no one o'erthrown;
Much gold has on the earth been strewn round,
But yet this Stone of Alchemist by none's found.[157]
Collyrium I know that doth increase light,
What use though is it if the eye doth lack sight?
I know that greatest kindliness in thee lies,
What use, though, when my fate doth ever dark rise?
Upon my gloomy fortune I no faith lay,
Impossible my hope appeareth alway.
Ah! though in this thou shouldest ever hard toil,
The end at length will surely all thy plans foil.
No kindliness to me my closest friends show;
Who is a friend to him whom he doth deem foe?
I know my fortune evil is and woe-fraught;
The search for solace is to me, save pain, nought.
There is a gazel that doth well my lot show,
Which constant I repeat where'er my steps go.

IX

From the Same

MEJNŪN'S GAZEL

Wefa her kimseden kim istedim andan jefa gurdum

FROM whomsoe'er I've sought for troth but bitterest
disdain I've seen;
Whome'er within this faithless world I've trusted,
all most vain I've seen
To whomsoe'er I've told my woes, in hope to find some
balm therefor,
Than e'en myself o'erwhelmed and sunk in deeper,
sadder pain I've seen.
From out mine aching heart no one hath driven
cruel grief away,
That those my friends of pleasure's hour affection did
but feign I've seen.
Although I've clutched its mantle, life hath turned
away its face from me;
And though I faith from mirror hoped, there persecuted
swain I've seen.[158]
At gate of hope I set my foot, bewilderment held
forth its hand,
Alas! whene'er hope's thread I've seized, in hand the
serpent's train I've seen.
A hundred times the Sphere hath shown to me
my darksome fortune's star;
Whene'er my horoscope I've cast, but blackest,
deepest stain I've seen.
Fuzulī, blush not then, should I from
mankind turn my face away;
For why? From all to whom I've looked, but reason
sad to wail I've seen.

X

From the Same

Zeyd's Vision

Her lahza qiliridi taze matem

His grief and mourning Zeyd renewèd alway,
From bitter wailing ceased he not, he wept aye.
That faithful, loving, ever-constant friend dear,
One night, when was the rise of the True Dawn near,[159]
Feeling that in his wasted frame no strength stayed,
Had gone, and down upon that grave himself laid.
There, in his sleep, he saw a wondrous fair sight,
A lovely garden, and two beauties, moon-bright;
Through transport rapturous, their cheeks with light glow;
Far distant now, all fear of anguish, pain, woe;
With happiness and ecstasy and joy blest,
From rivals' persecutions these have found rest;
A thousand angel-forms to each fair beauty,
With single heart, perform the servant's duty.
He, wondering, question made: « What Moons so bright these?
What lofty, honored Sovereigns of might these?
What garden, most exalted, is this parterre?
What throng so bright and beautiful, the throng there?»
They answer gave: « Lo! Eden's shining bowers these;
That radiant throng, the Heaven-born Youths and H*uri*s;[160]
These two resplendent forms, bright as the fair moon,
These are the ever-faithful — Leyl*i*, Mejn*u*n!
Since pure within the vale of love they sojourned,
And kept that purity till they to dust turned,
Are Eden's everlasting bowers their home now,
To them the H*uri*s and the Youths as slaves bow:
Since these, while on the earth, all woe resigned met,
And patience aye before them in each grief set,
When forth they fled from this false, faithless world's bound,
From all those pangs and sorrows they release found!»

FAZLI

971 [1563]

From his Gul u Bulbul, "Rose and Nightingale"[161]

Ki meger ruzgar-i mazida

ONCE, in times long ago, in ages of eld,
Over bright realms, the fairest man e'er beheld,
(These in Rome[162] lay) a King of fame ruled in state,
Prosperous, glad, of joy and fortune innate;
He, a King, high of rank, of auspicious part,
Fair of face, fair of nature, and fair of heart;
All his actions on justice sure did recline,
All his beauty and spirit perfect did shine;
Pure of mind, debonair, in council aright,
Heart-rejoicing, and graceful, the soul making bright,
He, a glorious, stately, most noble King,
Thus 'twas they named him, all his subjects:—King Spring.
Through the stream of his justice the earth blossomed fair,
Like to Eden the world through his mercy's air:
With benignity, grace, and kindness imbued,
With discretion and faultless justice endued:
All around spread his sway like the wind that blows,
Everywhere swept his law like the flood that flows;
Fair his equity e'en as the breeze of dawn,
Making earth's face a verdant, fresh-blooming lawn.
'Midst of his blest dominions none uttered wail,
Save it were 'mongst the flowers the sad nightingale;
'Gainst his neighbor did no one the dagger bare,
Save the fresh blooming lily within the parterre;[163]
To his neighbor did no one anguish impart,
Saving the thorn to the nightingale's heart;[164]
From his neighbor did no one the diadem seize,
The tulip's crown only was stol'n by the breeze.

Herbs, in mighty array, were spread o'er the ground,
Forming a host without limit or bound;
Leaves and fruits did these bear in numbers untold,
Even more than the leaves that the trees unfold.
'Midst of the mead narcissus-eyed guards did stand,
Sentries, gold-uskufed, a numberless band;
Tulip-like, ruby-beakered and ruby-crowned,
Many cup-bearers lovely did him surround;
Guards, like the lily, a thousand he had,
All of these sabre-wearing and armor-clad;
Like the cypress, uprearing proudly the head,
Many warriors valiant his banners spread;
Like the thorn, sharp-featured, wielding the dart,
His were spearsmen who'd pierce the dread lion's heart;
Many couriers his, like the zephyr in speed,
Like the crown-snatching life was each one indeed.
In the heaven of might, a Star bright he beamed;
In the casket of state, a Gem fair he gleamed.
'Midst his life's garden only one rose had blown,
One divine gift to him from God's lofty throne;
Him a daughter had granted the mercy divine,
Who in earth's garden, like the rose, fair did shine;
Though yet but a rosebud, her name was Rose —
In the parterre of grace a rosebud arose!
Many rosebuds, a thousand rosebuds most fair,
Heart-contracted, did envy her mouth in despair;
Ne'er a rival to her in beauty was found,
In her love was the world secure captive bound.

NISHANI

975 [1567]

Gazel

Fenn-i 'ishqa bashladim, diqqatla gurdum nije bab

I began love's art to study, divers chapters did
I read;
Longing's texts and parting's sections a whole book
would fill indeed;
Union formed a short abridgment, but the pangs of
love for thee
Have their commentaries endless made each
other to succeed.
O Nishani, hath the master, Love, thus truly
taught to thee:—
"This a question hard whose answer from the loved
one must proceed!"

SELÍMÍ

(SULTAN SELÍM II.)

982 [1574]

I

Gazel

Khalin ile zulfun el bir eylemish

Hand in hand thy mole hath plotted with thy hair,[166]
Many hearts made captive have they in their snare.
Thou in nature art an angel whom the Lord
In His might the human form hath caused to wear.
When He dealt out 'mongst His creatures union's tray,
Absence from thee, God to me gave as my share.
Thou would'st deem that Power, the limner, for thy brows,
O'er the lights, thine eyes, two *nuns* had painted fair.[167]
O Selími, on the sweetheart's cheek the down
Is thy sighs' fume,[134] which, alas, hath rested there.

II

Gazel

Leylī zulfun sihr-i gamzan 'aql u janim aldilar

Ta'en my sense and soul have those thy Leylí locks, thy glance's spell,
Me, their Mejnun, 'midst of love's wild dreary desert they impel.[154]
Since mine eyes have seen the beauty of the Joseph of thy grace,
Sense and heart have fall'n and lingered in thy chin's sweet dimple-well.[168]
Heart and soul of mine are broken through my passion for thy lips;
From the hand of patience struck they honor's glass, to earth it fell.
The mirage, thy lips, O sweetheart, that doth like to water show;
For, through longing, making thirsty, vainly they my life dispel.
Since Selími hath the pearls, thy teeth, been praising, sense and heart
Have his head and soul abandoned, plunging 'neath love's ocean-swell.

III

Gazel

Yuzunden zulfun sur, keshf-i hijabet

Thy veil raise, shake from cheeks those locks of thine then;
Unclouded beauty's sun and moon bid shine then.
But one glance from those soft and drooping eyes throw,
The heart through joy to drunkenness consign then.
Were I thy lip to suck, 'twould heal the sick heart;
Be kind, an answer give, Physician mine, then.
Beware lest evil glance thy beauty's rose smite,
From ill-eyed rival careful it confine then.
O heart, this is Life's Water 'midst of darkness,[53]
In night's gloom hidden, drink the ruby wine then.[23]
My love's down grows upon her rosy-hued cheek,
A book write on the woes it doth enshrine then.[51]
Thy wine-hued lip, O love, grant to Sel*i*m*i*,—
And by thy parting's shaft my tears make wine then.[169]

SHEMSI PASHA

988 [1580]

GAZEL

Raqibin ku-yi yarinden guzari var, benim yoq dur

THE rival entry free hath to the loved one's ward,
but none have I;
Regard unto the very dogs they there accord, but
none have I.
The heart doth seize the Magian's[245] hand; the cup-bearer,
his glass; but I—
For gentle love they grant to these their due
reward, but none have I.
To gain regard I would complain loud as the dogs
within thy ward,
For these have power their plight to show, their griefs
record, but none have I.
From all eternity have I to Mejnun taught the
pang of love,[154]
How then do all the folk to him renown award,
but none have I?
To God be praise that brightly shines the mirror of
my heart, Shemsi,
For more or less earth's glass with dust is soiled or marred,
but none have I.

YAHYA BEG

990 [1582]

I

From his Shah u Geda, "King and Beggar"

Suweyle ey tuti-i shirin-maqal

Parrot, sweet of voice, thy song now raise! 115
All thy words purify in Love's fierce blaze!
Every point of Love as whole book shows;
Every mote of Love as bright sun glows.
Drowned in one drop thereof Time, Space, in sooth;
Lost in one grain thereof Both Worlds, in truth.
Man becomes man through Love, pure, bright,
Teacher respected, guide of the right.
Through its beams everything man as chief owns,
Rays of sun into rubies turn black stones. 127

* * * * *

He who a Lover is on God relies;
On, on, upward still doth he rise.
One day he secrets all shall descry,
Love makes the soul from sleep raise the eye;
Unto him all things shall oped be and shown,
Off e'en the curtain from God shall be thrown.

MURADI

(SULTAN MURAD III.)

1003 [1595]

GAZEL

Lutf-i Rakmana istinadim var

YEA, on God's favor all my trust I place;
Ah! how my soul desireth His dear grace!
Since with the Lord I have my heart made right,
All of my hope upon His aid I base.
I upon troops and treasures no faith lay;
Nay, to the Hosts Unseen I leave my case.[38]
Bravely strive on, the Holy Warfare fight;
Firm, in God's cause to war, I've set my face.
By Him, I trust, received my prayer may be;
For, on acceptance I my whole hope place.

B*A*Q*I*

1008 [1600]

I

QA*I*SDA[17]

(In Praise of Sultan Suleym*a*n I.)

Hengam-i sheb ki kungure'-i cherkh-i asm*a*n

One night when all the battlements Heaven's
castle doth display,
Illumed and decked were, with the shining
lamps, the stars' array,
Amidst the host of gleaming stars the Moon lit up
his torch;[84]
Athwart the field of Heaven with radiance
beamed the Milky Way.
The Secretary of the Spheres had ta'en his
meteor-pen,
That writer of His signature whom men
and jinns obey.
There, at the banquet of the sky, had
Venus struck her lyre,
In mirth and happiness, delighted,
joyed and smiling gay.
Taking the keynote for her tune 'neath in
the vaulted sphere,
The tambourinist Sun her visage bright
had hid away.[171]
Armed with a brand of gleaming gold had leapt
into the plain
The Swordsman of the sky's expanse, of
heaven's field of fray.
To give direction to the weighty matters of the
earth

Had Jupiter, the wise, lit up reflection's
taper's ray.
There raised aloft old Saturn high upon the
Seventh Sphere
Sitting like Indian elephant-conductor on
did stray.[172]
« What means this decking of the universe ? »
I wond'ring said;
When, lo ! with meditation's gaze e'en whilst I
it survey,
Casting its beams on every side, o'er all earth
rose the Sun,
O'er the horizons, e'en as Seal of Suleym*a*n's
display.[173]
The eye of understanding looked upon
this wondrous sight;
At length the soul's ear learned the secret hid in
this which lay:
What is it that hath decked earth's hall with
splendors such as this,
Saving the might and fortune of the King who
earth doth sway ?
He who sits high upon the throne above
all crowned kings,
The Hero of the battlefield of dread
Key*a*n*i* fray,[174]
Jemsh*i*d[63] of happiness and joy,
Darius of the fight,
Khusrev[65] of right and clemency,
Iskender[53] of his day!

Lord of the East and West ! King whom the
kings of earth obey!
Prince of the Epoch ! Sultan Suleym*a*n!
Triumphant Aye!

Meet 'tis before the steed of yonder
Monarch of the realms
Of right and equity, should march earth's rulers'
bright array.

Rebelled one 'gainst his word, secure he'd
bind him in his bonds,
E'en like the dappled pard, the sky
chained with the Milky Way.
Lord of the land of graciousness and bounty,
on whose board
Of favors, spread is all the wealth that
sea and mine display;
Longs the perfumer, Early Spring, for the
odor of his grace;
Need hath the merchant, Autumn, of his bounteous
hand alway.[175]
Through tyrant's hard oppression no one
groaneth in his reign,
And though may wail the flute and lute,
the law they disobey.
Beside thy justice, tyranny's the code of
Key-Qub*a*d;[176]
Beside thy wrath, but mildness Qahram*a*n's
most deadly fray.[177]
Thy scimitar's the gleaming guide empires to
overthrow,
No foe of Isl*a*m can abide before thy sabre's ray.
Saw it thy wrath, through dread of thee would
trembling seize the pine;
The falling stars a chain around the heaven's
neck would lay.
Amidst thy sea-like armies vast, thy flags
and standards fair,
The sails are which the ship of splendid triumph
doth display.
Thrust it its beak into the Sphere, 'twould
seize it as a grain,
The 'anqa strong, thy power, to which 'twere
but a seed-like prey.[6]
In past eternity the hand, thy might,
it struck with bat,
That time is this time, for the Sky's Ball
spins upon its way.[178]

Within the rosy garden of thy praise the bird,
the heart,
Singeth this soul-bestowing, smooth-as-water-running lay.

If yonder mouth be not the soul,
O heart-enslaver gay,
Then wherefore is it like the soul,
hid from our eyes away?
Since in the casket of our mind thy ruby's
picture lies,[23]
The mine is now no fitting home for
gem of lustrous ray.
Thy tresses fall across thy cheek in many
a twisting curl,
"To dance to Hij*az* have the Sh*am*is tucked their
skirts," we'd say.[179]
Let both the youthful pine and cypress view
thy motions fair;
The gardener now to rear the willow need no
more assay.[32]
The dark and cloudy brained of men thine
eyebrows black depict,
While those of keen, discerning wit thy glistening
teeth portray.
Before thy cheek the rose and jasmine bowéd
in suj*u*d,
The cypress to thy figure in qiy*a*m did
homage pay.[180]
The heart's throne is the seat of that great monarch,
love for thee;
The soul, the secret court, where doth thy ruby's
picture stay.
The radiance of thy beauty bright hath filled
earth like the sun,
The hall, *BE! and it is*, resounds with love of
thee for aye.[181]
The cries of those on plain of earth have
risen to the skies,
The shouts of those who dwell above have found
to earth their way.

Nor can the nightingale with songs as sweet
as *Baqi*'s sing,
Nor happy as thy star can beam the garden's bright
array.
The mead, the world, blooms through thy beauty's rose,
like Irem's bower;[182]
On every side are nightingales of sweet,
melodious lay.
Now let us pray at Allah's court:
« May this for aye endure,
The might and glory of this prospered King's
resplendent sway;
Until the lamp, the world-illuming sun,
at break of dawn,
A silver candelabrum on the circling skies
display,[183]
Oh! may the Ruler of the world with skirt of
aid and grace
Protect the taper of his life from blast of doom,
we pray! »
Glory's the comrade; Fortune, the cup-bearer
at our feast;
The beaker is the Sphere; the bowl, the Steel of
gold-inlay![184]

II

Gazel

Mahabbat bahri dir, ahim yelinden mevj wurur yashim

'Tis love's wild sea, my sighs' fierce wind doth lash those
waves my tears uprear;
My head, the barque of sad despite; mine eyebrows twain,
the anchors here.
Mine unkempt hair, the den of yonder tiger dread,
the fair one's love;
My head, dismay and sorrow's realm's deserted
mountain-region drear.
At whatsoever feast I drain the cup thy rubies'
mem'ry to,
Amidst all those who grace that feast, except the dregs,
I've no friend near.
Thou know'st, O Light of my poor eyes, with t*u*ty*a* mixed are
gems full bright,
What then if weep on thy path's dust mine eyes that scatter
pearls most clear![42]
The Sphere, old hag, with witchcraft's spell hath parted me
from my fond love,
O B*aqi*, see, by God, how vile a trick yon jade hath
played me here!

III

Gazel

Yillar durur yolunda senin paymal dir

Years trodden under foot have I lain on that path of thine ;
Thy musky locks are noose-like cast, around my feet to twine.
O Princess mine! boast not thyself through loveliness of face,
For that, alas, is but a sun which must full soon decline!
The loved one's stature tall, her form as fair as juniper,[32]
Bright 'midst the rosy bowers of grace a slender tree doth shine.
Her figure, fair-proportioned as my poesy sublime,[185]
Her slender waist is like its subtle thought—hard to divine.[186]
Then yearn not, Baqi, for the load of love's misfortune dire ;
For that to bear mayhap thy soul no power doth enshrine.

IV

Gazel

Sallanan nazila ol serv-i semen-sima mi dir?

With her graceful-moving form, a Cypress
jasmine-faced is she?
Or in Eden's bower a branch upon the Lote
or T*u*ba-tree?[187]
That thy blood-stained shaft which rankles in my wounded
breast, my love,
In the rosebud hid a lovely rose-leaf, sweetheart,
can it be?[188]
To the dead of pain of anguish doth its draught
fresh life impart;
O cup-bearer, is the red wine Jesu's breath? tell,
tell to me![189]
Are they teeth those in thy mouth, or on the rosebud
drops of dew?
Are they sparkling stars, or are they gleaming pearls,
that there I see?
Through the many woes thou wreakest upon B*a*q*i*,
sick of heart,
Is't thy will to slay him, or is it but sweet disdain
in thee?

V

Gazel

Qaddin qatinda qamet-i shimshad pest olur

Before thy form, the box-tree's lissom figure dwarfed
would show;[32]
Those locks of thine the pride of ambergris would
overthrow.[43]
Who, seeing thy cheek's glow, recalls the ruby is
deceived;
He who hath drunken deep of wine inebriate
doth grow.
Should she move forth with figure like the
juniper in grace,
The garden's cypress to the loved one's form
must bend right low.
Beware, give not the mirror bright to yonder
paynim maid,[190]
Lest she idolater become, when there her face
doth show.
Baqi, doth he not drink the wine of obligation's
grape,
Who drunken with *A-lestu's* cup's o'erwhelming draught
doth go?[191]

VI

Gazel

'Arizin ab-i nab dir guya

THY cheek, like limpid water, clear doth gleam;
Thy pouting mouth a bubble round doth seem.
The radiance of thy cheek's sun on the heart
Like moonlight on the water's face doth beam.
The heart's page, through the tracings of thy down,[51]
A volume all illumined one would deem.
That fair Moon's sunny love the earth have burned,
It warm as rays of summer sun doth stream.
At woeful sorrow's feast my blood-shot eyes,
Two beakers of red wine would one esteem.
Baqi, her mole dark-hued like ambergris,
A fragrant musk-pod all the world would deem.

VII

Gazel

Dil derd-i 'ishq-i yar ile bezm-i belada dir

All sick the heart with love for her, sad at the feast
of woe;
Bent form, the harp; low wail, the flute; heart's
blood for wine doth flow.[77]
Prone lies the frame her path's dust 'neath, in union's
stream the eye,[192]
In air the mind, the soul 'midst separation's fiery glow.
O ever shall it be my lot, zone-like, thy waist to clasp!
'Twixt us, O love, the dagger-blade of severance
doth show!
Thou art the Queen of earth, thy cheeks are Towers
of might, this day,
Before thy Horse, like Pawns, the Kings of grace and
beauty go.[193]
Him hinder not, beside thee let him creep, O
Shade-like stay!
Baqi, thy servant, O my Queen, before thee
lieth low.

VIII

Gazel

(On Autumn)

Nam u nishane qalmadi fasl-i baharden

Lo, ne'er a trace or sign of springtide's beauty doth
remain;
Fall'n, midst the garden lie the leaves, now all
their glory vain.
Bleak stand the orchard trees, all clad in tattered
dervish rags;
Dark Autumn's blast hath torn away the hands from
off the plane.[99]
From each hill-side they come and cast their gold
low at the feet
Of garden trees, as hoped the streams from these some
boon to gain.[194]
Stay not within the parterre, let it tremble with
its shame:
Bare every shrub, this day doth nought of
leaf or fruit retain.
Baqi, within the garden lies full many a
fallen leaf;
Low lying there, it seems they 'gainst the winds
of Fate complain.

IX

Gazel

Lale-khadler qildilar gul-gesht-i sahra semt semt

TULIP-CHEEKED ones over rosy field and plain stray
all around;
Mead and garden cross they, looking wistful each way,
all around.
These the lovers true of radiant faces, aye, but who
the fair ?
Lissom Cypress, thou it is whom eager seek
they all around.
Band on band Woe's legions camped before the
City of the Heart,
There, together leagued, sat Sorrow, Pain, Strife,
Dismay, all around.
From my weeping flows the river of my tears
on every side,
Like an ocean 'tis again, a sea that casts spray
all around.
Forth through all the Seven Climates have
the words of Ba*qi* gone;
This refulgent verse recited shall be alway,
all around.

X

Gazel

Jemalin afitabinden olur uur

From thine own beauty's radiant sun doth light flow;
How lustrously doth now the crystal glass show!
Thy friend's the beaker, and the cup's thy comrade;
Like to the dregs why dost thou me aside throw?
Hearts longing for thy beauty can resist not;
Hold, none can bear the dazzling vision's bright glow!
United now the lover, and now parted;
This world is sometimes pleasure and sometimes woe.
Bound in the spell of thy locks' chain is *Baqi*,
Mad he, my Liege, and to the mad they grace show.

XI

Gazel

Peyale khusrev-i milk-i gama taj-i keyani dir

The goblet as affliction's Khusrev's[65] bright Keyani[174]
crown doth shine;
And surely doth the wine-jar love's King's Khusrevani
hoard enshrine.
Whene'er the feast recalls Jemshid, down from its eyes
the red blood rolls;
The rosy-tinted wine its tears, the beakers its
blood-weeping eyne.
At parting's banquet should the cup, the heart,
with blood brim o'er, were't strange?
A bowl *that*, to the fair we'll drain, a goblet filled full high
with wine.
O Moon, if by thy door one day the foe should sudden
me o'ertake—
A woe by Heaven decreed, a fate to which I must
myself resign!
The fume of beauty's and of grace's censer is thy cheek's
sweet mole,
The smoke thereof thy musky locks that spreading fragrant
curl and twine;
Thy cheek rose-hued doth light its taper at the moon that
shines most bright,
Its candlestick at grace's feast is yonder collar fair
of thine.
Of love and passion is the lustrous sheen of Baqi's
verse the cause;
As Life's Stream brightly this doth shine; but that,
th' Eternal Life Divine.

XII

Gazel

Jame-kh,ab ol afeti aldiqja tenha qoynuna

When the sheets have yonder Torment to their bosom ta'en to rest,[195]
Think I: «Hides the night-adorning Moon within the cloudlet's breast.»
In the dawning, O thou turtle, mourn not with those senseless plaints;
In the bosom of some stately cypress thou'rt a nightly guest.
Why thou weepest from the heavens, never can I think, O dew;
Every night some lovely rose's bosom fair thou enterest.
Hath the pearl seen in the story of thy teeth its tale of shame,
Since the sea hath hid the album of the shell within its breast?
Longing for thy cheeks hath Baqi all his bosom marked with scars,
Like as though he'd cast of rose-leaves fresh a handful o'er his chest.[92]

XIII

TERKIB-BEND

Elegy on Sultan Suleyman I.[196]

'Ey pa-yi-bend-i dam-geh-i qayd-i nam u neng!

O THOU! foot-bounden in the mesh of fame and glory's snare!
Till when shall last the lust of faithless earth's pursuits and care?
At that first moment, which of life's fair springtide is the last,
'Tis need the tulip-cheek the tint of autumn leaf should wear;
'Tis need that thy last home should be, e'en like the dregs', the dust;[197]
'Tis need the stone from hand of Fate should be joy's beaker's share.[198]
He is a man indeed whose heart is as a mirror clear;
Man art thou? why then doth thy breast the tiger's fierceness bear?
In understanding's eye how long shall heedless slumber bide?
Will not war's Lion-Monarch's fate suffice to make thee ware?
He, Prince of Fortune's Cavalier! he to whose charger bold,[199]
Whene'er he caracoled or pranced, cramped was earth's tourney-square!
He, to the lustre of whose sword the Magyar bowed his head!
He, the dread gleaming of whose brand the Frank can well declare!
Like tender rose-leaf, gently laid he in the dust his face,
And Earth, the Treasurer, him placed like jewel in his case.

In truth, he was the radiance of rank high and
glory great,
A Shah, Iskender-diademed, of *Dara*'s armied state; [200]
Before the dust beneath his feet the Sphere bent
low its head; [201]
Earth's shrine of adoration was his royal
pavilion's gate.
The smallest of his gifts the meanest beggar
made a prince;
Exceeding bounteous, exceeding kind a Potentate!
The court of glory of his kingly majesty most high
Was aye the centre where would hopes of sage
and poet wait.
Although he yielded to Eternal Destiny's
command,
A King was he in might as Doom and puissant
as Fate!
Weary and worn by this sad, changeful Sphere,
deem not thou him:
Near God to be, did he his rank and glory
abdicate.
What wonder if our eyes no more life and the
world behold!
His beauty fair, as sun and moon, did earth
irradiate!
If folk upon the bright sun look, with tears are
filled their eyes;
For seeing it, doth yon moon-face before
their minds arise! [202]

Now let the cloud blood drop on drop weep,
and its form bend low!
And let the Judas-tree anew in blossoms
gore-hued blow! [94]
With this sad anguish let the stars' eyes rain
down bitter tears!
And let the smoke from hearts on fire the heavens
all darkened show! [134]
Their azure garments let the skies change into
deepest black!

Let the whole world attire itself in robes of princely
woe!
In breasts of fairies and of men still let the
flame burn on —
Of parting from the blest King Suleyman
the fiery glow! [125]
His home above the Highest Heaven's ramparts
he hath made;
This world was all unworthy of his majesty,
I trow.
The bird, his soul, hath, huma-like, aloft
flown to the skies, [203]
And nought remaineth save a few bones on
the earth below.
The speeding Horseman of the plain of Time
and Space was he;
Fortune and Fame aye as his friends and bridle
guides did go.
The wayward courser, cruel Fate,
was wild and fierce of pace,
And fell to earth the shade of God the
Lord's benignant grace.

Through grief for thee, bereft of rest and tearful
e'en as I,
Sore weeping let the cloud of spring go wand'ring
through the sky!
And let the wailing of the birds of dawn
the whole world fill!
Be roses torn! and let the nightingale
distressful cry!
Their hyacinths as weeds of woe displaying,
let them weep,
Down o'er their skirts their flowing tears [204]
let pour — the mountains high!
The odor of thy kindliness recalling,
tulip-like,
Within the Tatar musk-deer's heart
let fire of anguish lie! [61]

Through yearning for thee let the rose
its ear lay on the path![205]
And, narcisse-like, till the Last Day the watch-
man's calling ply!
Although the pearl-diffusing eye to oceans
turned the world,
Ne'er into being should there come a pearl
with thee to vie!
O heart! this hour 'tis thou that sympathizer
art with me;
Come, let us like the flute bewail, and moan,
and plaintive sigh!
The notes of mourning and of dole
aloud let us rehearse;
And let all those who grieve be moved by
this our seven-fold verse.[206]

Will earth's king ne'er awake from sleep?—broke
hath the dawn of day;
Will ne'er he move forth from his tent, adorned
as Heaven's display?
Long have our eyes dwelt on the road,
and yet no news hath come
From yonder land, the threshold of
his majesty's array:[207]
The color of his cheek hath paled, dry-lipped he
lieth there,
E'en like that rose which from the vase of flowers
hath fall'n away.
Goes now the Khusrev of the skies[208] behind
the cloudy veil,
For shame, remembering thy love and kindness,
one would say.
My prayer is ever: "May the babes, his tears,
go 'neath the sod,
Or old or young be he who weeps not thee in
sad dismay."[209]
With flame of parting from thee let the sun burn
and consume;

And o'er the wastes through grief let darkness of the
clouds hold sway.
Thy talents and thy feats let it recall and weep
in blood,
Yea, let thy sabre from its sheath plunge in the
darksome clay.
Its collar, through its grief and anguish,
let the reed-pen tear!
And let the earth its vestment rend through
sorrow and despair!

Thy sabre made the foe the anguish dire of wounds
to drain;
Their tongues are silenced, none who dares to gainsay
doth remain.
The youthful cypress, head exalted, looked upon
thy lance,
And ne'er its lissom twigs their haughty heirs
displayed again.
Where'er thy stately charger placed his hoof,
from far and near
Flocked nobles, all upon thy path their lives to
offer fain.
In desert of mortality the bird, desire,
rests ne'er;
Thy sword in cause of God did lives as
sacrifice ordain.
As sweeps a scimitar, across earth's face on
every side,
Of iron-girded heroes of the world thou
threw'st a chain.
Thou took'st a thousand idol-temples,
turnèdst all to mosques;
Where jangled bells thou mad'st be sung the call
to Prayers' strain.
At length is struck the signal-drum, and thou hast
journeyed hence;
Lo! thy first resting-place is Eden's flowery,
verdant plain.

Praise is to God! for He in the Two Worlds hath blessèd thee,
And caused thy glorious name, *Hero and Martyr* both to be.[210]

Baqí, the beauty of the King, the heart's delight, behold![211]
The mirror of the work of God, the Lord of Right, behold!
The dear old man hath passed away from th' Egypt sad, the world;
The youthful Prince, alert and fair as Joseph bright, behold!
The Sun hath risen, and the Dawning gray hath touched its bourne;
The lovely face of yon Khusrev,[65] whose soul is light, behold!
This chace now to the grave hath sent the Behram of the Age;
Go, at his threshold serve, King Erdeshír aright, behold![212]
The blast of Fate to all the winds hath blown Suleyman's throne;[125]
Sultan Selím Khan on Iskender's[5] couch of might, behold!
The Tiger of the mount of war to rest in sleep hath gone;
The Lion who doth now keep watch on glory's height, behold!
The Peacock fair of Eden's mead hath soared to Heaven's parterre;[213]
The lustre of the Huma of high, happy flight, behold!
Eternal may the glory of the heaven-high Khusrev dwell!
Blessings be on the Monarch's soul and spirit:—and farewell!

‘ADLI

(SULTAN MUHAMMED III.)

1012 [1603]

Gazel

Yoq durur zulma rizamiz ‘adla biz mailleriz

Cruel tyranny we love not, nay, to justice we incline;
Full contentedly our eyes wait for the blest command divine.
Know we truly, for a mirror, world-reflecting, is our heart;
Yet conceive not us to Fortune's ever-changeful ways supine.
To the rule of God submissive, all concern we cast aside;
We indeed on Him confiding, on His providence recline.
Shall our heart anoint its eye then with the kuhl of Isfahan? [86]
Pleased it with this tutya: dust that doth the Fair One's pathway line. [42]
Since our heart, ‘Adli, within Love's crucible was purified,
'Midst the universe, from guile and guilt free, bright our soul doth shine.

BAKHTI

SULTAN AHMED I.)

1026 [1617]

GAZEL

Buy ersa jan meshammina fasl-i baharden

O that a fragrant breath might reach the soul from early spring!
O that with warbling sweet of birds the groves once more might ring!
O that in melody the songs anew might rose-like swell!
That fresh in grace and voice the nightingale be heard to sing!
O that the New Year's Day were come, when, minding times gone by,[214]
Should each and all from Time and Fate demand their reckoning!
In short, O Bakhti, would the early vernal days were here,
Then, 'midst the mead, ne'er should we part from brink of limpid spring.

FARIS*I*

(SULTAN 'OSM*A*N II)

1031 [1622]

GAZEL

Gurdugum gibi seni oldu gunul awara

SOON as I beheld thee, mazed and wildered grew
  my sad heart;
How shall I my love disclose to thee who
  tyrant dread art?
How shall I hold straight upon my road,
  when yonder Torment
Smitten hath my breast with deadly wounds by her
  eyelash-dart?
Face, a rose; and mouth, a rosebud; form,
  a slender sapling—
How shall I not be the slave of Princess such
  as thou art?
Ne'er hath heart a beauty seen like her of graceful
  figure;
Joyous would I for yon charmer's eyebrow with
  my life part.
Faris*i*, what can I do but love that peerless
  beauty?
Ah! this aged Sphere hath made me lover of
  yon sweetheart.

'ATA'I

1045 [1635]

Museddes

Ah kim bagrim peymane gibi doldu khun

AH! THAT once again my heart with blood is filled,
like beaker, high;
At the feast of parting from my love I fell,
and prostrate lie;
O'er this wildered heart the gloom of frenzy, conquering,
doth fly;
In the valley of distraction ne'er a guide can
I descry.
Heedless mistress! loveless Fortune! ever-shifting,
restless sky![114]
Sorrows many! friends not any! strong-starred foeman!
feeble I!

In the land of exile loomed dark on one side the
night of woe,
Nowhere o'er me did the lustrous moon of beauty's
heaven glow;
Yonder glared the Two Infortunes,[78] sank my
helping planet low;
Here did fortune, there did gladness, parting from me,
distant go.
Heedless mistress! loveless Fortune! ever-shifting,
restless sky!
Sorrows many! friends not any! strong-starred foeman!
feeble I!

Strange is't if the nightingale, my heart, in thousand
notes doth wail?
Fate to part it from the rosebud, the belovèd,
did prevail;

Whilst I'm on the thorn of anguish, rivals with my love
regale:
Why recite my woes, O comrades? space were none
to tell their tale!
Heedless mistress! loveless Fortune! ever shifting,
restless sky!
Sorrows many! friends not any! strong-starred foeman!
feeble I!

E'en a moment at the feast of woes from tears can
I refrain?
How shall not the wine, my tears, down rolling,
all my vestment stain?
Can it be with e'en one breath I should not like the
reed complain?
Sad, confused, like end of banquet,[215] why then
should not I remain?
Heedless mistress! loveless Fortune! ever-shifting,
restless sky!
Sorrows many! friends not any! strong-starred foeman!
feeble I!

Yonder Princess, though I served her, pitiless drave
me away,
Banished me far from her city, sent me from her
court's array:
When I parted from her tresses, black the world
before me lay;
Helpless 'midst the darkness did I, like unto
'At*a'i*, stray.
Heedless mistress! loveless Fortune! ever-shifting,
restless sky!
Sorrows many! friends not any! strong-starred foeman!
feeble I!

NEF'*Í*

1045 [1635]

Gazel

'Arif ol, ehl-i dil ol, rind qalender-meshreb ol

BE THOU wise and thoughtful, e'en as qalender in mind
be free ;[216]
Nor a faithless, graceless paynim, nor a bigot
Muslim be.
Be not vain of wisdom, though thou be the Plato of
the age ;[217]
Be a school-child when a learned man and righteous
thou dost see.
Like the world-adorning sun, rub thou thy face
low 'midst the dust ;
Overwhelm earth with thy planet, yet without a
planet be.[218]
Fret not after Khizar, rather go, and, like to
Nef'*í*'s heart,
At the channel of Life's Stream of grace drink full
contentedly.[58]

H*A*FIZ PASHA

(GRAND VEZ*I*R)

1041 [1632]

Gazel[219]

To Sultan Mur*a*d IV

Aldi etrafi 'aduv imdada 'asker yoq-mi-dir?

Round us foes throng, host to aid us here in sad plight,
is there none?
In the cause of God to combat, chief of tried might,
is there none?
None who will checkmate the foe, Castle to Castle,
face to face?
In the battle who will Queen-like guide the brave Knight,
is there none?[220]
Midst a fearful whirlpool we are fallen helpless,
send us aid!
Us to rescue, a strong swimmer in our friends' sight,
is there none?
Midst the fight to be our comrade, head to give or
heads to take,
On the field of earth a hero of renown bright,
is there none?
Know we not wherefore in turning off our woes ye
thus delay;
Day of Reckoning, aye, and question of the poor's plight,
is there none?
With us 'midst the foeman's flaming streams of scorching
fire to plunge,
Salamander with experience of Fate dight,
is there none?
This our letter, to the court of Sultan Mur*a*d,
quick to bear,
Pigeon, rapid as the storm-wind in its swift flight,
is there none?

MURADI

(SULTAN MURAD IV.)

1049 [1640]

I

Gazel

In Reply to the Preceding

Hafiza, Bagdada imdad etmege er yoq-mi-dir?

To relieve Bagdad, O Hafiz, man of tried might,
is there none?
Aid from us thou seek'st, then with thee
host of fame bright, is there none?
"I'm the Queen the foe who'll checkmate,"
thus it was that thou didst say;
Room for action now against him with the brave Knight,
is there none?
Though we know thou hast no rival
in vain-glorious, empty boasts,
Yet to take dread vengeance on thee, say, a
Judge right, is there none?
Whilst thou layest claim to manhood,
whence this cowardice of thine?
Thou art frightened, yet beside thee fearing no fight,
is there none?
Heedless of thy duty thou,
the Rafizis have ta'en Bagdad; 221
Shall not God thy foe be? Day of Reckoning,
sure, right, is there none?
They have wrecked Ebu-Hanifa's city
through thy lack of care; 222
O in thee of Islam's and the Prophet's zeal, light,
is there none?

God, who favored us, whilst yet we knew not,
with the Sultanate,
Shall again accord Bagdad, decreed of God's might,
is there none?
Thou hast brought on Islam's army direful ruin
with thy bribes;
Have we not heard how thou say'st: « Word of this
foul blight, is there none? »
With the aid of God, fell vengeance
on the enemy to take,
By me skilled and aged vezir, pious,
zeal-dight, is there none?
Now shall I appoint commander a vezir
of high emprize,
Will not Khizar [53] and the Prophet aid him?
guide right, is there none?
Is it that thou dost the whole world void and
empty now conceive?
Of the Seven Climes,[9] Muradi, King of
high might, is there none?

II

Lugaz[223]

Bir qal'a-i mu'allaq ichinda oldu derya

There's an o'erhanging castle in which there flows a main,
And there within that castle a fish its home hath ta'en;
The fish within its mouth doth hold a shining gem,
Which wastes the fish as long as it therein doth remain.
This puzzle to the poets is offered by Mur*a*d;
Let him reply who office or place desires to gain.

'AZIZI

1050 [1641 *ca.*]

From his Shehr-engiz[224]

SACHLI ZEMAN (FORTUNE THE LONG-HAIRED)

Zeman the Long-haired, 'midst these lovely ones see,
A wayward, wanton Torment of the world she.[195]
Like *Fortune*, she nor clemency nor grace knows;
The number of her *hairs* her lovers' tale shows.
The tribute from the realm of hearts her *curls* bore,
Seduced me have these *locks* that hang her neck o'er.

JIHAN BANU (LADY WORLD)

She whom they call Jihan's a damsel moon-faced,
Who, like the *World*, is faithless, and doth hearts waste.
Save faithlessness, though comes not from the *World* aught;
The heart from that love of the soul can pass not.
Let but her mind contented be with poor me,
Then may the *World* divorced from me for aye be.

LA'LP-ARA (RUBY-CHIP)

La'l-para as her name doth one of these own,
A girl whose heart is hard as is the flint-stone.
Her mouth in very truth's a *ruby* bright red,
Her teeth are pearls, so too the words by her said.
Strange were it, if my heart be by her love slaved?
For sooth her *rubies* bear the « coral-prayer » graved.[225]

AQ-'ALEM (WHITE UNIVERSE)

AND *Aq-'Alem* they one of yonder maids call,
For her the moon of heaven acteth jackal.
Is't strange if through her loveliness she famed be?
A *white* Rose on the earth is yonder H*uri*.
He who with that bright Moon as friend goes,
A *universe* enjoys more fair than earth shows.

NA'ILI

1077 [1666]

MUSEDDES

Firashim seng-i khara, pushishim shevk-i qatad olsun!

BE MINE for dress, the piercing thorn![226] be mine
for couch, the hard, hard stone!
Be mine for home, grief's cot! be mine for bread,
woe's tears! for work, pain's moan!
Be all my bleeding frame with wounds of cruel foeman's
hatred sown!
Be these rejoiced in heart and gay who make my grieving
soul to groan!
Be all those glad by whom my aching heart is tortured
and o'erthrown!
By those blest with their wish who say of me:
« Be all his hopes cast prone!»

Unfaithfulness is aye the rule which guides the Sphere
that loves to pain,
The inborn nature of the skies is but to manifest
disdain;[114]
Within the breasts of those who pleasure seek there lurks
some yearning vain;
O heart, blest is the practice of the thought enshrined
in this refrain:
Be all those glad by whom my aching heart is tortured
and o'erthrown!
Be those blest with their wish who say of me:
« Be all his hopes cast prone! »

When time is past, rejoiced shall swell the hearts of all my
comrades dear;
And through their cruelty — my choice — my foes shall
mourn in sorrow drear.

Let all those learn this verse of me who hap to come my
pathway near,
And let them from the tongues of that green sward which
decks my grave this hear:
Be all those glad by whom my aching heart is tortured
and o'erthrown!
Be those blest with their wish who say of me:
« Be all his hopes cast prone! »

Within this hostel of the world my portion is the
tray of dole;
My eye, the birthplace of the flame, refuseth health's
most pleasant stole;
Fatigue, the rest of my sad heart; anguish, the present
to my soul;
Ne'er through Eternity to gain my longing is my
longing's goal.
Be all those glad by whom my aching heart is tortured
and o'erthrown!
Be those blest with their wish who say of me:
« Be all his hopes cast prone! »

O Na'ilí, is't possible to change or alter Fate's
decree?
Annulled can ever be the edict writ by pen
of Destiny?
My heart is gladdened with this thought, that ne'er
an hour's delay can be
In whetting keen and sharp that axe of pain which rust
can never see.
Be all those glad by whom my aching heart is tortured
and o'erthrown!
Be those blest with their wish who say of me:
« Be all his hopes cast prone! »

SIDQ*I*

1115 [1703]

Gazel

Wasil-i bi-'llah olanlar gayri ihsan istemez

He who union with the Lord gains, more delight
desireth not!
He who looks on charms of fair one, other
sight desireth not.
Pang of love is lover's solace, eagerly he seeks
there-for,
Joys he in it, balm or salve for yonder blight,
desireth not.
Paradise he longs not after, nor doth aught
beside regard;
Bower and Garden, Mead, and Youth, and H*uri*
bright, desireth not.[160]
From the hand of Power Unbounded draineth he
the Wine of Life,
Aye inebriate with Knowledge, learning's light,
desireth not.
He who loves the Lord is monarch of an empire,
such that he—
King of Inward Mysteries—Suleyman's might,
desireth not.[125]
Thou art Sultan of my heart, aye, soul of my soul
e'en art Thou;
Thou art Soul enow, and Sidq*i* other plight
desireth not.

IQBALI

(SULTAN MUSTAFA II.)

1115 [1703]

MUNAJAT [227]

Allah! Rabb-i la-yezal, ya Wahid, ya Zu-'l-Jelal!

ALLAH! Lord who liv'st for aye! O Sole! O King of Glory's Ray!
Monarch who ne'er shalt pass away! *show Thou to us Thy bounties fair.*
In early morning shall our cry, our wail, mount to Thy Throne on high:
"Error and sin our wont," we sigh: *show Thou to us Thy bounties fair.*
If cometh not from Thee Thy grace, evil shall all our works deface;
O Lord of Being and of Space! *show Thou to us Thy bounties fair.*
Creator of security! to Thy Belovèd greetings be![27]
These words are in sincerity: *show Thou to us Thy bounties fair.*
Iqbali sinnèd hath indeed, yet unto him Thy grace concede;
Eternal, Answerer in need! *show Thou to us Thy bounties fair.*

NABI

1124 [1712]

I

Mukhammes

Bu gulistanda benim ichin ne gul ne shebnem var

ALAS! nor dew nor smiling rose within this
mead is mine;
Within this market-place nor trade nor coin for
need is mine;
Nor more nor less; nor power nor strength for act
or deed is mine;
Nor might nor eminence; nor balm the cure to
speed is mine.
O that I knew what here I am, that which indeed
is mine!

Being's the bounty of the Lord; and Life,
the gift Divine;
The Breath, the present of His Love; and Speech
His Grace's sign;
The Body is the pile of God; the Soul, His
Breath benign;
The Powers thereof, His Glory's trust; the Senses,
His design.
O that I knew what here I am, that which
indeed is mine!

No work, no business of my own within this
mart have I;
All Being is of Him alone — no life apart
have I;

No choice of entering this world, or hence of start have I;
To cry: « I am! I am! » in truth, no power of heart have I.
O that I knew what here I am, that which indeed is mine!

The Earth the carpet is of Power; the Sphere, the tent of Might;
The Stars, both fixed and wandering, are Glory's lamps of light;
The World's the issue of the grace of Mercy's treasures bright;
With Forms of beings is the page of Wisdom's volume dight.
O that I knew what here I am, that which indeed is mine!

Being is but a loan to us, and Life in trust we hold:
In slaves a claim to Power's pretension arrogant and bold;
The servant's part is by submission and obedience told;
Should He: « My slave » address to me, 'twere favors manifold.
O that I knew what here I am, that which indeed is mine!

I'm poor and empty-handed, but grace free is of the Lord;
Nonentity's my attribute: to Be is of the Lord;
For Being or Non-being's rise, decree is of the Lord;
The surging of the Seen and Unseen's sea is of the Lord.
O that I knew what here I am, that which indeed is mine!

Of gifts from table of His Bounty is my
daily bread;
My breath is from the Breath of God's benignant
Mercy fed;
My portion from the favors of Almighty
Power is shed;
And my provision is from Providence's kitchen
spread.
O that I knew what here I am, that which
indeed is mine!

I cannot, unallotted, take my share from
wet or dry;
From land or from the ocean, from earth or
from the sky;
The silver or the gold will come, by
Providence laid by;
I cannot grasp aught other than my fortune
doth supply.
O that I knew what here I am, that which
indeed is mine!

Creation's Pen the lines of billows of events
hath traced;
Th' illumined scroll of the Two Worlds' Creation's
Pencil graced;
Their garments upon earth and sky, Creation's woof
hath placed;
Men's forms are pictures in Creation's great
Sh*a*h-N*a*ma traced.[228]
O that I knew what here I am, that which
indeed is mine!

I cannot make the morning eve, or the dark
night the day;
I cannot turn the air to fire, or dust to water's
spray;

I cannot bid the Sphere stand still, or
mountain-region stray;
I cannot Autumn turn by will of mine to
lovely May.
O that I knew what here I am, that which
indeed is mine!

From out of Nothingness His mighty Power
made me appear;
Whilst in the womb I lay, saw He to all I
need for here;
With kindnesses concealed and manifest did
He me rear;
With me He drew a curtain o'er Distinction's
beauty dear.
O that I knew what here I am, that which
indeed is mine!

God's Revelation is Discernment's Eye,
if 't oped remain;
The picturings of worlds are all things changing
aye amain;
The showing of the Hidden Treasure is this
raging main,
This work, this business of the Lord, this
Majesty made plain.
O that I knew what here I am, that which
indeed is mine!

Now void, now full, are Possibility's store-houses
vast;
This glass-lined world's the mirror where Lights Twain
their phases cast;[229]
The blinded thing—in scattering strange fruits its
hours are past;
Ruined hath this old Vineyard been by autumn's
sullen blast.
O that I knew what here I am, that which
indeed is mine!

II

Gazel

Ashiyan-i 'andelib-i zara bir su qalmamish

Ne'er a corner for the plaintive bulbul's nest
remaineth now;
Ne'er a palm-tree 'neath whose kindly shade is rest
remaineth now.
Day and night some balm I've sought for, to relieve my
wounded heart;
Ne'er a cure within the Heavens' turquoise chest
remaineth now
From its source, through every country, searched have I
but all in vain —
Ne'er a single drop, in mercy's fountain blest,
remaineth now.
Empty earthen pots are reckoned one with jewels
rich and rare;
Ne'er a scale in value's mart the worth to test
remaineth now.
'Neath the earth may now the needy hide themselves,
Nabi, away;
Ne'er a turret on the fort of interest
remaineth now.

‘*A*RIF

1125 [1713]

I

MUN*A*J*A*T

Ya Rabb, ne intiha sana zahir ne ibtida

O Lord, to thee is never a beginning, neither end;
Thy mercy's ocean, limitless, doth over all extend.
E'en though the value-weighing hand of Thine unbounded might
Hath wrought astounding marvels that all numbering transcend,
Yet, Lord, Thou formedst Adam *in the best of symmetry*; [230]
Thou worthy of Thy grace to make this folk didst condescend.
Unfathomed and unsounded lies Thy mercy's ocean vast,
Which truly hath made earth beneath its surging waves descend:
O Lord, could any hurt or harm befall that shoreless deep,
Did Thou a single drop therefrom to this Thy servant send?
Since ‘*A*rif owns a Master kind in graciousness like Thee,
O Lord, before another's door were 't right for him to bend?
O Lord, thus ever doth in joy Thy blest device appear—
Thy greatest glory from the works of vileness Thou dost rear! [231]

II

Gazel

Derun-i sineya mihr-i rukhun tab-efken olmush dur

The sun of love for thy fair cheek the heart's core
floods with radiant light;
The soul's most secret court is filled with dazzling rays
at Thy sweet sight.
With union's joys though blest one be, or though with pangs
of absence torn,
Are still sad wail and plaintive cry the e'er-true signs of
lovelorn plight.
Then welcome, O thou gentlest breeze, that bear'st to
him who dwells midst woe,
As news from yonder absent maid the sweet scent of her
garment white.
Of gilded halls no need in sooth to libertines when
wine flows free;
Some ruined den beseems them more, like Jemsh*i*d's
hut of woeful site.[63]
The sparks raised by my passioned sighs' and plainings'
smoke are each one quenched;
For every tear that rolleth down upon my robe's a
rich pearl bright.
O '*A*rif! this poor captive bird hath grown to love th'
entangling snare;
For curling locks to careworn hearts afford a refuge
sure from fright.

III

Museddes

Veda'iyya (Farewell Poem)

A ! Safa, 'azm edip aldin dil-i nalani bile

Ah, my Joy! thou'rt gone, and my sad weeping heart
hast borne indeed,
And my breast by bitter parting's raging fires
all worn indeed;
Grief for thee in hundred pieces hath my raiment torn
indeed;
Be thy escort on the journey tears I weep,
forlorn indeed.
Thou art gone, and longing for thee makes my
heart to mourn indeed;
Without thee, banquets where friends meet, all I have
forsworn indeed.

Wheresoe'er thy footsteps wander, be the aid of
God thy guide;
As the pilot to thy wishes be His grace aye
at thy side;
Shadow for thy crown of glory may the huma's
wing provide; 203
Ah! may ever joyous, happy fortune
on thy path abide.
Thou art gone, and longing for thee makes my
heart to mourn indeed;
Without thee, banquets where friends meet,
all I have forsworn indeed.

O thou Source of joy and quiet unto my poor
grieving breast!
Hence forever I with separation's fires am
sore opprest;
Thou, Crown of my joy! my Treasure!
mercy show to me distrest!

Now, my Lord, to whom shall Master's title
be by me addrest?
Thou art gone, and longing for thee makes my
heart to mourn indeed;
Without thee, banquets where friends meet,
all I have forsworn indeed.

Ever in thy court of service may th' inconstant
Heavens be!
I am fallen, soul and body, to woe's depths
by their decree;
From a kindly master like thee, merciless,
they've sundered me;
And into the dreary vale of exile have they
driven thee.
Thou art gone, and longing for thee makes my
heart to mourn indeed;
Without thee, banquets where friends meet,
all I have forsworn indeed.

Though I'm far now from the shadow of thy love,
O Cypress straight,
Still my prayers I may offer for thy happiness
of state.
Think at times upon thy servant '*A*rif
sitting desolate;
Him from near thy skirt of kindness taken
hath his darksome fate.
Thou art gone, and longing for thee makes my
heart to mourn indeed;
Without thee, banquets where friends meet,
all I have forsworn indeed.

NED*Í*M

1140 [*1727 ca.*]

Gazel

Tahammul milkini yiqdin Helagu Khan mi sin, Kafir?

The realm of patience thou'st laid waste, Hel*agu*[232]
hight art thou, Paynim?[190]
O mercy! thou'st the world consumed, a blazing light
art thou, Paynim?
A maiden's grace, is that thy grace, a conquering hero's
voice, thy voice;
Thou Woe, I know not, maid or youthful lord of might art
thou, Paynim?
What mean those hidden, secret sighs, and tears, and
saddest grievings, pray?
The wailing lover of some wanton gay and bright,
art thou, Paynim?
Why on the polished mirror dost thou thus so frequent
cast thine eyes?
Bewildered and distraught at thine own beauty's sight
art thou, Paynim?
I've heard that poor Ned*í*m hath been by cruel Paynim
captive ta'en—
That fierce oppressor of the Faith, and foe of right,
art thou, Paynim?

SABQATĪ

(SULTAN MAHMŪD I.)

1168 [1754]

Gazel

Kerem-bakhsh olmaz, ey dil, halini janana suweylersen

O heart! e'en though thou tell'st thy woes, yon maid will ne'er compassion deign:
When constancy and troth thou seek'st, dost thou address the barren plain?
The student of the course of tyranny is yonder wanton wild;
To look for faith or grace from her who enmity desires is vain.
That paynim glance doth hold in hand a dagger sharp of point and keen;
And yet, O babe, my heart, thou dost to thousands sing her praises' strain.
In hope that it would yield the soul a breath of favor's odor sweet,
How yonder rosebud-mouth effaceth all, thou dost thereto explain.
O Sabqatī, what wondrous science hath thy magic talent learnt,
That thou right royally inditest every joyous, glad refrain?

BELIG

1170 [1756 *ca.*]

I

GAZEL

Oi al fes kakul uzre berg-i gul dur sunbul ustuna

A ROSE LEAF o'er the spikenard fall'n — the red fes lies
on her dark hair;[233]
The perspiration studs her cheeks — the dew-drops
which the roses wear.[147]
Since mirrored in th' o'erflowing bowl did yon cup-bearer's
chin beam bright,
My eyes were fixed upon that wine, like bubbles which
that wine did bear.
Behold thou, then, her braided locks, as musk, all dark and
sweet perfumed;
Like ambergris, her tresses shed abroad an odor rich
and rare.
Those who set forth on Mystic Path behind soon leave the
earth-born love;
The Bridge, as home, within this world of ours,
no man hath taken e'er.[234]
Now, O Belig, that steed, thy reed, doth caracole
across this page;
Thy finger-points, the Hayder bold whom that Duldul
doth onward bear.[235]

II

Gazel

On a Dancing-Girl

El aldiqja o chengi guzeli charpara

When that beauty of a dancing-girl her castanets
hath ta'en,
Should the sun and moon behold her, jealous,
each were rent in twain.
Patience from my soul is banished when beginneth
she to dance;
Leaps with her my heart; my eyesight, faltering,
is like to wane.
When the moon looks down upon her, must it not be
seared of heart?
Yonder moon-fair one her crimson skirt for halo
bright hath ta'en.
In her motions and her pausings what varieties
of grace!
While her lovely frame doth tremble, like to
quicksilver, amain! [236]
Full delighted at her motions, loud as thunder
roars the drum;
Beats its breast the tambourine, its bells commence to
mourn and plain.
When she cometh, like a fairy, begging money
from the crowd,
In her tambourine, had one a hundred lives,
he'd cast them fain.
Deck her out on gala-days, and take her by
the hand, Belíg;
Yonder spark-like Idol hath consumed my soul
with fiery pain.[237]

SAMI

1170 [1756 *ca.*]

I

Gazel

Mevj-khiz oldu yene eshk-i terim seyl gibi

Surge in waves my streaming tears, e'en like a rushing
flood, once mo;
From their smallest drop, the sources of a hundred
Niles would flow.
Overwhelm the raging billows of my tears the heart's
frail barque,
Though the mem'ry of her cheek, like to the beacon,
radiance throw.
What my pen writes down appeareth, in the eyes
of brutish men,
Like the needle to the blinded, of discerning clear
the foe.[238]
One the beggar's bowl would be with the tiara of
the King,
Were it but reversed, for then like to the royal crown
'twould show.[239]
Though it be coarse as a rush-mat, is that soul the
seat of grace,
Which doth, like the wattle-basket, freely bread to
guests bestow.
"Yonder hair-waist I encircled," did the braggart
rival say;
But her waist exists not — hair-like slight his boasting's
truth doth show.[240]

O thou vain one! see, what anguish to the head of
Nimrod brought
Was by one gnat's sting, which like to trunk of
elephant did grow.[241]
Sami, it is thy intention to compare to Heaven's
bowers
These thy distichs eight, with shining flowers of
rhetoric that glow.[242]

II

Fragment

Medh-i Kevserle gunul sanma dusher me'mula

Think not that with Kevser's praises hearts become of joy full;[50]
Preacher, rather doth the tale of mouth and kiss the soul rule.
Thinking of her rubies red, whene'er I drink tobacco,
The nargila's a flask of wine, the pipe-bowl is a sumbul.[243]
Know how holy is her land: — who dwelleth in Edirna,
Ere he to the Ka'ba bends, doth turn him to Istambul.[244]

NEV-RES

1175 [1761 *ca.*]

Gazel

Devr-i la'linda bash egmem bade'-i gul-fama ben

Near thy rubies ne'er I bow my head to wine of rosy hue;
'Neath the shadow of the Magian priest, I ne'er the glass eschew.[245]
Now it makes me exile's prisoner, now the comrade close of pain —
What to do I know not, what with this sad fate of mine to do!
E'en the Home of Peace it turneth to the cot of woe for me,
Through the longing for thy dusky mole, when Sh*a*m I journey through.[246]
Since 'tis needful midst the people that I still reside and move,
If the days ne'er suit me, I shall suit myself the days unto.
Never unto Nev-res, never, will thy sweet words bitter seem;
Speak thou, then, for I'm contented all reproach to hearken to.

SHAHIN GIRAY

(KHAN OF THE CRIMEA)

1205 [1789]

Gazel [247]

Yar gelip 'ashiqin menzilini qilsa jay

If the fair one would but come in her lover's
home to stay,
Were his eyes not filled with light by her face
as bright as day?
Or would yonder Moon but dart that her glance as
dagger keen,
And my rival's bosom pierce that, like flute,
he breathe dismay! [248]
Fly not this poor one, Moon-face, who hath drunken
deep of woe;
Order not that I be burned in the fire of love,
I pray.
If the grace of God the Lord to a slave
should aider be,
Though he lack a single groat he'll the Sphere
as monarch sway.
Rush the tear-drops from my eyes through their
longing for thy face;—
By its power thy sun-like face doth the dew-drops
steal away.[249]
By the Mystic Pathway's side, if thou'rt wise,
a hostel build,
For the travelers of Love, as a caravanseray.
Proud and noble mistress mine, with those eyebrows
and those eyes,
Where a need of bow and shaft this thy lover
fond to slay?

Thou hast loosed thy tresses dark, o'er thy day-face
spread a veil—
Or in House of Scorpio is the Moon
eclipsed, say?[144]
Should my loved one pierce my breast,
right contented sooth were I;
Only worthy of her grace let that
Moon-face me survey.
Write, O pen, that I desire, like the
salamander, fire;
Thus declare, should she it will, yonder
lovely Queen Humay.[250]
Is it then the shining moon that the
world doth silver o'er,
Or the radiance of thy face that doth
earth in light array?
Did the caviller dispute and thy
sun-bright face decry,
Would thy lover, like the mote,
to that fool the truth convey.[251]
Lovers surely for their loves do
their talents aye employ;
Is it thine thy tribute now to present,
Shahin Giray?

GALIB

1210 [1795]

I

From his Husn u 'Ishq, "Beauty and Love"[252]

THE SONG OF LOVE'S NURSE

Ey mah uy uy ki bu sheb

O MOON! sleep, sleep thou, for this night
The cry "O Lord!" upon thine ear shall smite;
Though formed, its purpose is yet hid from sight,
It shall be seen — the stars' potential might.
Thou'lt be the roast upon the spit of pain!

O Rosebud! sleep thou then this little while;
The Sphere's design against thee sooth is vile,
For pitiless is it and strong in guile;
Ah! never trust it, even though it smile.
Thou'lt have, I fear me, reason oft to plain!

O Love's Narcissus! sleep the sleep of peace!
Fall at the skirt of Fate and beg surcease;
Thy soul's eye ope — and, lo! thy fears increase!
Guard thee against the end of woe, nor cease.
Thou'lt be as plaything by Misfortune ta'en!

Come, in the cradle of repose thee rest
A few short nights, by sorrow undistrest;
Bid care and all it brings leave thee unprest;
In place of milk, blood shall be thy bequest.
Thou'lt need the goblet of despite to drain!

O Jasmine-breast! within the cradle lie;
Thus will not long remain the rolling Sky:
The stars do not aye in one circle hie;
See what they'll do to thee, Love, by-and-by.
  Thou'lt be the mill on sorrow's torrent's train!

From slumber do not thou thine eyelids keep,
If aid can reach thee, it will come through sleep;
The Sphere will give a draught of poison deep,
Then will thy work, like Galib's, be to weep.
  Thou'lt be the rebeck at the feast of pain!

II

From the Same

Love's Song

Ey khosh o zeman ki dil olup shad

Sweet were those moments when the heart was gay,
And the soul's realm, the court of joy's array;
Thoughts of those times now o'er my spirit stray,
For love of God! O Heavens! mercy! pray!
The pride of both the day and night was I.

A garden fair was that my soul's repose;
Like those in Eden's bower, its every rose;
But parting comes and all of that o'erthrows,
Now in my heart nought but its mem'ry glows.
With honor's wine then drunken quite was I.

Then to the Sphere I never uttered prayer;[114]
Feast, music, and delight — all mine — were there;
Moved ever by my side my Cypress fair;
Unopened then my secret and despair.
The envy of the springtide bright was I.

Now before grief and woe I'm fallen prone;
Like nightingale in early spring, I moan.
Through fire I've past and to the shore have flown.
And, like the shattered glass, to earth am thrown.
Sipping the wine, the fair's despite, was I.

Ah me! alas! those happy hours are past;
The spring is past; the rose, the flowers, are past;
The smiles of her who graced the bowers are past;
The thirsty soul remains, the showers are past.
Drinking with her the wine so bright was I.

I with my loved one feast and banquet made,
Wild as the whirlpool then I romped and played;
At wine-feasts I myself in light arrayed,
And with my songs the nightingales dismayed.
  Like Galib, blest with all delight was I.

FITNET KHANIM

1215 [1800 *ca.*]

I

Gazel

Khiyal-i gamzasini sineda nihan buldum

The mem'ry of his glance hid in my breast deep
laid I found;
It seemed as though a fawn within the lion's
glade I found.
O heart! a parallel unto those eyebrows and that
glance,
In Rustem's [199] deadly bow and Qahraman's [177] bright
blade I found.
When, through my grieving at thine absence,
dead of woe was I,
That mem'ry of thy rubies' kiss new life conveyed
I found.
My heart's wound, through the beauty of the
spring of love for thee,
By turns, rose, tulip, Judas-tree of crimson shade,
I found.[92]
Is't strange, O Fitnet, if my soul around do
scatter gems?
Within the ink-horn's vault a hidden treasure
laid I found.

II

Museddes

Sahab-i nev-bahar 'alema guher-nisar oldu

The fresh spring clouds across all earth their glistening pearls profuse now sow;
The flowers, too, all appearing, forth the radiance of their beauty show.
Of mirth and joy 'tis now the time, the hour to wander to and fro;
The palm-tree o'er the fair ones' picnic gay its grateful shade doth throw.
O Liege, come forth! from end to end with verdure doth the whole earth glow;
'Tis springtide now again, once more the tulips and the roses blow.

Behold the roses, how they shine, e'en like the cheeks of maids most fair;
The fresh-sprung hyacinth shows like to beauties' dark, sweet, musky hair.
The loved one's form behold, like cypress which the streamlet's bank doth bear;[253]
In sooth, each side for soul and heart doth some delightful joy prepare.
O Liege, come forth! from end to end with verdure doth the whole earth glow;
'Tis springtide now again, once more the tulips and the roses blow.

The parterre's flowers have all bloomed forth, the roses, sweetly smiling, shine;
On every side lorn nightingales, in plaintive notes discoursing, pine;

How fair, carnation and wallflower the borders of the garden line!
The long-haired hyacinth and jasmine both around the cypress twine.
O Liege, come forth! from end to end with verdure doth the whole earth glow;
'Tis springtide now again, once more the tulips and the roses blow.

Arise, my Prince! the garden's court hath wondrous joys in fair array;
O hark, there midst the rose's boughs, the wailing nightingale's fond lay;
Thy bright cheek show the new-oped rose and make it blush with shamed dismay;
With graceful air come then, thy cypress-mien before the mead display.
O Liege, come forth! from end to end with verdure doth the whole earth glow;
'Tis springtide now again, once more the tulips and the roses blow.

Enow! thy lovers pain no more, of faithful plight the days are now;
On streamlet's banks, of mirth and joy and gay delight the day are now;
In hand then take the heart's dear joy, the goblet bright, its days are now;
O Fitnet, come, and these thy verses sweet recite, their days are now.
O Liege, come forth! from end to end with verdure doth the whole earth glow;
'Tis springtide now again, once more the tulips and the roses blow.

ILHAM*I*

(SULTAN SEL*I*M III.)

1222 [1807]

I

Gazel

Ruz u sheb didelerim derdin ile qan aglar

Ah! through grief for thee mine eyes blood, every night
and day, weep;
Those who know my bitter sorrow's secret pang for
aye weep.
When they see me blood-besmearèd by my bosom's red
wound,
Pitying my doleful plight, the garden's flowerets
gay weep.[92]
When he viewed my bleeding heart, ruth had yon
physician;
Quoth he: "Doth the cure for thee, Sick of love-dismay,
weep."
Yet to me doth yonder Torment of the Soul no
grace show;
For my plight do all my friends, who me thus sick
survey, weep.
E'en as gazeth on thy cheek, amidst his
woes, Ilham*i*,
Though his face may smiling be, his heart doth
blood alway weep.

II

Gazel

Bag-i 'alem ichre zahirda safa dir saltanat

Midst the orchard of the world though empire may
appear delight,
Still, if thou wouldst view it closely, empire is but
ceaseless fight.
Vain let no one be who ruleth kingdoms in these
woeful days;
If in justice lie thy pleasure — then is empire truly
right.
Reacheth e'en one lover union in the space of thousand
years?
Let whoever sees it envy — empire is of faithless
plight.
Think, O heart, alas! the revolutions of the rolling
Sphere!
If at times 'tis joy, far oftener empire bringeth
dire affright.
Do not envy, do not covet, then, the Kingship
of the world;
O! take heed, Ilhami, empire bides not, swift
indeed its flight.

FAZIL BEG

1225 [1810]

I

Gazel

Giydi shejer 'imame siyah u sefid u surkh

The trees and flowers their turbans roll of black and
white and red;
The garden fastens on its stole of black and white
and red.
With sable eve and ermine dawn and fes of sunset
bright,
The sky doth all its pomp unroll of black and white
and red.
The pupils of my eyes are points upon the gleaming
page,
With tears of blood I've writ a scroll of black and
white and red.[254]
The youthful Magian's[245] locks and breast were
shadowed in the wine;
It seemed as though they filled the bowl with black
and white and red.
Is't ambergris, or is it pearl, or coral, Fazil, say,
This poesy thy reed doth troll, of black and white
and red?[255]

II

From the Zenan-Nama [256]

Description of Circassian Women

Ey rukhi dide-ruba-yi khurshid

Ah! her cheek doth rob the fair sun of its sight,
And her sweet grace envy brings to Venus bright.
Like to moons are the Circassian damsels fair;
Whatsoe'er the lover seeks he findeth there.
Like to tall palm-trees their slender forms in grace,
Or a ladder to the clear moon of the face.
With the two feet of the eyes doth one ascend,
But the vision of the mind too one must bend.
Since their lips and cheeks are taverns of wine,
Is it strange their eyes inebriate should shine?
Since like rubies are created their two lips,
Doubly seared the lover's heart, like the tulip's.[257]
Since their bodies are distilled from moon and sun,
How an equal to their pure frame find can one?
Though they lovelier than Georgians may be,
Still in Georgians one will great attractions see.
Closely curtained sit they all in virtue's place;
Pure of skirt is ever this unrivaled race;[258]
Pure and free from stain is every act of theirs;
Not a soil the vestment of their honor bears;
Marked with chastity indeed, of noble heart,
Ever seeking to fulfill the righteous part;
Bright with bounty and fidelity and sense,
How that blessèd nature glows with light intense!
Think not with this race that any can compare
Upon earth, unless it be the Georgian fair.

III

From the Same

Description of Greek Women[259]

Ey kelisa-yi bela naqusi

Oh! thou the Bell upon the church of pain!
Thou the Pride of all the Messianic train![260]
Source of being! if a mistress thou should seek,
Then, I pray thee, let thy loved one be a Greek.
Unto her the fancies of the joyous bend,
For there's leave to woo the Grecian girl, my friend.[261]
Caskets of coquetry are the Grecian maids,
And their grace the rest of womankind degrades.
What that slender waist so delicate and slight!
What those gentle words the sweet tongue doth indite!
What those blandishments, that heart-attracting talk!
What that elegance, that heart-attracting walk!
What that figure, as the cypress tall and free—
In the park of God's creation a young tree!
What those attitudes, those motions, wondrous fair!
What that glance inebriate that showeth there!
Given those disdainful airs to her alone,
And her legacy that accent and that tone.
All those letters on her sweet tongue's tip are rolled,
And those words with many graces she'll unfold;
Strung the regal pearls of her enchanting speech,
Pounded seem they when her gentle mouth they reach;
To her tongue if come a letter harsh to say,
Then her sweet mouth causeth it to melt away;
Her mouth would fain the words conserve in sooth,
For her mouth is speech-conserves in very truth;[262]
Speaking parrots are they surely one and all,[115]
To their portion doth the birdies' language fall.[263]
With a thousand graces saith her rosebud-lip:
« Zee vine, O noble Lord, vill zou no sip;[264]

When thy glass is empty, fill it full again,
To my love drink, O my Pasha, drink amain!»[265]
To the soul add life her ways and charms so dear,
Surely thus is it a mistress should appear.
E'en the old misogynist would conquered be,
Saw he yonder maid, uxorious were he.
So symmetrical the line her body shows,
One would it a balanced hemistich suppose.
Other women seek to imitate her grace,
As their pride and frontispiece she holds her place.
What that figure tall, and what that graceful mien!
Fair-proportioned is her body ever seen.
Moving lithely, she from side to side will turn,
That the hearts of all her lovers she may burn.
That cap which on one side she gaily wears;
That jaunty step; those joyous heedless airs;
Those motions — they are just what me delight;
And her tripping on two toes — how fair a sight!
'Twere as though with fire her pathway were inlaid,[266]
That would burn the feet of yonder moon-like maid.
Thou wouldst deem her lovers' hearts upon her way,
Burning with their love for her, all scattered lay.

* * * * *

Is't herself they call «Qoqona» let us see?[267]
Or her locks? — how wondrous sweet their odors be!
As the sash trails on the ground beneath thy feet,
So will she thy feet salute with kisses sweet.
Misbeliever, thou dost sense steal from the heart;
Torment thou — I know not what a Woe thou art;
Know not I if thou be *huri* or *peri*,[268]
Know not I of Mary what is found in thee;
Art thou Mary's child of 'Imran's, rosebud bright?[269]
Of the dwelling of the monks art thou the light?
Envy bearing to her hinna-crimsoned hand,
Doth the red egg covered o'er with blushes stand.[270]
With the Greek cannot thy genus e'er compare,
Deem I, be thou genius or *huri* fair![271]

WASIF

1236 [1820 *ca.*]

I

TERJI'-BEND[272]

On the Defeat of the French in Egypt by the Qapudan Huseyn Pasha

Ey jedel-gah-i jihanin Nirem-i jeng-averi!

O thou Nirem, battle-waging, of the world's fierce field of fight! [273]
O thou Sam, fell dragon-visaged, of the age's plain of might!
Thou art he in whom the favors of the Lord Most High unite;
Earth and ocean thou hast conquered, waging war on left and right!
Gold, in Islam's cause, thou pouredst like to water down a height;
Legions like the Nile on Egypt's shore thou madest to alight.
With thy sabre's blow right fiercely thou the foeman's head didst smite;
Giddy made thy sword the misbelievers' chieftains with affright.
Midst the earth's oak-grove a valiant lion like to thee in might,
Since the days of Rustem, ne'er hath passed beneath the Heavens' sight.
«Bravo! Champion of the Epoch! rending ranks in serried fight!
O'er the 'Arsh hang now thou sabre, sparkling like the Pleiads bright!» [274]

Lion! Alexander![53] had he seen that battle thou
didst gain,
Crown and throne to thee to offer Key-Qubad
were surely fain!
O most noble! thou a Vezir to such fame that
dost attain,
That the God of Hosts did surely Lord of Fortune
thee ordain!
Like to flame, the fiery blast scathed foemen's lives,
it blazed amain;
Threw'st thou, cinder-like, the misbelievers' ashes
o'er the plain.
"Conqueror of the Nations' Mother" as thy title
should be ta'en:[275]
Since thou'st saved the Nations' Mother, all the
nations joy again.
Wishing long ago, 'twould seem, to sing thy splendid
glory's strain,
Nef'i wrote for thee this couplet—for thy deeds a
fit refrain:[276]
"Bravo! Champion of the Epoch! rending ranks in
serried fight!
O'er the 'Arsh hang now thy sabre, sparkling like the
Pleiads bright!"

When the misbelieving Frenchman sudden swooped
on Egypt's land,
Thither was the army's leader sent by the Great King's
command:
But at length o'erthrown and vanquished by the foe
his luckless band,
Then thou wentest and the vile foe scatter'dst wide on
every hand;
Then, when they thy lightning-flashing, life-consuming
cannon scanned,
Knew the hell-doomed misbelievers vain were all things
they had planned.
Hundred vezirs, joy-attended, countless foemen did
withstand;

Day and night, three years the misbelievers fought they
brand to brand;
Worn and wretched fell those at thy feet, and quarter
did demand:
It beseems thee, howsoever high in glory thou mayst
stand!
"Bravo! Champion of the Epoch! rending ranks in
serried fight!
O'er the 'Arsh hang now thy sabre, sparkling like the
Pleiads bright!"

Through this joy beneath thy shade the world doth
its desires behold;
With thy praises eloquent the tongues of all, both
young and old.
Thou to Faith and Empire then didst render
services untold
Hurling down to earth the foeman's house in one assault
right bold!
O Vezir! Jem-high! think not that flattery my words
enfold;—[277]
Though a poet, not with false or vaunting boasts I've
thee extolled.
Midst the fight for Egypt's conquest firm in stirrup
was thy hold,
Under thy Egyptian charger trod'st thou foemen like the
mould.[278]
From the handle of thy sword, like water, down the
red blood rolled;
Thou the foe mad'st turn his face, mill-like, in terror
uncontrolled.
"Bravo! Champion of the Epoch! rending ranks in
serried fight!
O'er the 'Arsh hang now thy sabre, sparkling like the
Pleiads bright!"

Those who sing thy glories, like to Wasif, wildered
aye must be;
Sayeth Wasif: "None on earth like Huseyn Pasha
I shall see."

If there be who has in vision seen a peerless one like thee,
As a dream all void of meaning, let him it relate to me.
Cannon-ball like, 'gainst the foe thou threw'st thyself from terror free;
Like the winter blast thou mad'st the foeman shake in front of thee.
Claim to manliness forsaking, even as the blind was he,
Sword in hand despairing stood he, like to one who nought can see;
Quick his throat thou seizedst, like the dragon direful in his glee,
'Neath thy sabre's wave thou drown'dst the misbeliever, like the sea!
"Bravo! Champion of the Epoch! rending ranks in serried fight!
O'er the 'Arsh hang now thy sabre, sparkling like the Pleiads bright!"

II

SHARQI[179]

Ey goncha'-i bag-i meram

O ROSEBUD of joy's flowery lea!
O graceful one with step so free!
If thou wilt yield thee not to me,
On earth the glass of mirth and glee
To me's forbid, apart from thee.

Behold my breast, by guile unprest,
Is't not mid thousand treasures best?
Until thou tak'st me to thy breast,
On earth the glass of mirth and glee
To me's forbid, apart from thee.

O Rose-leaf fresh! concealed from sight
With thee till morn a livelong night
If I may not enjoy delight,
On earth the glass of mirth and glee
To me's forbid, apart from thee.

Yearning for union fills my soul,
Patience and peace have no control;
O wanton one! my longing's goal!
On earth the glass of mirth and glee
To me's forbid apart from thee.

Seek, Wasif, her who hearts doth snare
Yon maid with bosom silver-fair;
Until thou thither dost repair,
On earth the glass of mirth and glee
To me's forbid, apart from thee.

III

SHARQÍ

Kim gursa ol la'l-i muli

To whom that wine-red ruby's shown
Is captive by those locks o'erthrown;
'Tis meet like nightingale I moan:
A lovely Scio Rose is blown.[280]

Unmatched yon maid with waist so spare,
Unrivaled too her wanton air;
Her ways than e'en herself more fair:
A lovely Scio Rose is blown.

The roses like her cheeks are few;
That rose — blush-pink its darling hue;
This summer ere the roses blew,
A lovely Scio Rose is blown.

The rose — the nightingale's amaze;
The rose the nightingale dismays;
A smile of hers the world outweighs:
A lovely Scio Rose is blown.

O Wasif, on the rosy lea,
The nightingale thus spake to me:
"Be joyful tidings now to thee —
A lovely Scio Rose is blown."

RAMIZ PASHA

1236 [1820 *ca.*]

GAZEL

Gunul oldusa da misdaq-i nass-i Esrefu', *ya* Rabb

ALTHOUGH my heart the truth of *Those who wrong themselves* doth show, O Lord![281]
In virtue of the words *Do not despair*, Thy love bestow, O Lord!
Beside the mead of truth and calm make aye my soul to go, O Lord!
My virtue's rose to tint and scent as captive do not throw, O Lord!
From vain attachments' stain wash pure and clean my heart as snow, O Lord!
Against me place not Thou the loathsome pool of lies of foe, O Lord!
The burning pain of exile no relief can ever know, O Lord!
Enow, if Thou the camphor-salve, the dawn of hope, did show, O Lord!
Thy slave is Ramiz; unto none save Thee doth he bend low, O Lord!
Before Thy mercy's gate his tears from eyes and eyelids flow, O Lord!

‘IZZET MOLLA

1252 [1836 *ca.*]

From the Mihnet-Keshan [282]

Gazel

Meyl edermi kukne sevba qamet-i bala-yi ‘ishq

After old rags longing hath the figure tall and
slight of Love?
Fresh and fresh renews itself aye the brocade
fire-bright of Love.
’Gainst the flames from thorns and thistles ne'er a
curtain can be wove,
Nor ’neath honor's veil can hide the public shame,
the blight of Love.
Through a needle's eye it sometimes vieweth far-off
Hindustan —
Blind anon in its own country is the piercing
sight of Love.
It will turn it to a ruin where naught save the
owl may dwell,
In a home should chance be set the erring foot of
plight of Love.
Will a single spark a hundred thousand homes
consume at times:
One to me are both the highest and the lowest site
of Love.
Never saw I one who knoweth — O most ignorant
am I!
Yet doth each one vainly deem himself a learnèd wight
in Love.
Rent and shattered — laid in ruins — all my caution's
fortress vast
Have my evil Fate, my heart's black grain, the rage,
the blight of Love.[283]

In its hell alike it tortures Musulman and infidel,
'Izzet, is there chance of freedom from its pangs,
this plight of love?
Of reality hath made aware the seeker
after Truth,
Showing lessons metaphoric, He, the Teacher
bright St. Love!

‘ADLÍ

(SULTAN MAHMÚD II.)

1255 [1839]

Gazel

Mubtelasi oldugu ol nev-juwan bilmezlenir

That I'm fall'n her conquered slave, yon maiden bright
feigns not to know;
Thus pretending, she who doth the soul despite feigns
not to know.
Though I fail nought in her service, she doth me
as alien treat;
Know not I why yonder Darling, earth's Delight,
feigns not to know.
If I dare to speak my eager longing those her
lips to kiss,
Friendship she disclaims, in sooth with cruel slight
feigns not to know.
That she whets her glance's arrow and therewith doth
pierce the heart,
E'en her bow-like eyebrow, yonder Ban of might
feigns not to know.[284]
Well the loved one knows the Sphere doth keep no
faithful troth; but, ah!
How she copies it, that Heart-ensnarer bright
feigns not to know.
There is ne'er a refuge, ‘Adlí, from the grief of
rivals' taunts;
I my love conceal not, still yon maiden slight
feigns not to know.

LEYLA KHANIM

1275 [1858]

I

TARIKH

On the Death of 'Andelib Khanim[285]

Akhiretlik 'Andelib Khanim fenaden gitdi, ah!

'ANDELIB, th' adopted sister, from this transient
world hath flown,
Yonder midst the flowers of Eden whilst still in her
youth to stray.
No physician, neither charmer, on the earth her pain
could ease;
So that youthful beauty bided not to smile on earth's
mead gay.
With her two-and-twenty summers, cypress-like
was she, ah me!
But the sullen blast of autumn smote her life's bright,
lovely May.
For its tyranny and rancor might have blushed the vile,
hard Sphere,
As the sister of earth's Monarch pined in grief
without allay.
Though her kind friend never parted from her eye's
sweet, gentle beam,
Still did she to God her soul yield, and the call,
Return, obey.[286]
Down the wayward Sphere hath stricken that bright
Jewel to the earth; —
What avail though men and angels tears of blood shed
in dismay?

Length of days to that great Sultan grant may He,
the God of Truth!
And yon fair Pearl's tomb make rival His own
Eden's bright display!
With the dotted letters, Leyl*a*, thou the year tell'st
of her death—
*C*a*l*m amongst *deli*ghtsome bowers may
'An*deli*b her nest array!

II

TAKHMIS

On a Gazel of Baqi[287]

Beni ser-mest u hayran eyleyen ol yar-i janim dir

'Tis yonder Darling of my soul that wildering my sense o'erthrows;
My waving Cypress 'tis that freshness to the garden doth disclose;
The bird, my heart, my gardener is in Love's fair parterre of the rose:
Mine eyes' field with thy cheek's reflection as my flowery orchard shows;
For long my heart the picture of thy palm-like figure doth inclose.

The world seems in my eyes as prison that doth my dear love control;
Through love for thee my heart acquireth many a scar, and that's the whole;
From hour to hour thine absence makes my tears like rushing waters roll:
The heart bows down through grief for thee, and constant weeps the life, the soul;
The fountain of this vineyard is the stream that from my weeping flows.

As well thou know'st, through fire of love for thee how sad my plight of woe,
My smiling Rosebud, wilt thou ne'er a glance of pity toward me throw?
My sighs and wailings thou dost see, O but for once compassion show:
Through gazing on the rose and bower, my heart repose shall never know,
The ward where doth my loved one dwell alone can yield my soul repose.

O how I think upon thy box-tree form in sorrow's
night so drear!
My story would Mejnun's and Ferhad's tales from mind
make disappear.
My groans and sighs and wails thus high do I unto
the Heavens uprear,
*By reason of the sparks my sighings raise that steely
bowl, the Sphere,*
*Revolves each night, my gold-enameled beaker at the
feast of woes.*

From thought of yonder witching eye my heart is ne'er
a moment free;
When flow thy tears recall not thou to mind, O Leyla,
'Oman's Sea.
Beneath thy shade my own heart's blood is all that hath
been gained by me:
*My tears, an ocean vast; my lashes, coral branches,
O Baqi!*
*The mem'ry, 'tis of thy palm-form that as my Judas-
tree bright glows.*

REF'ET BEG

SHARQI[288]

Amalimiz efkarimiz iqbal-i watan dir

OUR hopes, our thoughts, are for the weal of our dear native land;
Our bodies form the rampart strong to guard our frontier strand:
We're Ottomans — a gory shroud our robe of honor grand.
« God is Most Great! » we shout in rush and charge on field of fight;
We're Ottomans! our lives we give, our gain is glory bright.

The name of Ottoman with terror doth the hearer thrill;
The glories of our valiant fathers all the wide world fill;
Think not that nature changeth — nay, this blood is yon blood still.
« God is Most Great! » we shout in rush and charge on field of fight;
We're Ottomans! our lives we give, our gain is glory bright.

A sabre on a blood-red field — our banner famed behold! [289]
Fear in our country dwelleth not, in mountain or in wold:
In every corner of our land croucheth a lion bold.
« God is Most Great! » we shout in rush and charge on field of fight;
We're Ottomans! our lives we give, our gain is glory bright.

Then let the cannon roar, and shower its flames
on every side!
For those our brothers brave let Heaven ope its
portals wide!
What have we found on earth that one from death
should flee or hide?
"God is Most Great!" we shout in rush and charge
on field of fight;
We're Ottomans! our lives we give, our gain is
glory bright.

ZIYA BEG

1296 [1879 *ca.*]

I

Gazel

Alir her lahza zevqa 'umr bir mey-khane dir 'alem

A tavern which each moment takes a life as pleasure's
pay is earth;
A glass which for a thousand souls doth sell
each drop of spray is earth.
The world's a Magian that adores the flame of power
and fortune high;
If thou should brightly shine, a moth about thy taper's ray
is earth.
Anon one is, anon is not — thus ever runs the
course of time;
From end to end a warning-fraught, a strange,
romantic lay is earth.
'Twixt sense and frenzy 'tis indeed right hard to draw
the sund'ring line,
Ah me! if understanding's wise, demented sooth
alway is earth.
The desolation of the world beside its weal is
truth itself;
Just as prosperity it seems, so ruin and
decay is earth.
How many Khusrevs and Jemshids have come,
and from its bower have past!
A theatre that vieweth many and many an act and
play is earth.[290]
Ziya, a thousand caravans of wise men through
its realms have past;
But yet not one can tell its tale, and all unknown
this day is earth.

II

TESD*I*S

On a Beyt of Mahm*u*d Ned*i*m Pasha

Gunul, gunul, ne bu huzn ve elem bu gam ta key?

HEART! heart! how long shall last this sorrow,
anguish and dismay?
All things upon earth's ruin-cumbered waste must
needs decay.
What was the splendor of Jemsh*i*d? where Khusrev
and where Key? [291]
Hold fast the goblet and the wine, let chance not
fleet away!
"Our coming to this world is one; man must
reflect, survey;
Care must one banish, and look out for calm
and quiet aye."

Be he Khusrev, or Rustem, or Ner*i*m*a*n,
or Jemsh*i*d,
Or be he beggar; be Isl*a*m or heathenesse
his creed;
A few days in earth's inn a guest is he,
then must he speed:
Something to render gay that time is surely
wisdom's need.
"Our coming to this world is one; man must
reflect, survey;
Care must one banish, and look out for calm
and quiet aye."

When viewed with understanding's eye, the mote
hath no repose;
The world must thus be imaged for exemption
from its woes:

Of my coming and my going it no lasting
picture shows —
That a departure surely is which no returning
knows.
"Our coming to this world is one; man must
reflect, survey;
Care must one banish, and look out for calm
and quiet, aye."

Events the workings of the Lord Most High make
manifest;
Being the mirror is in which the Absolute's
exprest;
He who this mystery perceives in every
state is blest;
The exit of each one who enters earth decreed
doth rest.
"Our coming to this world is one; man must
reflect, survey;
Care must one banish, and look out for calm
and quiet aye."

See that thou grievest not thyself with sorrows
all unwise;
'Tis need all pleasure to enjoy as far as
in thee lies;
Alike is he who lives in joy and he whom
trouble tries;
If thou be prudent, ne'er thine opportunities
despise.
"Our coming to this world is one; man must
reflect, survey;
Care must one banish, and look out for calm
and quiet aye."

Since first the banquet fair, this world, was cast
in form's designs,
How many rakes have passed away! how
many libertines!

As counsel meet for revelers, when he
perceived those signs,
Around the goblet's rim the Magian priest
engraved these lines:[245]
"Our coming to this world is one; man must
reflect, survey;
Care must one banish, and look out for calm
and quiet aye."

At length, *Ziya*, shall joy beam forth, and grief an
end shall find;
But yet, O man, these ever enter Fortune's
feast combined.
This hidden mystery learn thou, by Mahm*u*d
Beg defined,
Who has the secret of the same within this
verse enshrined:
"Our coming to this world is one; man must
reflect, survey;
Care must one banish, and look out for calm
and quiet aye."

THOSE DEAR WOMEN!

Photogravure after the painting by de Beaumont.

BIOGRAPHICAL NOTICES

BIOGRAPHICAL NOTICES

THE following Biographical Notices are, for the most part, compiled from Von Hammer's *Geschichte der Osmanischen Dichtkunst*. The greater length of the sketches of the earlier poets is accounted for by the fact that the materials for drawing out such sketches are much more accessible in their case than in that of the more modern authors. The originals of the verses translated in some of the Notices will be found in the *Tezkeras* of Latífí and Qinali-Zada. The dates immediately following a poet's name show the year of his death, the first, according to the Hijra; the second, to the Christian era.

'ASHIQ PASHA (733=1332) is the earliest writer of the Ottomans; he flourished as far back as the reign of Orkhan, second monarch of the nation; and consequently, as may be imagined, his work is of great interest as a specimen of the language at that distant period. He lived where he was born, in the town of Qir-Shehr in Anatolia. His title of *Pasha* is a spiritual one; he was not a leader of warriors, but a chief among mystics; in the same way the great Sheykh Bukhara is called *Emir*, and the son of Mevlana Jelalu-'d-Dín, *Sultan* Veled. The following is one of 'Ashiq's sayings, recorded by Latífí: «He is a dervish who forsakes the world; he is a beggar whom the world forsakes.»

AHMEDÍ (815=1412) is the first and perhaps the greatest of the Ottoman epic poets. He does not, however, owe this high position to elegance of diction, for his words and phrases are not unfrequently rough and uncouth, but to the immense sweep of subject contained in his great work, the *Iskender-Nama*, which is an epitome not only of Oriental history from the earliest times down to the period when he wrote, but also of Eastern mysticism, philosophy, and science. He was born at S*i*v*a*s, and flourished during the reigns of Mur*a*d I. and B*a*yez*i*d I. The biographers relate that when Ahmed*i* took his *Iskender-Nama* to his patron, Prince Suleym*a*n, the ill-fated son of B*a*yez*i*d, he met with but a poor reception, being told that an elegant *qasida* would have been preferable to so ponderous a work. Ahmed*i*, deeply chagrined at this, went and complained to the great poet Sheykh*i*, with whom he lived; so Sheykh*i* that night composed a *qasida* in Ahmed*i*'s name and gave it to the latter to take to his patron. The Prince, at once perceiving the difference between the graceful diction of Sheykh*i* and the unpolished style of Ahmed*i*, said smilingly to the poet: « If this *qasida* is thine, then yonder book is not; and if yonder book is thine, then this *qasida* is not.» When T*i*m*u*r in his Anatolian campaign, which so very nearly proved fatal to the Ottoman power, arrived at Am*a*siya, he made the acquaintance of Ahmed*i*; for he was fond of the society of men of letters, and the exploits of Ahmed*i*'s hero, Alexander the Great, were congenial subjects to the T*a*t*a*r conqueror. One day, in the public bath, the monarch said to the poet: « Value me these fair boys thou seest here.» Ahmed*i* valued them, some, at the world filled with gold and silver, others, at the tribute of Egypt in pearls and jewels. « And at how much dost thou value me?» said the mighty conqueror. « At eighty *aqchas*,» * replied the poet. «The towel I have about me is alone worth eighty *aqchas*,» said T*i*m*u*r. Ahmed*i*'s answer was bold: « It was therefore I valued thee thereat, and above that thou art worth nothing; for the Commanding Soul † is not worth a red farthing.» T*i*m*u*r, instead of being angry,

* An aqcha is a small coin, one-third of a para, and consequently $\frac{1}{120}$th of a piastre, or the $\frac{1}{35}$th of a penny.

† There are three states of the passions in Muslim ethics — (1) *Nefs-i Emmare*, «the Commanding Soul or Flesh,» that state of the passions when they habitually control and compel the individual to obey

was pleased with this reply, and rewarded the poet. Besides the *Iskender-Nama*, Ahmedi left a romantic poem called *Jemshid and Khurshid* and a *Diwan* of *gazels* and *qasidas*. He had a brother, who wrote in twenty-four volumes the romantic history of Hemza, the uncle of the Prophet. This work earned for its author the surname of Hemzavi; and to this day the fabulous tales and poems wherewith the *Meddahs*, or public story-tellers, amuse the guests in the coffee-houses are called in Turkey *Hemza-Namas*.

SHEYKHI (830=1426 *ca.*), the first of the Ottomans to write a romantic poem, was born, during the reign of Bayezid I., in Germiyan in Asia Minor. His name was Sinan, the *takhallus*, or surname, of Sheykhi being given to him partly on account of his advancement in the mystic path, and partly by reason of his being the Sheykh, or chief, of the poets of his age. He studied for a time at Brusa with Ahmedi the author of the *Iskender-Nama*, and then under the celebrated Sheykh Haji Beyram, founder of the Beyrami Order of dervishes. To gain his livelihood, Sheykhi undertook the study of medicine, giving particular attention to the diseases of the eye, a branch of the science to which he may have been attracted by some such malady in himself. Anyhow the story is told of a patient, to whom he had for an *aqcha* given an ointment for the eyes, making him a present of another *aqcha* that he might prepare a further supply for his own organs of vision. Sheykhi was the trusted medical adviser of Sultan Muhammed I. Things had not gone very well with that monarch on one of his military expeditions, and in consequence thereof he had lost both his spirits and his health. The physician, perceiving what was the cause of the Sultan's indisposition, promised him complete recovery with the news of the first victory. This was not long of coming, and with it returned the sovereign's heart and health. Muhammed, pleased with his doctor's penetration,

their exigencies; (2) *Nefs-i Levwama*, «the Upbraiding Soul,» that state when the passions can be controlled, though they still strive to make their voice heard; *Nefs-i Mutma'inna*, «the Peaceful Soul,» that state when the passions are totally subdued.

rewarded him with the rich fief of Toquzlu. This, however, did not meet with the approval of the then possessor of that demesne, who waylaid Sheykh*i* on his road thither, robbed him of all he had about him, and give him a severe cudgelling into the bargain. The poet brought this incident under the Sultan's notice by means of a satire written in verse and entitled *Khar-Nama*, «The Ass-Book,» in which he related the whole adventure. Sultan Mur*a*d II. held the poet-doctor in even higher esteem than had done his predecessor, Muhammed; for he desired to make him his vez*i*r. This the enemies of Sheykh*i* prevented: under guise of zeal for literature they represented to Mur*a*d how much better it would be to first employ such a distinguished poet in some great literary work, and then to reward him with the vez*i*rate. The Sultan was deceived; he requested Sheykh*i* to translate into Turkish some of the works of the great Persian poet Niz*a*m*i*. *Khusrev and Shirin* was the poem selected; but Sheykh*i* did not live to finish it; he died during the reign of Mur*a*d II., to whom his translation is dedicated, and lies buried at K*u*t*a*hiya. His nephew, Jem*a*l*i*, the author of several poems, completed the work. Five Ottoman poets besides Sheykh*i* have sung the story of Sh*i*r*i*n: *Ahi*, Jel*i*l*i*, Khal*i*fa, and Mu'eyyed-z*a*da composed *Khusrev and Shirins;* whilst L*a*m*i*'*i* wrote the tale of her adventures with Ferh*a*d under the name of *Ferhad-Nama*, «The Book of Ferh*a*d.» We are told that once, shortly after the capture of Constantinople, when the great Sheykh, Aq Shemsu-'d-D*i*n, was seated in deep meditation amongst his disciples, he repeated over and over again, as it were from the depths of his soul, the words, «O Germiy*a*n! O Germiy*a*n!» When his wondering pupils asked him what he meant thereby, he said to them that the exclamations had been wrung from him by admiration of these lines of the great poet of Germiy*a*n:

Ne'er can Reason, of the caravan of God's might, news convey
Through that means, not e'en the tinkling of its bell can reach the soul.*

* *Kibriyanin karabaninden khaber vermez 'uqul;*
Ermez andan jan qulagina meger bang-i jeres.

YAZIJI-OGLU (853=1449), called also Ibn-Katib — the first name being Turkish, the other Arabic, for the *Scribe's Son* — lived at Galipoli with his brother Bijan, who was, like himself, a mystic poet. The first, who had studied under the celebrated Sheykh Haji Beyram, founder of the order of dervishes, called the Beyrami, wrote in Arabic a great theological work entitled, *Magaribu-'z-Zeman fi Gara'ibi-'l-Eshya fi-'l-'Ayn ve-'l-'Ayan*, which his brother translated into Turkish under the name *Envaru-'l-'Ashiqin*, « The Lights of Lovers.» Both brothers then took the *Magarib* as material for new works: Bijan compiled from it the *Durr-i Meknun*, « The Hidden Pearl,» and the other, known as Yaziji-Oglu, the great poem of the *Muhammediyya*. This immense work, which consists of 9,109 couplets, comprises the whole doctrine of Islam, as well as the history of the Prophet. It was completed in 853 (1449), four years before the capture of Constantinople.

SULTAN MURAD II. (855=1451), sixth sovereign of the House of 'Osman, is notable as being the earliest of the Ottoman Monarchs who encouraged poetry by personal example, the first of the long line of poet-sultans. The principal events of Murad's reign are, an unsuccessful siege of Constantinople, and the memorable victory of Varna, where a host of forsworn Christians under Hunyades met in an utter and ignominious rout, the just reward of treachery. In this battle the standard of the Ottomans consisted of a lance on which was reared a copy of the treaty violated by the Christians, who, having seen Murad occupied in Asia, pounced upon his European territories, after swearing upon the Gospels to leave them undisturbed. Murad II. twice abdicated and was twice recalled to the throne, the first time to gain the battle just spoken of. More to his taste than the pomp of sovereignty was his quiet and pleasant retreat at Magnisa, where twice a week he held re-unions of savants and poets, at which the guests discussed literary questions and recited verses of their own composition. Murad died in Adrianople, after a glorious reign of thirty years.

'AVNI: SULTAN MUHAMMED II. (886=1481) was girt with the scimitar of 'Osman when twenty-one years of age

Two years later Constantinople, and with it the last vestige of the Roman Empire, fell before his victorious legions. When, after the capture of this great city, the Sultan entered the deserted palace of the Emperors, gazing upon the scene of desolation, and pondering on the transitoriness of the glories of earth, he repeated this famous Persian couplet:—

> Midst the palace of the Cæsars doth the spider weave her toil;
> And the owl stands sentry o'er the turrets of Efrasiyab.*

Many conquests mark his reign: the Principality of Sinub and the Empire of Trebizond were annexed to the Ottoman dominions; and the Kingdom of Qaraman, which had been the rival of the 'Osmanli power from its earliest days, was finally subdued. Sultan Muhammed II. fought and overthrew the Vallachian Prince, Vlad the Impaler, one of the most cruel tyrants of whom history makes mention. The Ottoman admiral, Gedik Ahmed Pasha, toward the close of this Sultan's reign landed in Italy and captured Otranto. Muhammed II. died at the age of fifty-two, having in his thirty years' reign conquered 2 empires, 7 kingdoms, and 200 towns. M. Servan de Sugny, who ought to have known better, gives credence to the fable of Irene (who never existed), and even goes so far as to connect one of the Sultan's poems with this mythical tragedy! Sultan Muhammed II., himself a poet, was a great patron and protector of literature and men of letters; thus, as his many and brilliant achievements in war have earned for him the title of *Ebu-'l-Feth*, "Father of Victory," so have his zeal and liberality in building *medresas*† and the like gained for him the surname of *Ebu-'l-Khayrat*, "Father of Good Works." Thirty Ottoman poets were pensioned by him, and every year he sent 1,000 ducats a-piece to the Indian Khoja'-i Jihan and the Persian Jami, the latter of whom composed an ode in his honor. Muhammed II., like many

* *Perde-dari mi-kuned der qasr-i Qaysar 'ankebut; Bum bang mi-zened der gumbed-i Efrasiyab.*

Efrasiyab is the name of a Turanian Prince, the chief opponent of the Persian Rustem his exploits are detailed in the Shah-Nama.

† A *medresa* is a college for the study of law and divinity.

other of the Ottoman Sultans (who resemble in this respect the old Khalifas of Bagdad), delighted exceedingly in the society of poets. Persians especially had for him a great attraction; and the story is told of a Turk who, to gain admittance to the Imperial circle, gave out that he was a native of *Iran*; he was however detected and summarily dismissed. Muhammed wrote most of his *gazels* under the *takhallus* of 'Avni. Many of his vezirs were poets; among whom may be mentioned Ahmed Pasha, Mahmud Pasha, and Jezeri Qasim Pasha; the two latter wrote under the names 'Adeni and Safi, respectively. These, like their master, were men of action as well as of letters.—Sultan Muhammed II. had full, round cheeks, tinted red and white; and a firm mouth; the moustachios that adorned his lips were «like leaves over two rosebuds, and every hair of his beard was as a thread of gold»; while his hooked nose over his red lips was like «the beak of a parrot above a cherry.»

The practice of imperial fratricide, though not originated by Muhammed II., was by him made into a state maxim. If it be true that it is better one should die than many, that «an insurrection is more grievous than an execution,»* then was this otherwise atrocious custom altogether justifiable; for as surely as an Ottoman Prince had the power to assault his brother's throne, he did so with might and main; and even if he had not the power, so long as he lived there was always a host of restless spirits and disappointed adventurers ready to make his detention the excuse for an attack upon the existing authority. For an empire, surrounded by inveterate and powerful foes, and containing within its own borders a conquered, and therefore hostile, population, to be periodically exhausted by furious and useless fratricidal wars would have been simply ruin. The sagacity of Muhammed foresaw this, and his grim fortitude did not shrink from applying the only possible remedy. In this case, as in many another, a swift stern blow dealt uncompromisingly at the root of the evil was, in the long run, the most merciful course that could be adopted. It need scarcely be said, that with the necessity for it, this custom died out. With the Jagatay Turkish Emperors of

* Qur-an, ii., 187.

Dihlí this rule did not hold; and, as a consequence, the empire of the «Great Moguls» was rarely free from civil war. It would seem that nothing less than a crown could satisfy the lofty ambition of a Turkish Prince.

'ADENÍ: MAHMÚD PASHA (879=1474), the conqueror of Negroponte, one of the poet-grand-vezírs of Sultan Muhammed II., was the son of an Illyrian father and a Byzantine mother. He constructed many public buildings in Constantinople, some of which remain to this day. His bounty and liberality are highly praised by the Ottoman biographers. Qinali-Záda tells us that on the completion of the college he built in the capital, he gave to each of the students two turbans, a piece of scarlet cloth (for a garment), and 500 *aqchas*. Every Friday he held an entertainment of savants, and regularly among the dishes served was a plate of rice and peas, a great number of the latter being of pure gold; every guest kept those he took up in his spoon. Mahmúd fell eventually under the Sultan's displeasure, was dismissed from office, imprisoned in the Seven Towers, and there, after a little, put to death. Shortly before his disgrace he said: «I came to the threshold of the Pádisháh with a horse, a sword, and 500 *aqchas;* whatsoever I possess besides has been gained in the service of the Pádisháh; and in the shade of his good fortune have heart and soul attained each hope and wish.»

*Á*FITÁBÍ (880=1475 *ca.*) was a native of the city of Amásiya. He gained admittance to the court of Sultan Báyezíd II.; but there «the fraternity of envy, to force and expel him from the court of the Pádisháh, blocked up the path of propriety with the thorns and thistles of spite and rancor, and drove him far from the Imperial presence; and in the time of old age shattered the glass, his tender heart, with the stone of cruelty.» In his retirement he composed a *qasída* giving an account of his misfortunes. Latífí says that «his *Díwán* is composed of flowery poesies; and his sweet expositions, of the delicious flavor of expressions.»

ZEYNEB (886=1481 *ca.*), according to Latífí, was born in Qastamúní but, '*A*shiq Chelebi states that Amásiya, where her father was *qadi*, was her native town. Perceiving her talent, her father made her study the Persian *Diwans*, and the Arabic *qasidas*, with happy result; for she herself composed a *Diwan* of Turkish and Persian poems, which she dedicated to Sultan Muhammed II. She seems never to have been married. Latifi says of her: «She was a lady of virtue and chastity, a maiden, modest and pure; in the female sex, in the class of womankind, a wonder of the age, one renowned and covered with fame.» And thus Qinali-Zada: «The bride, her learning and poetry, is not hidden and concealed by the curtain of secrecy and the veil of bashfulness; but the rosiness of her beauty and the down and mole of her comeliness are beheld and esteemed of the public, and the object of the gaze of every man and woman.»

Prince Jem (901=1495) was the younger brother of Sultan Bayezid II., with whom (after the wont of Turkish Princes) he contested the Imperial throne. Being defeated at Yeni-Shehr, he fled to the court of the Sultan of Egypt, where he was hospitably received, and whence he made the pilgrimage to Mekka. Next year he renewed the war and was again defeated; and this time, unfortunately for himself, he sought refuge in Christian lands. He fled with thirty followers to Rhodes and begged protection from the Knights of St. John. D'Aubusson, the Grand Master, received him, not out of any kindliness, but for the sake of the coffers of the Order. The Knights soon came to the conclusion that their prisoner would be safer in one of the *commanderies* owned by the Order in France, so they shipped the Prince and his few retainers off to Nice. The Grand Master then made an arrangement with Sultan Bayezid, whereby the former was to receive a yearly payment of 45,000 ducats, ostensibly for the maintenance of the Prince, but in reality as a bribe for his compulsory detention in some possession of the Order. On Jem's arrival at Nice, he composed his celebrated *gazel* which begins with the lines:—

Come, O Jem, thy Jemshid cup drain; 'tis the land of Frankistan;
Aye, 'tis fate, and what is written on his brow must hap to man.*

* *Jam-i Jem nush eyle, ey Jem, bu Firenkistan dir;*
Her qulun bashina yazilan gelir, devran dir.

He was detained for some months in that city under various pretexts, and most of his Turkish followers were forcibly separated from him; then he was removed to the interior, where he was transferred from castle to castle. At one of these, that of Sassenage, the beautiful Philipinne Hélène, daughter of the châtelain, fell in love with the Turkish Prince, and by her kindness did much to cheer the dreary hours of his captivity: long after his removal from Sassenage his only solace was in correspondence with this fair friend. During his thirteen years of captivity among the Franks, so far as history tells, Prince Jem received no sincere kindness from any Christian, except this lady. Knights, Kings, and Popes, though they treated him with outward respect, and flattered him with false promises of aid to gain his father's throne, made him an object of barter among themselves for the sake of the ducats that could be got from Stamboul for his safe custody.

From the hands of the Rhodian Knights, Jem was transferred to those of Pope Innocent VIII., who, dying shortly afterward, was succeeded by the infamous Alexander Borgia. This pontiff sent an ambassador to Constantinople to arrange about the continuation of the payment of the 45,000 ducats; but he also stipulated that he was to have the option of receiving 300,000 ducats down, if he effectually relieved Bayezid from all further anxiety on the score of Jem, by putting an end to that Prince's life. Charles VIII., King of France, invaded Italy, entered Rome, and acquired possession of Jem. Borgia saw that his chance of profit through the maintenance of the Ottoman Prince was gone, so he chose the still more profitable alternative, and caused the unfortunate fugitive to be poisoned.

The biographers record that, when at the Egyptian Court, Jem sent to his brother this verse:—

Thou liest on couch of roses, smiling with delight;
Whilst I am fall'n mid suff'ring's fires—O wherefore is it so?*

* *Sen bister-i gulda yatasin, shevq ile khandan;*
Ben kul dushinem kulkhan-i mihnetda, sebeb ne?

to which Bayezid replied:—

Since from eternity to us hath Kingship been decreed,
To destiny yield'st thou thee not? O wherefore is it so?
«I pilgrim am to Holy Shrine,» 'tis thus thou dost declare;
O why then such desire for earthly empire dost thou show? *

Prince Jem was endowed with a large share of the poetic talent by which his House is so distinguished; many of his verses are full of fire, grace, and originality; he was indeed a poet in the most restricted meaning of the term.

AHMED PASHA (902=1496), the son of Veliyyu-'d-Din, a *Qaziyyu-'l-'Asker* † under Murad II., is the first really great lyric poet of the Ottomans. Quick at repartee and highly endowed with the poetic genius, he was raised to the rank of vezir by the poet-fostering Sultan, Muhammed II., whose tutor he had been in earlier days. As an instance of his ready wit the biographers relate that one day when he and the Sultan were together, the latter, a great lover of literature, and as such naturally well versed in the most famed productions of the East, repeated with much admiration the following couplet of the Persian poet, Hafiz of Shiraz:—

Those who can make, with but one look, the dust elixir grow,
O that a sidelong glance they would toward us in kindness throw! ‡

whereupon Ahmed at once improvised in Persian and in the same metre:—

Those who can make, with but one look, the dust elixir grow,
To tutya turn the pearly dust where'er thy footsteps go! §

* *Chun Ruz-i ezel qismet olunmush bize devlet,*
Taqdira riza vermeyesinbuyle sebeb ne?
Hajju-'l-Haremeynim deyipin da'wa qilirsin,
Bu saltanat-i dunyeviya bunja taleb ne?

† «Judge of the army,» the title of two high legal functionaries, subordinate only to the *Sheykhu-'l-Islam*.

‡ *Anan ki khakra be-nazar kimiya kunend, Aya buved ki gushe-i cheshmi be-ma kunend!*

§ *Anan ki khakra be-nazar kimiya kunend, Khak-i jevahir-i qademet tutiya kunend!*

Kimiya is properly the «Philosopher's Stone,» not «elixir.»

So delighted is the Sultan said to have been with this ready answer, that he ordered the Vezir's mouth to be filled with jewels.

Ahmed, however, did not continue in the Sultan's favor. Qinali-Zada gives the story of his fall in this wise (Latifi tells it somewhat differently): Among the pages of the Seraglio was a beautiful boy of whom the Vezir was very fond; Muhammed suspected this, but not being sure, resolved to put the Pasha to the test. He ordered the boy's beautiful hair to be cut off, and sent him with a cup of sherbet to the Vezir, who was in the bath. Ahmed, when he saw the boy shorn of his locks, gave utterance to his sorrow and dismay in these words:—

> Yon Idol hath removed his locks, his infidelity disclosed;
> The Magian hath his girdle rent, but yet no Musulman is he; *

which, being reported to the Sultan, at once confirmed his suspicion, and, in his rage, he ordered his minister to be shut up in the Chamberlain's apartment, there to be put to death. Imprisoned there, in the hope of moving the clemency of the Sultan, Ahmed Pasha composed and sent out to him his famous *Kerem Qasidasi*, "Grace Qasida," so called because the word *kerem* "grace" forms its *redif*. It commences thus:—

> O a drop from grace's ocean! thou that art the Main of grace!
> Fills thy hand's cloud bounty's flowery garden with the rain of grace.
> Should the slave do wrong, what harm then if the King of kings forgive?
> Were my two hands steeped in blood, blood's dye away were ta'en of grace!
> What the grace that can be vanquished, aye, and even slain of sin!
> What the sin not to be vanquished, aye, and even slain of grace?
> Water drowns not, no, it fosters these things which itself hath reared;
> Wherefore then should overwhelm me ruin from the Main of grace?

This poetical petition had the desired effect, for Muhammed, who was a sort of Harunu-'r-Reshid, was so pleased that he not only forgave the Pasha, but presented him with the page; he, however, banished him to Brusa, with the appointment of director of the legacies of the Mosque of Sultan

***Zulfun gidermish ol sanem kafirligin qonar henuz;*
Zunnarini kesmish mugbeche veh Musulman olmamish.

Murad. After a while he was named *Sanjaq-Begi* of Sultan-Unu; and under Muhammed's son and successor, Bayezid II., he was appointed governor of Brusa, an office which he held during the remainder of his life.

At one time Ahmed Pasha stood high in the favor of the Great Conqueror of Constantinople, who, himself a poet, was always very partial to those who cultivated his favorite art; he gave him the revenues of the village of Ekmekji near Adrianople, along with one of his slave-girls, called Tuti, «Parrot,» by whom Ahmed had a daughter, who died in childhood. Von Hammer, in his «History of the Ottoman Empire,» tells the following anecdote, taken from the work of Seyyid Isma'il, who is known as «the Rhetorician of Brusa.» One day, when Sultan Muhammed, Ahmed Pasha, and one of the pages of the Seraglio were out riding, annoyed by the dust which blew in their faces, the Pasha repeated the words of the Qur'an: «Would that I were dust!»* The Sultan, not hearing exactly, asked: «What does he say?» whereupon the boy, witty as handsome, repeated Ahmed's quotation, but with the words which in the verse come immediately before: «Saith the *Kafir* («infidel,» «scoundrel»), 'would that I were dust!'»

As already stated, Ahmed Pasha is the first Ottoman lyric poet with any claim to greatness; but he was soon eclipsed by Nejati and Zati, who, in their turn, paled before the brilliancy of Baqi, the sun of 'Osmani lyric poetry. Ahmed's poems lack polish and, still more, originality; most of them being close imitations, if not indeed translations, of Persian models.

NEJATI (914 1508), whose real name was 'Isa (*i. e.*, Jesus), was, according to Qinali-Zada, born at Adrianople, but brought up at Qastamuni. At Brusa, where he dwelt with the lyric poet, Ahmed Pasha, whose adventures form the subject of the preceding notice, he gained his first laurels by the composition of two *gazels*, imitating, but surpassing in merit, one by a poet called Nuh, which was then much spoken of in the town. His poetical talent began to show itself toward the close of the reign of Sultan Muhammed II., to

* Qur'an, lxxviii., 41.

whose notice he chose a singular method of introducing himself. He wrote a *gazel* in praise of the Conqueror, and fastened it in the front of the turban of one of that monarch's favorites who was in the habit of playing chess with his master. The first time they seated themselves to play, the Sultan noticed the piece of paper on his friend's turban, took it, read it, and admired it, and forthwith appointed the poet Secretary of the Divan. Shortly after obtaining this post, Nej*ati* dedicated to the Conqueror his Winter Qas*i*da, and, a little later, his Spring Qas*i*da. On the death of Sultan Muhammed he composed a poem of the same class in honor of that monarch's son and successor, B*a*yez*i*d II. An extract from all three of these *qasidas* will be found among the translations from Nej*ati*'s works in the present volume.

Nej*ati* accompanied B*a*yez*i*d's son, Prince 'Abdu'-ll*a*h, to the province (shortly before the kingdom) of Qar*a*m*a*n, of which the latter had been appointed Governor; and there, on that Prince's death, he wrote an elegy in which occur these lines:—

> O heart! from out Love's register thy name erase;
> Go, be a qalender,* those like thee hermits praise;
> Look thou no more upon the world, for from the eyes of him
> Tears roll, who would straight at the sun's bright visage gaze.

Nej*ati* now entered the service of Prince Mahm*u*d, another of B*a*yez*i*d's sons, with whom he went to Magn*i*sa in the capacity of *nishanji*. On the occasion of this promotion he composed some lines which begin thus:—

> That turn of time has changed or altered me, conceive thou ne'er;
> It has but moved a ringlet of its dark musk-shedding hair.
> The secretary, Fate, from out of Destiny's Divan
> Has marked and set me forth as sign before the whole world's stare.

Nej*ati* collected his poems into a *Diwan*, which he dedicated to his master, Prince Mahm*u*d, at whose suggestion he translated into Turkish Gaz*a*l*i*'s famous ethical treatise *Kimiya-yi Sa'adet*, "The Alchemy of Happiness,"† and

* A wandering dervish.

† This has been translated into English by Mr. H. A. Homes, of New York.

Jemalu'-d-Din Muhammed's historical work, *Jami'u-'l-Hikayat ve Lami'u-'r-Riwayat*, «The Collector of Stories and the Illuminator of Traditions.» On the death of this Prince, Nejati again wrote an elegy in which are found the words:

This world is but the home of pain, sorrow, and decay;
That which they call the court of joy is the palace of dismay.
At last a winding-sheet shall shroud us every one:
Alike the beggar's lowly plight, the emperor's display.
Thus would the grave's mouth cry to thee, had it a tongue to speak:
«False! vain! is all that I about this monster dare to say!»*

Sultan Bayezid, to whom he brought this elegy, gave him his choice of a public appointment; but Nejati, who above all things preferred leisure and freedom from business, contented himself with a monthly pension of 1,000 *aqchas*. He built himself a house in Constantinople, where he lived almost entirely alone. He had several sons, all of whom died before him, and one daughter, who was married to a distinguished philologist.

Nejati was a true poet; he wrote indeed no *mesnevis*, only *gazels* and *qasidas*, but in these he surpassed all his predecessors, including the friend of his youth, Ahmed Pasha, who till then had been regarded as the greatest of the Ottoman lyric poets. His immediate successor Zati, if he equaled, which is doubtful, certainly did not surpass him; it was reserved for Baqi, Sultan of all Turkish lyrists, to excel Nejati, even as he had himself excelled all those who had preceded him.

MESIHI (918=1512), who was born at Pirishtina, near Uskub, was a poet of high merit, and is held in great repute by the biographers. His strength, like that of Lami'i, lies in elegant descriptions of the beauties of nature, but unlike that great poet, he wrote no *mesnevis*—if we except one *shehr-engiz* composed, as this style of poem always is, in the *mesnevi* form—confining himself to *gazels* and the like. According to Qinali-Zada, his *takhallus* of Mesihi, «Messianic,» or «Follower of the Messiah,» was well chosen: «it is fit that he should have fame through that name, for

*It has not dared to tell the whole truth; the monster is Death.

his Jesus-like words would raise the dead, and from the channel of his musky reed he caused the Water of Life to flow; and it is meet that that poet of eloquence should be styled a second Messiah by reason of his soul-nurturing poesies and his verses that life bestow." * He became Secretary of the Divan to the Grand Vez*i*r 'Al*i* Pasha the Eunuch, who gave him a fief, on the revenues of which he lived. He owed this post to a petition in verse, a *qasida*, a few distichs of which are translated in this book. This poem, in which he showed unmistakable signs of genius, was addressed to the Nish*a*nji T*a*j*i*-Z*a*da Ja'fer Chelebi.

However, according to the biographer '*A*shiq, on the authority of the poet Ned*i*m*i*'s father, likewise a servant in 'Al*i* Pasha's employ, Mes*i*h*i* was very negligent of the duties of his office and much more frequently to be found in taverns and other places of amusement than in the minister's cabinet, which, on being learned by the Sultan, was the cause of a considerable reduction of the poet's salary. On 'Al*i* Pasha's death Mes*i*h*i* sought employment from the Grand Vez*i*r Y*u*nus Pasha, and then from T*a*j*i*Z*a*da Ja'fer Chelebi, but without success in either case.

Zati, the poet-laureate, who was jealous of Mes*i*h*i*, charged the latter with having appropriated some of his ideas; the accusation was conveyed in this form: —

O Mes*i*h*i* who doth honor steal must surely be a thief;
Thou art King of verse's city, yet somehow is this thing clear.
That from *Zati*'s realm of poems certain thoughts have stolen been,
And that these thy D*i*w*a*n ent'ring, there in altered guise appear.

Mes*i*h*i* thus replied: —

Do not think that I stretch forth my hand unmeaning thoughts to grasp;
I'm no infant, food by others mashed and chewed that I should eat;
Knowing that the soul within me is to me nought save a loan,
For my life each day a thousand times I blush with shame complete.

Besides his *Diwan*, Mes*i*h*i* wrote an *Insha* † called *Gul-i Sad-Berg*, "The Hundred-Leaved Rose," and, as has been said, a *Shehr-engiz*.

* See Note 189.

† A collection of epistolary forms.

HARIMI : PRINCE QORQUD (918=1512) was son of Bayezid II. and brother of Selim I. When that fierce monarch prevailed upon his father to abdicate the throne, Prince Ahmed, another brother, raised the standard of revolt, with the result of his own defeat and death, besides affording Selim an excuse for ordering the execution of his five nephews. When Prince Qorqud in his government of Sari-Khan heard the tidings of this massacre, he knew what was sure to be Selim's purpose regarding himself, and tried hard to gain to his side the janissaries and Sanjaq-Begis, vainly hoping to ward off the coming blow. Selim heard of his attempt, and, professing to go upon a hunting expedition, arrived suddenly with a formidable body of horsemen before Magnisa, the capital of Qorqud's province. The Prince had barely time to escape with a single attendant and take refuge in the hills. After hiding among the rocks for twenty days, their retreat was discovered by some Turkmans, who informed the Imperial officers. No sooner was the Sultan made aware of the discovery of his brother than he ordered Sinan, the *Qapiji Bashi*, or Grand Chamberlain, the officer of the Imperial Court in whose charge is the bow-string, to go and perform his duty. Sinan arrived in the middle of the night, awakened Qorqud, and announced to him the death-sentence passed upon him by the Sultan; the Prince asked for an hour's respite, which, being granted, he occupied in writing a letter in verse to his brother, in which he bitterly reproached him for his cruelty; and then gave his neck to the fatal cord.

Qorqud, though not possessing the talent of his uncle, Prince Jem, was nevertheless a fair poet; he was besides well versed in Muslim Law and compiled a highly valued collection of *Fetwas*, called *Qorqudiyya;* he encouraged poets and legists by every means in his power, filling many of the offices of his provincial court with men of letters; he was, moreover, very fond of music, and composed an air known as *Gada-yi Ruh*, "The Nourishment of the Soul."

MIHRI (920=1514 *ca.*) was a poetess of Amasiya, whose *gazels*, breathing ardent love, fully justify her *takhallus*, which means at once "Follower of Love" and "Follower of the Sun." Von Hammer styles her the Ottoman Sappho. She was deeply in love with the fair Iskender Chelebi, son of Sin*a*n Pasha, whom she frequently alludes to — sometimes even mentions by name — in her verses. The first of her poems in this book is an example. Though she thus sang aloud her love, the voice of slander was never raised against her: she was as famed for virtue as for talent. She carried on a literary correspondence with several of the poets of her time, notably with *Zati* and Guv*a*h*i*, to the latter of whom she dedicated a poem, thanking him for all his kindnesses toward her. She appears never to have been married. The biographers do not mention the year of her death.

SEL*I*M*I*: SULTAN SEL*I*M I. (926=1520) ascended the throne in the year 918 (1512), on the abdication of his father, B*a*yez*i*d II. Like his grandfather, Muhammed II., Sel*i*m was a great warrior; in a short reign of less than nine years he doubled the extent of the Ottoman Empire. At first he spared his brothers, but some of them, revolting against him, were defeated, captured, and executed. His first great foreign victory was on the field of Ch*a*ldir*a*n, where he totally defeated Sh*a*h Ism*a*'*i*l and the chivalry of Persia. He afterward led his victorious legions to Cairo, overthrew the Circassian dynasty of the Meml*u*ks, and added Egypt with its dependencies, Syria and Hij*az*, to the Ottoman dominions.

Sel*i*m I. is the only Ottoman Sultan who shaved his beard after ascending the throne; the Imperial Princes wear only mustaches, but whenever one succeeds to the throne, he lets the whole beard grow. On being asked by a Muft*i* why he departed from the established custom, Sel*i*m facetiously replied that he shaved his beard in order that his vez*i*rs might not find anything whereby to lead him. This Sultan changed, likewise, the Imperial turban; he abandoned the pointed cap, the top of which appeared above the surrounding shawl, that had been worn by his predecessors, and adopted in its place a head-dress modeled after the tiara of the ancient Kings of Persia. This turban received the name of *Selimi*, "Sel*i*mean." A glance at the portraits of Muhammed II. and Selim I., in this volume, will show the difference between the two head-dresses.

Sultan Selim I., though often fierce and ruthless, was a great lover of literature and patron of men of learning. He left a *Diwan* of poems in the Persian language, which, for literary purposes, he seems to have preferred to Turkish.

By his conquest of Egypt, Selim gained the Khalifate for the House of 'Osman. *Khalifa*, «Caliph,» *i. e.*, «Successor of the Prophet in the government of the Muslims,» is properly an elective, not a hereditary, office. The titular Khalifa of the Muslim world at this time was a descendant of the House of 'Abbas, who was resident in Cairo when that city was taken by Selim. An arrangement, at once recognized by the Qureyshi Sherif of Mekka, was arrived at between this Prince and the Sultan, whereby the former conferred upon Selim the rank and title of Khalifa, together with all the influence which that office commands. The title of Khalifa has ever since been borne by the Sultans of Constantinople, and their claim thereto is, and ever has been, acknowledged by the world of Sunni Islam, Morocco, Masqit, and Zanzibar alone excepted.*

MUHIBBI: SULTAN SULEYMAN I. (974=1566), surnamed *Qanuni*, «the Lawgiver,» the most illustrious of the Ottoman monarchs, succeeded his father, Selim, the conqueror of Egypt, in 926 (1520). It would occupy too much space to recount the many glories of Suleyman's reign. The people, weary of the vexatious severity of Selim, hailed with delight the accession of a prince known to be at once generous and brave: they saw in his name—that of the greatest of the Jewish Kings—a happy augury, and they were not deceived. His first military exploits were the reduction of Belgrade and the capture of Rhodes, two strongholds which had foiled even his illustrious ancestor, Muhammed II. Then followed the subjugation of Hungary, the king of which country died with all his chivalry on the battlefield of Mohacz. Three years later the Sultan laid siege to Vienna; but not even his happy star and

*See Mr. Redhouse's «Vindication of the Ottoman Sultan's Title of Caliph.» London: Effingham Wilson. 1877.

the valor of the Ottomans prevailed to capture that famous city. Suleyman's attention was not, however, confined to Christian foes; he led several expeditions against Persia, and added Erivan, Van, Mosul, and Bagdad to his empire.

These were likewise halcyon days for the Turks upon the seas: the crescent flag waved proudly over the blue waters of the Mediterranean, and the Christian mariners trembled when they heard the name of Torgud, who, after a glorious career, died, with countless others of the beleaguering Ottomans, on the blood-stained shores of Malta; or of Piyala Pasha, who announced his victory at Jerba by a vessel which entered the Golden Horn with the high standard of Spain trailing in the sea from the stern. But no Ottoman Qapudan* ever inspired the foes of Islam with greater terror, or rendered his sovereign more valuable services, than Khayru-'d-Din Pasha, whom the Italians called the Corsair Barbarossa;—Tripoli, Tunis, and Algiers were added by him to the Sultan's dominions. The Admiral Sidi 'Ali planted the Ottoman standard on the shores of India. This Sidi 'Ali was a poet and a man of science as well as a sailor; several works by him on geography, mathematics, and navigation still remain. Suleyman died in his tent before Szigeth, in Hungary, a few days too soon to hear the glad tidings of that stronghold's fall.

This monarch is perhaps the brightest ornament of the House of 'Osman; he was endowed with almost every quality which goes to make a great sovereign: a soul noble and generous; a genius vast and enterprising; warlike courage; love of justice; and respect for humanity. His greatest weakness was his blind passion for the Russian slave-girl Khurrem, who was all unworthy of her master's devotion; it was through her intrigues that, led to believe his gifted and noble-minded son, Mustafa, was about to rise in revolt against his authority, he gave the order for his execution, and, in so doing, deprived Turkey of one who bade fair to be among her most illustrious sovereigns. Among the brightest jewels in Suleyman's crown is the encouragement which he always extended to letters; his reign

* From the Italian *capitana*, a naval captain; the Lord High Admiral is called *Qapudan Pasha*.

is the golden era of his nation's literature. A poet himself, as well as a friend of poets, he has left a *Diwan* of *gazels*, in which he takes the name of Muhibbi.

Suleyman I. had a grave, calm cast of countenance, a high, wide forehead, and rather dark skin. He modified the head-dress adopted by his father, Selim I., making it higher and not so round ; it was surmounted by two heron plumes, and the point of the cap was visible above the muslin that formed the turban. This fashion of head-dress is called *Yusufi*, "Josephean," probably after the patriarch Joseph, who is a type of wisdom as well as of beauty.

FIGANI (933=1526), of Qaraman, was a secretary to Prince 'Abdu-'llah, one of Sultan Bayezid's sons. The most noteworthy incident in his career is its close. When the Grand Vezir Ibrahim returned from the capture of Ofen, among the spoils that he brought to Constantinople were certain statues which had adorned the royal palace of the Hungarian city; these statues, which the Turks looked upon as idols, were set up in the Hippodrome in front of Ibrahim's mansion. Figani, playing on the Vezir's name Ibrahim, the Oriental form of Abraham, and referring to the well-known story in the Qur'an where that patriarch destroys his father's idols, composed this couplet :—

Two Ibrahims have upon the earth appeared ;
Idols were o'erthrown by one, by one upreared. *

This witticism cost the poet dear; for the offended Vezir caused him to be paraded through the streets of Constantinople on the back of a donkey with his face toward its tail, and then put to death. Figani wrote an *Iskender-Nama*, and a *Heft-Peyker*, "Seven Faces," in imitation of Nizami's poems of the same names.

LAMI'I (928=1531), one of the very best and, at the same time, most fruitful writers of the Ottomans, passed, so far as we know, a quiet and uneventful life; all his time and attention seem to have been sedulously devoted to

* *Du Ibrahim amed be-deyr-i jihan;*
Yek but-skiken shud diger but-nishan.

study, and very great indeed is the success which he achieved in the domain of poesy. In grace and originality his poetry almost rivals that of Baqi, while it far exceeds it in quantity.

Muhammed-bin-'Osman-bin-Naqqash (which is Lami'i's name in full) was born in Brusa. The word *Naqqash*, which means both « painter » and « embroiderer," may in this instance bear either signification, indeed it was probably chosen on that account; for we are told that the grandfather of the poet, besides being a celebrated painter, studied the art of embroidery in Semerqand, and brought thence into Turkey the first embroidered saddle. After studying for a time in his native city (we do not hear that he ever left it), Lami'i turned his thoughts to the mystic doctrines of the dervishes, and entering the Naqishbendi Order, was for long a disciple of the Sheykh Seyyid Ahmed Bukhari; eventually he became himself the Dervish-Sheykh of Brusa.

Among his prose writings are: translations of Jami's famous work, *Nefahatu-'l-Uns*, « Breaths of Friendship," under the title of *Futuhu-'sh-Shahidin fi Tervihi-'l-Qulubi-'l-Mujahidin*, « Disclosures of the Witnesses for Perfuming the Hearts of the Champions," and of the same author's *Shewahidu-'n-Nubuvvet*, « Witness-bearers of the Apostleship.» He likewise translated into Turkish the *Sherefu-'l-Insan*, « The Nobility of Man," Fettahi of Nishapur's mystic romance, *Husn u Dil*, « Beauty and Heart,» * and a collection of anecdotes, called '*Ibret-numa*, «Example-Shower.»

Instead of choosing as subjects for his *mesnevis* the oft-told stories of Leyli and Mejnun, Yusuf and Zuleykha, and Khusrev and Shirin, Lami'i selected three of the most ancient romances of Persia as the threads upon which to weave the web of his poetry: *Wamiq and 'Azra*, *Veysa and Ramin*, and *Ebsal and Selaman* are, all three, tales belonging to a remote antiquity; indeed some see in Wamiq the old Hindu poet Valmiki, and in Veysa the sage Vyasa. Among other poetical works are: a *Shehr-engiz* of Brusa, *Shem' u Perwana*, « The Taper and the Moth," *Gu u*

* Translated into English by Price. 1827.

Chevgan, «The Ball and Bat,» *Heft-Peyker*, «The Seven Faces,» and *Maqtel-i Hüseyn*, «The Martyrdom of Huseyn.» Besides all these, Lami'i left a large *Diwan* of *gazels*, *qasidas*, and such like; and, at the command of Sultan Suleyman, translated the Persian poets Ansari and Jurjani. In prose and verse he composed two *Munazarats* or «Disputes,» one between *Nefs u Ruh*, «Flesh and Spirit,» the other, from which our extracts are taken, between *Behar u Khizan*, «Spring and Autumn.» Von Hammer devotes 174 pages of his «History» to this poet and his works.

KEMAL PASHA-ZADA (941=1534). Ahmed the son of Kemal Pasha is a writer of great note in the annals of Ottoman literature. One day, while still a boy, he accompanied his father, who was a pasha of eminence under Muhammed II., to the Grand Vezir's divan, when the son of one of the foremost men of the Empire, Ahmed Evrenos-Oglu (a famous name, this Evrenos, in old Turkish history), entered the council-chamber in grand array, and was there received with all due deference. Shortly afterward, in came an old man meanly attired in a worn-out dress, to whom the Grand Vezir paid a yet higher respect than that which he had shown to the descendant of the ancient and noble house. This was the great legist Molla Lutfi of Toqat. There, on the spot, the admiring Ahmed resolved to abandon the military profession and devote himself to the Law. He found a patron and a helper in the poet Mu'eyyed-Zada, then *Qaziyyu-'l-'Asker* of Rum-Eyli, through whose influence he obtained several professorships, one after another, and at whose suggestion the Sultan ordered him to write a history of the Ottoman Power. Under Selim I., Kemal Pasha-Zada attained the highest legal position in the Empire, and, as holder of such, accompanied that Sultan on his Egyptian expedition. By the imperial command he translated on the march the historical work entitled, *Nujumu-'z-Zahira fi Muluki-'l-Misri ve'l-Qahira*, «Shining Stars concerning the Kings of Egypt and Cairo»; day by day he gave his royal master the pages as they were finished, in this way acquainting him with the details of the history of that country he was about to conquer.

The biographers have preserved many stories of Kemal Pasha-Zada's ready wit and clever answers, one of which, related by Qinali-Zada, will suffice here. One day when Sultan Selim, with the poet in his retinue, was passing by Qaraman, he observed a whirlwind, whereupon he inquired whether there was any reason for the frequency of whirlwinds in the land of Qaraman. "The capital of this province of Qaraman," answered Ahmed, "is Qonya; there dwelt Mevlana Jelalu-'d-Din, and therefore do the very hills and stones and dust of this land perform the Mevlevi dance." Ahmed Kemal Pasha-Zada lies buried at Constantinople, outside the Adrianople Gate. He left a collection of historical anecdotes, called the *Nigaristan*, "The Picture Gallery," also a poem on the favorite subject of Yusuf and Zuleykha, which is regarded as his master-work.

GAZALI (941=1534) is the *takhallus* of Muhammed Chelebi, a distinguished poet of Brusa, whose jovial but dissolute habits gained for him the nickname *Deli Birader*, "Mad Brother." He commenced his career as a *muderris*, or teacher, at the *medresa* of Sultan Bayezid in his native city; but being introduced to Qorqud, the gifted but unfortunate son of Bayezid II., he entered the circle of that Prince's boon companions, and was one of those who accompanied him on his mission to Egypt. On the execution of his patron, Gazali retired to a cell at the foot of Olympus, near his native Brusa, and there, for a time, devoted himself to the solitary life of a dervish. But tiring of seclusion, he again sought office, and was appointed professor at various colleges, one after another; finding teaching, however, as little suited to his taste as meditation, he wrote a petition to the Sultan and received a monthly allowance of 1,000 *aqchas*. He then took up his abode at Beshik-Tash on the Bosphorus, where he built a mosque, a cell, and a bath. His patron at this time was the Defterdar Iskender Chelebi, on whose death he deemed it best to retire to Mekka, where he built a mosque, and laid out a garden, in which he entertained pilgrims and lived pleasantly till his death. He is buried in the sacred city, in the court of his own mosque.

Gazali wrote for Prince Qorqud a work entitled *Dafi'u-'l-Hummum ve Rafi'u-'l-Gummum*, "The Dispeller of Cares and the Remover of Griefs," which was so licentious that the Prince dismissed the author from his court. The bath which he afterward built at Constantinople was a meeting-place for all the dissolute and profligate of the capital, and a den of every vice; in consequence of which the Grand Vezir Ibrahim Pasha, as soon as he heard of the way in which it was conducted, sent a hundred janissaries who leveled it with the ground. Shortly afterward, Deli Birader got himself into another difficulty which necessitated his journey to Arabia.

This poet was not without talent; he was a beautiful calligraphist, understood music, had a ready store of wit, and knew something of medicine. In the gardens of his bath (for the building of which the Sultan as well as the Vezir, who afterward pulled it down, had subscribed) he provided all manner of pleasures for his guests; fruits, sweet-meats, coffee, opium, and all the other delights of the Eastern voluptuary were there in abundance.

Ishaq Chelebi (944=1537), the son of a sword-cutler of Uskub, was noted for his drunken and abandoned life. Along with two other poets he was summoned to attend Sultan Selim on his Egyptian campaign, in order to afford some amusement to that monarch during the tedious march; but so awkwardly did Ishaq and his companions behave themselves on their introduction to Selim, even pushing him with their swords, that that passionate Sultan ordered them to be beheaded with their own unmanageable weapons. This sentence, however, he immediately commuted to the bastinado. The next day, again summoned to the Imperial presence, the three, in unseemly ragged garments, came before the Sultan: thinking to amuse him, they began to repeat ribald verses, whereupon Selim turned his back on them, saying: "I desired companions, not buffoons."

Zati (953=1546), one of the poetic lights of the reigns of Bayezid II. and Selim I., was born in the province of

Qarasi, where his father followed the occupation of a shoemaker. The youthful poet, not relishing his father's trade, set out for Constantinople, where, after many struggles, he succeeded in making his fortune. During the early period of his life in the capital, he used to sell his poems to gain his daily bread, and to further eke out his livelihood, he exercised the calling of a geomancer, or diviner, by means of figures traced in sand. On some of his writings coming into the hands of Sultan B*a*yez*i*d and his ministers, Z*a*t*i*'s abilities were recognized, and he was forthwith suitably provided for. During the reigns of B*a*yez*i*d and his son Sel*i*m, Z*a*t*i* enjoyed the favor of the great; but the second of these sovereigns had an unamiable fancy for executing his ministers, and Z*a*t*i*'s patrons were put to death with the rest; in consequence of which the poet found himself, on the accession of Suleym*a*n, without a friend. Certain fiefs had been made over to him by Sultan B*a*yez*i*d, on the revenues of which he lived; but early in Suleym*a*n's reign a decree was issued requiring all who did not render military service to give up their holdings; so in his old age Z*a*t*i* was left once more resourceless. He again had recourse to geomancy; but he died in a few months, and was buried by the Adrianople Gate, where so many poets rest.

Of Z*a*t*i*'s lengthy poems may be mentioned, *Shem' u Perwana*, "The Tapir and the Moth," *Ferrukh Nama*, "The Book of Ferrukh," *'Ashiq u Ma'shuq*, "The Lover and the Loved," and *Gul u Nev-Ruz*, "The Rose and the New-Year."

LUTF*I* (957=1550), the Grand Vez*i*r and brother-in-law of Sultan Suleym*a*n, was by birth an Albanian. Unlike his predecessor, *Ayaz* Pasha, Lutf*i* Pasha entertained a profound contempt for women. A quarrel with his wife, in which he was guilty of outrageous misconduct, occasioned his disgrace. Suleym*a*n, highly displeased, took the Princess away from him, dismissed him from office, and banished him to Demitoka, where he died. Lutf*i* wrote several works during his exile, conspicuous among which is a history of the Ottoman Empire brought down to twelve years before his own fall.

Mukhlisi: Prince Mustafa (960=1552). This Prince, whom all accounts represent as being talented, courageous, generous, and refined, was heir to Suleyman's throne, having been born before any of the children of the slave-girl Khurrem. That crafty Russian, desirous of securing the succession for her own son Selim, contrived, in collusion with her son-in-law the Grand Vezir Rustem Pasha, to persuade the Sultan, when on the point of setting out on a Persian campaign, that Mustafa was about to head a revolt for the purpose of placing himself upon the throne, and that the only way to secure his crown during his absence was to crush the germ of the evil by the execution of his son. Suleyman most unhappily fell into the snare; it was the great mistake of his life: it took the reins of the empire from the hands of a brave and skillful soldier and placed them in those of a wretched profligate. When the army reached Eregli on its eastward march, Prince Mustafa was conducted to one of the Imperial tents, and there, instead of being received in audience by his father as he expected, he was set upon by the Mutes, the private executioners of the Imperial Court, and strangled.

Khiyali (964=1556), a native of Asia Minor, came to Constantinople as a *qalender* of the Order of Baba 'Ali. He found a patron in the Defterdar Iskender Chelebi, who introduced him to Ibrahim Pasha, the Grand Vezir, through whose influence he gained admission to the innermost circle of Sultan Suleyman's companions. He excused the silence which he displayed when before the great Padishah and his favorites, the most illustrious poets of the golden period of Ottoman literature, with these lines:—

To such a lofty circle hath Khiyali entrance gained,
That there the rose of Eden had for shame unoped remained.

Shahi: Prince Bayezid (969=1561), one of the sons of Sultan Suleyman I., who after the murder of the unfortunate Mustafa, led astray by the treacherous promptings of his tutor Lala Mustafa, sought to oppose the succession of his brother Selim. He raised an army wherewith to make good his claim; but being totally defeated on the plain of

Qonya, fled into Persia. There he was at first kindly received, but the Shah, pressed by the Sultan, whose mind was poisoned against his son by lying stories and dark intrigues, gave up the hapless refugee to the Ottoman messengers, by whom he and his followers were put to death. This Prince is described as being most amiable and accomplished, and beloved by the people and the soldiery, many of the latter accompanying him in his Persian exile, where they shared his fate.

FUZULI (970=1562), of Bagdad, is one of the ten great poets of Sultan Suleyman's reign. The biographers give no particulars of his life, save that he was resident in Bagdad when that city was taken by the Ottomans under Suleyman. Judging from the great number of words and phrases belonging to the Persian-Turkish dialect that are to be met with in his poems, Fuzuli would seem to have been an *Azerbayjani* Turk. The fact that he was living in Bagdad at the time of the Ottoman conquest gives color to this supposition; for before its capture by Suleyman that city had formed part of the dominions of the Shah of Persia.

Fuzuli's *Leyli and Mejnun* contains many touching passages of great beauty; and his *Diwan* is distinguished, even among those of Turkish poets, by its flowery and picturesque imagery; the reader frequently comes upon passages of great profundity, which prove the writer to have been an earnest thinker and a learned scholar as well as an elegant poet. He translated the famous Persian work of Huseyn Kashifi on the death of 'Ali and his sons, entitled *Ravzatu-'sh-Shuheda*, «The Parterre of the Martyrs,» into beautiful prose, under the name *Hadiqatu-'s-Su'ada*, «The Garden of the Blest.» He further wrote a mystic poem called *Beng u Baba*, «Opium and Wine.»

FAZLI (971=1563) — whose real name was Muhammed — nicknamed *Qara Fazli*, «Black Fazli,» was son of a saddler of Constantinople. In youth he was a dervish of the Khalveti Order, and in civil occupation a clerk; his love of poetry, however, attracted him first to Nejati, and then to the poet-laureate, Zati, whose disciple he became. At the great festival with which Sultan Suleyman I. celebrated the circumcision of his three sons Muhammed, Mustafa, and Selim, *Zati*, after reciting a *qasida* of his own, requested permission to recite one by his pupil Fazli. Suleyman recognized and appreciated the student's talent, and when Prince Muhammed was shortly afterward appointed governor of Magnisa, Fazli accompanied him as Secretary of Divan. On the death of Muhammed, Fazli became Secretary to Prince Mustafa (whose brief career has already been noticed), with whom he remained till his tragic end. He then entered the service of Prince Selim (afterward Sultan Selim II.), who, in the year 970 (1562), appointed him Secretary of State. Next year Fazli died at Kutahiya, aged about 50.

Fazli wrote a romantic poem, entitled *Huma'i and Humayun*, founded on a Persian model. Two others of his works are imitations of the Persian, *Matla'u-'l-Envar*, «The Rising-Point of Lights,» modeled after Nizami's *Lujjetu-'l-Esrar*, «The Ocean of Secrets,» and the *Nakhlistan*, «The Palm-Grove,» after Sa'di's famous *Gulistan*, «Rose-Garden.» He wrote besides, *gazels*, *qasidas*, and *ruba'is*. The gem of his works, and his chief title to glory is his romantic poem *Gul u Bulbul*, «The Rose and the Nightingale,» the simple but impassioned story of which is clad in the richest and most beautiful language. In this work, called by Von Hammer his swan-song, for he finished it but two years before his death, he is in no way indebted to any Persian or Arab master; it is a genuine Ottoman poem, original alike in conception and expression.

NISHANI (975=1567), Jelal-Zada Mustafa, was the great historian of Suleyman's reign, during which he occupied some of the highest offices of state. He was an eyewitness of many of the events recorded in his history. In 1524 he was promoted to the rank of Re'is Efendi, and, ten years later, in the Bagdad campaign, to that of *Nishanji*, or «Cipher-writer to the Sultan.» This office still exists in Turkey, but the holder is now called *Tugra-kesh*.* Nishani is another form of Nishanji, and its employment here offers

*See Mr. W. A. Clouston's «Arabian Poetry for English Readers,» page 434.

an example of a poet choosing his *takhallus* from his occupation, not an uncommon thing, as we have seen in the Introduction.

SELÍMÍ: SULTAN SELÍM II. (982=1574). One day, near the beginning of the First Rebí' of the year 974 (September, 1566), the cannons of Leander's Tower announced to the people of Constantinople that the great Suleyman was no more, and that his son Selím was Sultan in his stead — very bad news, had they known it. Selím's mother was the Russian slave-girl known by the Persian name of Khurrem, "Gay,"* who had gained a great and pernicious influence over her master, and, after a series of dark and cruel intrigues, culminating in the murder of the gallant Prince Mustafa, had managed to secure the succession for her son. The character of this son was the very opposite to that of his illustrious father. A dissolute drunkard, who, instead of attending to the affairs of his empire, shut himself up in his harem, Selím II. is notable in history as the first Ottoman Sultan who shrank from leading his armies in person. But the empire of Muhammed the Conqueror and Suleyman the Lawgiver was too strongly built to fall to pieces even under the rule of so effeminate a sovereign; it maintained all its splendor and even extended its limits by the conquest of Cyprus from the Venetians; — the wine of the island is said to have been the attraction in the eyes of the despicable semi-Russian Sultan. Toward the close of his reign a combination of all the Christian powers of the Mediterranean gained a naval victory over the Ottomans at Lepanto. Although these Christians made a great noise about this, it was for them but a barren triumph; for when, a year or two later, the Venetians sued for peace, they had not only to agree to the retention of Cyprus by the Sultan, but to pay him all the expenses of the conquest.

SHEMSÍ Pasha (988=1580), the confidant and governor of the palace of Selím II. and Murad III., was born in Hungary. He was the last scion of the House of Qizil-Ahmedli, which, on the partition of the Seljuqí Empire,

*Europeans call her Roxelana.

had reigned on the southern coast of the Black Sea. This family — whose lands, like those of all the other petty Turkish chiefs in these parts, had been swallowed up by the ever-growing Empire of Orkhan and his successors — traced its descent from Khalid-bin-Velid, the famous general of the Khalifa 'Osman. Shemsi, whose talents had brought him under the notice of Sultan Suleyman, became the intimate friend of Selim II., and under Murad III. he grew to be one of the most powerful men in the Empire. He is notorious as the introducer of corruption among the high officers of the Ottoman State. The historian 'Ali relates, that one day, when Shemsi was coming out of his cabinet, he heard him say with joy to his *kyahya* (steward): «At length have I avenged the dynasty of Qizil-Ahmedli on that of 'Osman; if the latter has brought about our ruin, I have prepared its too.» «How?» asked the aged *kyahya*. The minister replied: «By inducing the Sultan to sell his favors; to-day the Sultan will himself set the example of corruption; and corruption will destroy the empire.» 'Ali, not very prudently, remarked: «Your Excellency is indeed the worthy descendant of your glorious ancestor, Khalid-bin-Velid, who, as history tells us, gave to the chamberlain of the Khalifa 'Osman two pieces of gold to be introduced to his master before his antagonist; and was thus the first to bring corruption into Islam.» Shemsi Pasha merely bent his head and said: «You know many things, 'Ali.»

Yahya Beg (990=1582) was an Albanian janissary who devoted himself with success to literature. He had the courage to compose an elegy on his friend Iskender Chelebi, put to death by the Grand Vezir Ibrahim, and the still greater audacity to write another, bewailing Prince Mustafa, executed by order of his father, Sultan Suleyman. This last one, coming to the knowledge of the Grand Vezir Rustem Pasha, Ibrahim's successor, and an enemy to all poets, he reported it to the Sultan, at the same time advising him to put Yahya to death; but this Suleyman refused to do. Rustem then summoned the poet-officer to the Imperial presence, hoping to make him say something which would offend the Sultan. «What meanest thou,» asked the Vezir, «by undertaking to censure the death-sentence on Mustafa, and degrading the deeds of the Padishah before the people?» Yahya answered: «With the Padishah's judgment have we judged the Prince; but with those who wept his death have we wept.» Though unable to bring about his death, Rustem succeeded in procuring his dismissal from the posts he held under Government; later on, however, he received a large fief of 27,000 *aqchas*. He used to frequent the parties of learned men and was acquainted with many of the great writers of his day; among others with the poet Khiyali, with whom he had a quarrel, arising from that author's charging him with the appropriation of certain of his verses. When 'Ashiq wrote his biographical work, Yahya was with «the Heroes of the Faith fighting the Holy War at Temeswar.»

He wrote several poetical works besides the *Shah u Geda*, of which the best known are, the *Usul-Nama*, the *Genjina'-i Raz*, «The Casket of Mysticism,» and a *Yusuf and Zuleykha*.

Muradi: Sultan Murad III. (1003=1595), who succeeded his father, Selim II., in 982 (1574), was a mild and well-meaning prince, but destitute of those high qualities which are necessary for the guidance of a mighty empire. His favorite wife, Safiyya, a Venetian lady of the noble house of Baffo, who had been captured by Turkish cruisers along with three other women, one of whom was Murad's mother, had the chief voice in the direction of the Imperial affairs. The most prominent features of his reign were wars with Persia and Austria, and the rapid progress of corruption and military insubordination. Murad III.—unworthy namesake of the valiant Khudavendigar, who died by an assassin's hand on the plain of Kosova after laying the pride of Servia in the dust—found his chief pleasure in the society of his ladies and eunuchs, jesters and dancers. Though a voluptuary, he was a protector of poets and philosophers, with whom he was fond of conversing. His own poems are mostly religious or mystical, and he is remarkable as the only one of the Ottoman Sultans who has written an ascetic work. On the morning of the last day of his life, he was lying in a beautiful kiosque that looked out upon the Bosphorus, watching the vessels sailing to and fro, when, feeling the presentiment of approaching death, contrary to his custom of allowing his minstrels to choose what airs they pleased, he told them to play him that one, of which the appropriate words commence thus: —

I am sick, O Death, this night come thou and watch keep by my side;*

just then two Egyptian galleys arrived and saluted the Seat of Empire; the glass dome of the kiosque where the dying Sultan lay was shattered by their cannon-fire. «Formerly,» said Murad, bitterly weeping, «the salute of all the fleet would not have broken this glass, which now falls at the noise of the cannon of these galleys: thus is it with the kiosque of my life.»

B*a*Q*i* (1008=1600), whose full name was Mahm*u*d 'Abdu-'l-B*a*q*i*, is, according to the unanimous verdict of the Ottoman critics, the greatest lyric poet that their nation has produced. Part of his *Diwan* has been translated into German by Von Hammer: when that illustrious Orientalist published this translation, he was under the impression that it comprised the whole of B*a*q*i*'s poems: but, as he afterward pointed out in his *Geschichte der Osmanischen Dichtkunst*, it really contains less than half of the great Ottoman poet's works, the manuscripts which he made use of being very imperfect. B*a*q*i* was born in Constantinople in the year 933 (1526). His father, who was *Mu'ezzin*, or summoner to prayer, at the Mosque of Muhammed the Conqueror, died in 973 (1565) while on the pilgrimage to Mekka. In his youth B*a*q*i* was a saddler, but he soon gave up this trade to devote himself to literature. He entered the service of Qaram*a*n*i*-Z*a*da Muhammed Efendi, to whom he dedicated his *Hyacinth Qasida*. His verses soon attracted the attention of Sultan Suleym*a*n, who conceived a great esteem for him, conferred upon him many favors, and even wrote a poem in his honor.

* *Bimarim, ey Ejel, bu geje bekle yanimda.*

Under Selim II. Baqi rose to even greater eminence; but during the reign of Murad III., certain of his rivals procured a *gazel*, by an old writer called Nami, in which the poet openly avows his love of wine; this they altered, by substituting Baqi's name for that of Nami, and brought it to Murad, saying, that the highly-favored poet had composed it for Selim II., who was by no means a strict Muslim. The enraged Sultan dismissed Baqi from office and ordered him to be banished; however, before the sentence of exile was carried out, the *gazel* in question was found in an old collection of Nami's poems, and Baqi was pardoned and reinstated in his position. On quitting his trade as a saddler Baqi had studied Law, and he gradually rose in the profession till he attained the highest legal position in the Empire. This celebrated poet died on Friday, 23 Ramazan, 1008 (11 April, 1600). The Sheykhu-'l-Islam recited the burial-service over his remains in the Mosque of Muhammed the Conqueror, where his father had been *Mu'ezzin;* and they buried him outside the Adrianople Gate, on the way to the suburb of Eyyub.

Qinali-Zada says, the first verses that brought Baqi into notice were these:—

When the mem'ry of the fair one's cheek across my heart doth stray,
Beams it brightly as reflected sunbeams in the mirror play.
Should I die through longing for the form of yonder Cypress fair,
Where the juniper shall shade me, in some spot, I pray, me lay.
For this reason go I never to thy ward, that weeping sore,
Fear I, O my Life, my tears should wet the dust that lines thy way.

The same biographer gives the following story, referring to the above poem, from the mouth of Baqi himself: "When I brought this *gazel* to Mevlana Zati, the chief of the Roman* poets of the time, he refused to believe that this fair poem was the offspring of my genius, I being very young. Throwing gems of advice from the mine, his heart, and scattering pearls of counsel from the shell, his soul, he said: 'If, like the plane tree, thou stretchest forth thy hand to the pocket of the words of other people and to the treasury of their verses, there is no doubt that the constable, Fate, will

* See Notes 64 and 259.

cut off the hand,* thy being; nor is there any uncertainty that he whose thoughts, his brides, thou through violence pressest to thy breast, will make thee the object of punishment and castigation.' I through bashfulness and confusion had no power to utter many words, and could only say: 'No, the verses are my own.' Then he showed me some places in his own *Diwan*, and, to try me, asked: 'Which are the spots of elegance, the nooks of grace?' As I had ever applied the finger of criticism to the pages of his poems, I pointed out with my finger the nooks of elegance in these verses. Although from this reception perfect confusion overcame me, still in my heart I rejoiced for that my verses had been worthy of acceptance and had attained the rank of approbation. When hereafter I brought him two *gazels*, he gave them perfect credence, and, from the depths of his heart, bestowed numberless blessings and scattered the jewels of approval." By-and-by *Zati* himself took a distich of B*a*q*i*'s as the foundation for a *gazel*, saying, that it was no shame to steal from such a poet.

A marginal note in Von Hammer's copy of Qinali-Z*a*da says that the following Persian distich was engraved on B*a*q*i*'s seal, the impression of which is found on several legal documents:—

Fleeting is the earth, therein no faith lies;
He doth alone endure, all else dies.†

B*a*q*i* has never lacked admirers; during his lifetime he was the valued friend of four Sultans, Suleym*a*n I., Sel*i*m II., Mur*a*d III., and Muhammed III., one of these, Suleym*a*n, the most magnificent emperor of the Ottomans and one of the greatest sovereigns the world has ever known; he filled, as we have seen, some of the highest offices of state, and all the poets of his time, even Z*a*t*i* himself, acknowledged him as master;—the later critics and biographers cannot

* Alluding metaphorically to the punishment of thieves in Muslim countries by cutting off the hand.

† The Persian of this verse, which, as Von Hammer says, would do equally well for the seal of a Fanny, is:—

*Fanist jihan der*u *wef*a *nist*,—*Baq*i *hema ust jumla fanist.*

Fleeting (*Fani*) is the world, in it fidelity is not;
All that endures (*Baqi*) is He, all (else) is fleeting (*Fani*).

find words to express their admiration; and so long as Ottoman literature shall exist, one of its most brilliant ornaments must be that poet whose very name signifies *Enduring*.

'Adlí: Sultan Muhammed III. (1012=1603), son of Murad III. and the Venetian Safiyya, succeeded his father on the throne. He was, unfortunately for his country, another of those *rois faineants* whose feeble arms had no strength to wield the scimitar of 'Osman. As in his father's days, so in his own, corruption held high carnival, and revolt and anarchy laid waste the land; and thus continued till crushed by the grim justice of Murad IV., to whom, whatever may be said of his severity, belongs the eternal glory of having saved the Empire from dissolution. The Battle of Keresztes was the great event of the reign of Muhammed III. The war in Hungary was going hard with the Ottomans; and the great historian Sa'du-'d-Dín had much ado in getting the Sultan to place himself at the head of his army and make an effort to retrieve the fortunes of the campaign. At length he was successful; and Muhammed was present at the three-days' battle on the marshy plain of Keresztes. At the beginning of the conflict fortune was adverse to the Muslim troops, and the faint-hearted Sultan wished to flee, but Sa'du-'d-Dín prevailed upon him to keep the field; and when the battle was over, Muhammed saw the Christian army scattered in every direction, and its leaders, Prince Sigismund and the Archduke Maximilian, flying for their lives. No share of the credit for this splendid victory is due to the Sultan; the day was won by the firmness of Sa'du-'d-Dín and the valor of Cicala, a noble Genoese who had embraced Islam, and who is known in Ottoman history as Jigali-Zada. One day, a dervish met Muhammed going into his palace, and prophesied to him that fifty-five days thence he would meet with a great misfortune — a prediction which made a great impression upon the Sultan, and may perhaps have tended to work its own fulfillment, since he died on the fifty-fifth day after this singular incident. Sultan Mahmud II. used 'Adlí for his *takhallus* as well as Muhammed III.

BAKHTI: SULTAN AHMED I. (1026=1617) succeeded his father, Muhammed III., when only fourteen years old. His reign is one of the most barren periods in Ottoman history. It may be remarked that tobacco was introduced into Turkey in the second year of his reign; coffee had come into use before this, in the days of the great Suleyman. This Sultan died in the twenty-eighth year of his age, and the fourteenth of his reign. He was succeeded by his half-witted brother, Mustafa I., who was speedily desposed in favor of 'Osman II., Ahmed's eldest son.

FARISI: SULTAN 'OSMAN II. (1031=1622). When the imbecile Mustafa I. (one of whose amusements consisted of throwing gold coins into the Bosphorus for the fish) was removed from the throne, his young nephew Prince 'Osman, then in the fourteenth year of his age, was named Sultan in his stead (1027—1618). This monarch formed a plan, bold enough in design, but which he lacked vigor to carry out, for destroying the Janissaries and Sipahis, whose insolence had grown beyond all bounds. These fierce Pretorians got word of the Sultan's scheme, and dashing into the Seraglio, seized 'Osman and dragged him off to the famous prison of the Seven Towers. There they slew their sovereign with circumstances of insolent cruelty; and thus were the Ottoman annals for the first time stained with the crime of regicide.

'ATA'I (1045=1635). 'Ata'i Nev'i-Zada, the most distinguished man of letters of his time, was born in 991 (1583). He studied first under his father, Nev'i, who had been tutor to Sultan Murad III., and afterward under the celebrated savant and biographer, Feyzu-'llah Efendi. He entered the legal profession, and was successively appointed judge at many places of note, amongst others, at Silistria, Rusjuk, Monastir, and Uskub. He died shortly after his return from Uskub to Stamboul. His greatest work is the continuation of Tash-Kupru-Zada's biography of learned men, known as *Sheqayiqu-'n-Nu'maniyya*, "The Red Anemone." Besides this prose work he left several poems: *Suhbetu-'l-Ebkar*, "The Converse of Virgins"; *Heft Kh,an*,

"The Seven Trays"; *Nefhatu-'l-Ezhar*, "The Breath of Flowers"; *Saqi-Nama*, "The Cup-Bearer Book," and a complete *Diwan*.

NEF'I (1045=1635), of Erzerum, was the greatest poet of the reign of Murad IV. His principal work is a collection of satirical verses known as *Siham-i Qaza*, "The Shafts of Fate." Once when Murad was reading this book, a thunderbolt fell at his feet; regarding this as a sign that the work was displeasing to Heaven, the Sultan tore it up, and banished the author from Constantinople. Nef'i was shortly afterward recalled; but having given mortal offense to the Vezir, Beyram Pasha, by a violent satire, he was condemned to death. The execution was carried out in the wood-store of the Seraglio; the headsman, a rough provincial, when leading him thither, called out: "Come, Nef'i, we are going to a wood where thou mayest cut thy darts!" "Wretched Turk,"* responded the poet, "do thy business, and meddle not thou with satire." He was beheaded, and his body cast into the sea.

HAFIZ PASHA (1041=1632), the Grand Vezir who, early in the reign of Murad IV., made an unsuccessful attempt to recover Bagdad from the Persians. A melancholy interest is attached to this brave and gifted but unfortunate officer, by reason of his tragic fate—a fate which, unhappily, has been the lot of too many Ottoman ministers. The story runs thus: The disaffected sipahis of the capital, incited, it is said, by Rejeb Pasha, a rival of Hafiz, broke into open revolt and demanded the head of the Vezir, along with those of many of his associates. The following day they forced their way into the sacred precincts of the Seraglio itself, and there repeated their demand. Murad, the recently-ascended Sultan, loved Hafiz and would fain have saved him; and he in vain tried to appease the infuriated rebels. The noble Vezir, who, in an adjoining apartment, had made the ablution of those about to die, now came forth

* The word *Turk* is a term of reproach among the Ottomans, implying a rude, uncultured, country boor; they always called themselves '*Osmanli*, *i. e.*, Ottoman.

and stood before the Sultan, and said: «My Padishah, may a thousand slaves like Hafiz die for thee.» Stooping, he kissed the ground, and repeated the words used by the Muslim in the last extremity: «In the name of God, the Merciful, the Compassionate! There is no strength nor any power save in God, the High, the Mighty: God's we are, and verily to Him we return.» Then he strode forward toward his murderers; a well-aimed blow laid the foremost on the ground, the next instant the Pasha fell pierced by seventeen wounds. A janissary knelt upon his breast and severed his head from the body. Before the Sultan retired he addressed to the assassins these bold words: «If God wills, vile murderers, ye shall meet with terrible vengeance—ye who fear not God, nor are shamed before the Prophet!» They little heeded the threat; but they soon discovered that he who uttered it never menaced in vain; and many were doomed to die ere the blood of Hafiz Pasha was avenged.

MURADI: SULTAN MURAD IV. (1049=1640) ascended the throne when but twelve years of age, at a time when the Empire was in a state of woeful disorder. The imbecile Mustafa had been raised a second time to the imperial dignity, to take the place of 'Osman II., the victim of the janissaries; but the Empire needed a very different hand to guide it through the dangers which threatened it on every side. Ever since the days of Selim II., things had been going from bad to worse: each Sultan had been more effete than his predecessor; corruption was rampant in every branch of the government, and military insubordination threatened to overthrow the state. A stern will and an iron arm were needful to save the Empire from dissolution;—Murad possessed them both. The Persians, having taken Bagdad, were victorious along the eastern frontier; revolts and insurrections were starting, or threatening to start, into existence on every hand; and the troops of the capital itself were in open mutiny (we have just seen how they compelled the youthful Sultan to deliver his Vezir into their murderous grasp). The promised day of vengeance was not long delayed: adroitly and boldly Murad disposed of the leaders of the mutineers, then heavily fell his hand upon the rest. He was a great monarch, though severe. He tolerated no corruption, and sternly repressed every incipient revolt; no petty oppressor or provincial tyrant was permitted to vex the people while he held sway; and whenever, during his progresses through Asia with his army, he heard of an unjust judge or tyrannical governor, the death of the guilty was the instant and inevitable issue. Thus, during his reign, though he was himself ruthless and unsparing, the Empire was in far better plight than under those feeble Sultans whose meekness, or weakness, was the cause of confusion and revolt.

In 1045 (1635) he took Er*i*v*a*n; and three years later he marched from Constantinople to redeem Bagd*a*d from the Persians. We are told that at Mosul he received an Indian ambassador, who brought him, amongst many splendid gifts, a shield, said to be proof against sword and bullet, made of the ears of elephants covered with rhinoceros hide; this the Sultan placed before him, and, with one blow of his battle-ax, cleft in two the «impenetrable» buckler. Bagd*a*d was retaken after forty days of bloody battle, in which many a noble Ottoman fell, notably the Vez*i*r Tayy*a*r Pasha, who, when reproached by Mur*a*d on the failure of an assault, replied: «Would to God, my P*a*dish*a*h, it were as easy for thee to take Bagd*a*d as it is for thy slave Tayy*a*r to give his life in serving thee!» and the next day, scaling the ramparts in the first rank of the assailants, fell dead, shot through the throat. Quarter had been granted to the defenders; but a mine, treacherously sprung, whereby eight hundred janissaries were killed, was the signal for a general massacre. Thirty thousand Persians, say the Eastern historians, perished beneath the Ottoman scimitars. A Persian musician named Sh*a*h-Q*u*l*i*, brought before Mur*a*d, played and sang so sweetly, first a song of triumph, then a dirge, that the Sultan, moved to pity by the music, gave orders to stop the massacre. Mur*a*d died in Stamboul, in the twenty-ninth year of his age.

'Az*i*z*i* (1050=1641 *ca.*), the poetic pseudonym of a certain Mustafa of Constantinople, who held the appointment of Provost of the Seven Towers. He is principally known from his *Shehr-engiz*, a few extracts from which are translated in the present volume.

Na'ili (1077=1666). Of this poet little is known save that he was a native of Constantinople, that his real name was Yeni-Zada Mustafa Efendi, and that he held a position under government.

Sidqi (1115=1703) was a daughter of Qamer Muhammed Efendi, a member of the *'ulema* of the time of Sultan Muhammed IV. She lies buried by her father's side without the Adrianople Gate, not far from the convent of Emir Bukhara. Besides her *Diwan*, she wrote two mystic poems, entitled *Genju-'l-Envar*, « The Treasury of Lights »; and *Mejma'u-'l-Akhbar*, « The Collection of Information.» Several poets have written under the name of Sidqi.

Iqbali: Sultan Mustafa II. (1115=1703). When Sultan Mustafa II., son of Muhammed IV., the great hunter, succeeded his uncle, Ahmed II., in 1106 (1695), he set himself vigorously to redress the many corruptions which had crept into the state during the last reigns. He placed himself at the head of his army, and was for a time successful against the Austrians; but being eventually worsted, he was obliged, by the Treaty of Carlowitz, to leave almost the whole of Hungary in the hands of the Imperialists. Shortly before his death, in 1115 (1703), Mustafa II. abdicated in favor of his brother Ahmed, who became third Sultan of that name.

Nabi (1124=1712), who was born at Roha, came to Stamboul in the reign of Muhammed IV., where he attached himself to that monarch's favorite, Mustafa Pasha, whom he accompanied through his Morean campaign. On the death of his patron, Nabi made the pilgrimage to Mekka, and on his return from the Holy City, fixed his residence at Aleppo, where he made the acquaintance of Baltaji Muhammed Pasha, who, after his first Grand-Vezirate, had been appointed governor of that town. This minister conceived a great attachment for Nabi, and on his recall to Constantinople, to resume the highest office of the Empire, he accorded to the poet an important official position. Nabi, who was over eighty years of age when he died, left an immense number of works, partly in prose and partly in verse; many of the latter are *qasidas* in praise of the various vezirs who befriended him. His *Diwan* contains nine thousand couplets. The *Khayriyya* and the *Khayr-Abad*, two long ethical poems addressed to his son, are considered his masterpieces.

'Arif (1125=1713), a distinguished member of the legal profession, famed for his great erudition and the elegance with which he wrote the *ta'liq* character. Besides some prose works on metaphysics and syntax, he composed a long poem on the *Mi'raj*, or Night-journey of the Prophet, also a complete *Diwan*. He founded a *medresa* at Eyyub; and left a sum of money in order that, on every anniversary of the Prophet's Night-journey, his poem on that subject might there be read.

Nedim (1140=1727 *ca.*). Regarding this poet we have very few particulars. He was patronized first by the Grand Vezir 'Ali Pasha, after whose death, on the battlefield of Peterwardein, Ibrahim Pasha, third famous Grand Vezir of the name, took him under his protection. Nedim was appointed librarian of the library founded by this minister.

Vehbi (1146=1733 *ca.*). This name has been adopted by several Ottoman poets. The author, of whose *gazels* a specimen is given in this work, flourished during the reign of Sultan Ahmed III.; but the most famous Vehbi is the poet styled, for distinction's sake, Sumbul-Zada Vehbi, who lived some seventy years later.

Sabqati: Sultan Mahmud I. (1168=1754). The reign of this monarch, who succeeded his uncle Ahmed III. in 1143 (1730), is marked by an attack made by Russia and Austria upon the Ottoman Empire. The first of these powers was on the whole successful, but the second was unfortunate, and, by the Treaty of Belgrade, compelled to restore to the

Porte several provinces she had taken from it by the Peace of Passarowitz. It is to the honor of Sultan Mahmud that he did not join in the attack made by many of the European powers on Austria when the youthful empress Maria Theresa succeeded to the throne: the opportunity for avenging himself upon the hereditary enemy of his country was a golden one, but he was too generous to take advantage of it.

BELIG (1170=1756 *ca.*). Little is known of this poet, save that he was the son of a certain Qara Bag 'Ali Efendi of Qaysariyya, and that he came to Constantinople in 1115 (1703), and dwelt there in one of the *medresas* of the Mosque of Muhammed II.

SAMI (1170=1756 *ca.*) is the annalist, whose history, along with those of Shakir and Subhi, forms one of the volumes of the Imperial Historiographers. Many of his poems contain pretty and original ideas, which are usually conveyed in graceful and appropriate language. He is particularly strong in *mufreds*. A *mufred* is a single *beyt*, or couplet, the hemistichs of which may or may not rhyme with one another; it stands by itself, unconnected with any other piece of verse, and must contain some *bon mot* neatly and briefly expressed. Sami has a great number of these; the following will serve as a specimen:

Stone about its middle fastened, and with iron staff in hand,
Tremblingly the compass-needle seeketh for the darling's land.*

NEV-RES (1175=1761). Nev-res 'Abdu-'r-Rezzaq was a poet of the times of Mahmud I. and Mustafa III., the

* *Bagrin tash basip, almish elina ahen 'asa Ku-yi janani arar titreyerek qibla-numa.*

The allusion in the first line is to the *qana'at tashi*, or contentment-stone; a stone which dervishes and Arabs, when going on a journey, sometimes tie tightly against the pit of the stomach to repel the pangs of hunger.

The following is the most celebrated of all Sami's *mufreds*, but it does not admit of translation:—

Bend-i shalwarin chuzup, upsem kus-i nermi nola ?
Yarma sheftalisi bag-i vusletin gayet leziz !

16

praises of whom are sung in many of his verses. Von Hammer has no particulars regarding him, save that on account of some offense given to a contemporary savant, called Hashmet Efendi, he was banished, in 1761, to Brusa, where shortly afterward he died.

SHAHIN GIRAY: KHAN OF THE CRIMEA (1205=1789). When the vast empire of Jengiz fell in pieces, the Khans who governed that portion of it which is now the southern half of Russia became independent monarchs. This territory was divided into three Khanates; Kazan, Astrakhan, and the Crimea. For centuries the princes of the last of these bore the surname of Giray; the origin of which is stated to be as follows. It was a custom of the Crimean Khans to send their sons in their youth to nomad tribes to receive a warrior's education. A certain Khan who had been thus brought up by the tribe Giray happened to meet his foster-father who was returning from Mekka, and at the earnest request of his old guardian named his infant son Giray, in honor of the tribe, and further ordered that all future princes of his house should bear that style as surname.

Shortly after the capture of Constantinople, the Crimean Khans declared themselves vassals of the Ottoman Sultans, and such they continued to be till within a few years of the theft of their territory by Russia, which put an end alike to their sovereignty and to the freedom of their people.

Shahin Giray, the last of the line, seems to have been a talented and accomplished prince, but totally wanting in political foresight; he had a difficult game to play, and played it badly. The Russians had penetrated into the Crimea by force and fraud, and, seeing their arms everywhere victorious over the Turks, and importuned and flattered by their agents, he very foolishly and wrongly forsook his old allegiance and proclaimed himself the vassal of Catherine. He was speedily deposed and sent into Russia; his country was formally annexed, and the last gleam of Tatar freedom drowned in the blood of 30,000 men, women, and children, massacred by the Russian soldiers. The treatment of those Crimean Princes, who placed themselves under Stambbul and St. Petersburg respectively, shows well the difference between Turk and Russian. Refused the pension that had been promised him, and insulted by his cruel captors, Shahín Giray fled to Constantinople; but desertion of his liege and betrayal of his people were crimes too great for the Sultan to overlook: the hapless Prince was sent to Rhodes and there executed as a traitor.

GALIB (1210=1795), son of a musician in a Mevlevi convent, was born in Constantinople in the year 1171 (1757). From his youth he was much given to study, and to frequenting the society of learned men. In his twenty-fourth year he compiled his *Diwan*, and two years later composed his most celebrated poem, a beautiful mystic romance, named *Husn u 'Ishq*, « Beauty and Love.» Sultan Selím III. conferred upon Galib the office of Sheykh of Galata, in return for which that poet composed a magnificent *qasida* in honor of his royal patron. In 1795, Galib undertook the pilgrimage to Mekka, on his return from which he died in Damascus, where he is buried. This author, who is frequently styled *Galib Deda*, «Father Galib,» is regarded as one of the greatest of modern Ottoman poets; he left a large number of works, principally on religious subjects.

FITNET KHANIM (1215=1800 *ca.*). Of this poetess I can find no particulars save that she was the daughter of a Mufti named Es'ad. 'Izzet Molla mentions her in one of his poems as being married to some one who was unworthy of her.

ILHAMI SULTAN SELIM III. (1222=1807). During the reign of this monarch, who ascended the throne in 1203 (1789), the star of the House of 'Osman was at its nadir. On his accession the Empire was engaged in a disastrous war with Austria and Russia. Peace was made with the former, but Catherine continued the struggle on her own account, until the intervention of Prussia and England secured a respite for the Ottoman State. Selím maintained neutrality during the European wars occasioned by the French Republic, till Napoleon's wanton assault upon Egypt compelled him to take up arms in his own defense. Familiar to every Englishman is the story of this war—how England went to her ally's aid; how the veterans of France, under the eyes of Bonaparte himself, dashed time after time against the walls of St. Jean d'Acre, only to be repelled by Jezz*a*r Pasha and his valiant comrades; and how Nelson destroyed Napoleon's fleet, and with it all his dreams of Eastern Empire, at the never-to-be-forgotten battle of Aboukir.

Sel*i*m, seeing that the constantly-recurring defeats sustained by the Ottoman troops resulted from their weapons and organization being those of the Middle Ages rather than of modern times, resolved to adopt the arms and tactics of the nations of Western Europe. This he began to accomplish, and the reason of the exceeding weakness of the Empire throughout his reign was this change of front in the face of powerful foes. That these reforms were absolutely necessary, is beyond question—they have saved the Empire. And now, after nearly a hundred years, we see the result: the Ottoman soldiers of to-day have shown on many occasions that, when at all fairly matched, they are able to cope successfully with the best-equipped troops in Europe; but it was very different in Sel*i*m's time. That monarch's reforms, however, met with violent opposition, especially from the Janissaries, and eventually cost him his life: a revolution, occasioned by his innovations, hurled him from the throne, and shortly afterward he was strangled in his private apartments. Thus perished Sel*i*m III.; but the reforms which he originated have been nobly and successfully carried out by his son Mahm*u*d II. and his successors.

F*a*zil Beg (1224=1810) was the son of T*a*hir Pasha (the Sheykh Daher of Volney and Savary), the accomplice of 'Al*i* Beg of Egypt in his revolt against the Ottoman Porte. Though for a time successful, 'Al*i* Beg was at length defeated, and T*a*hir was driven into 'Akka, where he defended himself till killed in a sortie (1775).

Fazil, who, with his younger brother, Kamil Beg, likewise a poet, was brought up in the Imperial Seraglio, early devoted himself to literature, and after holding several official appointments, was eventually made one of the *Khojagan*, or Members of the Divan. Besides the *Zenan-Nama*, "Book of Women," he wrote the *Khuban-Nama*, "Book of Fair" (*i. e.*, Youths), the *Defter-i 'Ishq*, "Register of Love," and the *Chengi-Nama*, "Book of the Public Dancer." The *Defter-i 'Ishq* comes first in the little volume of his works, next follow the *Khuban* and *Zenan Namas*, companion poems, and then lastly, the *Chengi-Nama*. He left also a *Diwan* of *gazels*.

In his little work on Turkish Poetry, Mr. Redhouse cites an elegy on the death of a lady, which is so pretty that I cannot forbear offering a translation of it. The verse is said to be by one Fazil, but whether he be the same Fazil as composed the *Zenan-Nama*, I have failed to ascertain; that author is, however, the only poet of the name mentioned in Von Hammer's work:—

ELEGY ON A LADY. BY FAZIL

Ah! thou'st laid her low, yet flushed with life, Cup-bearer of the Sphere!
Scarce the glass of joy was tasted when the bowl of Fate brimmed o'er;
Hold her, O thou Earth! full gently, smile on her, O Trusted One!*
For a wide-world's King this fair Pearl as his heart's own darling wore.†

WASIF (1236=1820 *ca.*). Von Hammer makes Wasif, the poet, identical with the historian of the same name; but, as the latter died in the year 1221 (1806), while the former has in his *Diwan* some *tarikhs* as late as 1236 (1820), the great Orientalist must be mistaken. I have been unable to gain any information concerning the poet, save that in his *Diwan* he is styled *Wasif-i Enderuni*, which shows that he was brought up in the Imperial Seraglio.

* See Note 7.

† *Hayf! ol mest-i 'hayata qiydin ey Saqi-i Cherkh!*
Jam-i kama qanmadan dolmush Ejel peymanesi:
Ey Zemin, khosh tut! nuwazish eyle, ey Ruhu-'l-Emin!
Kim bu gevher-para bir shah-i jihan jananesi.

Ramiz Pasha (1236=1820 *ca.*) was the *Qapudan*, or Lord High Admiral, and intimate friend of Sultan Mustafa IV. The revolution which dethroned that monarch compelled Ramiz to flee to Russia for his life; he lived for some time in that country, and there he wrote his *gazels*, which show how sorely he yearned for his friend and his native land. The original of the poem translated in this work may be found in the *Mines de l'Orient*.

'Izzet Molla (1252=1836 *ca.*) was one of Sultan Mahmud the Second's Vice-Chancellors. « At some time,» says Mr. Redhouse, « during the calamitous days of the Greek insurrection, before the epoch of the destruction of the Janissaries, Navarino, and the Russian War that led to the treaty of Adrianople — namely, at about the date when the Prince, afterward the Sultan, 'Abdu-'l-Mejid was born, in 1823 or 1824 — 'Izzet Molla had incurred the displeasure of a powerful colleague, and had been banished from Constantinople to the town of Keshan, situated between Rodosto and the Lower Maritza. At his death, a poem of about seven thousand couplets, and entitled, according as its name, *Mihnet-Keshan* (*Mihnet-i Keshan*), may be read or understood, 'The Suffering,' 'The Sufferers,' or 'The Sufferings of Keshan,' was found among his papers, and published by his grandson, Nazim Bey.» * Fu'ad Pasha, the celebrated statesman, was the son of 'Izzet Molla; like his father, he cultivated poetry: a few lines by him will be found in Mr. Redhouse's work, from which the preceding remarks have been taken.

'Adli: Sultan Mahmud II. (1255=1839). When the Janissaries deposed Sultan Selim III., they placed upon the throne his cousin Mustafa, the eldest son of 'Abdu-'l-Hamid I. This prince was not long allowed to enjoy the honors of royalty, for Mustafa Bayraq-dar, the Pasha of Rusjuq, a loyal adherent of the unfortunate Selim entered the capital with an army of 40,000 men, and proceeded to storm the Seraglio. Sultan Mustafa IV. gave orders for the immediate execution of his cousin, the deposed Selim, and

* « On the History, System, and Varieties of Turkish Poetry,« p. 5.

his own brother, Prince Mahm*u*d, hoping by this means to secure his own life and throne, as he knew no one would dare to injure the sole male representative of the House of 'Osm*a*n. The Pasha and his followers were a few minutes too late to save Sel*i*m, but in time to rescue Mahm*u*d, whom a faithful slave had hid in the furnace of a bath. Sultan Mustafa was at once deposed, and the youthful Prince raised to the throne. Mahm*u*d resolved to follow the example of his cousin, and energetically proceeded with the reforms inaugurated by the latter. One of the most remarkable incidents of his reign was the Destrution of the Janissaries; this once most formidable body of troops, which had been founded 500 years before, in the days of Sultan Orkhan, had turned into a horde of military tyrants, who set up and pulled down sultans as they pleased, and whose lawless violence not unfrequently drenched Constantinople with blood. As these men consistently and bitterly opposed every attempt at reform, and as there was, and could be, no security either for the monarch or for any of his subjects so long as their power was unbroken, Mahm*u*d determined on the bold, but most necessary, stroke of their annihilation. The story of how he effected this is too well known to need repeating here; suffice it to say that it was an act which was justified, as it could alone have been, by extreme necessity. Many reverses, such as the loss of Greece and Algiers, the defeat of Navarino, the Egyptian rebellion, and the Russian invasion, fell to this Sultan's lot; but he met all with the undaunted calmness of one who is conscious that his cause is just. Worn out with continual anxiety and ceaseless labor, Sultan Mahm*u*d II. died in 1839, when, to use the words of Sir Edward Creasy, the English historian of the Ottoman Empire, "as gallant a spirit left the earth, as ever strove against the spites of fortune — as ever toiled for a nation's good in preparing benefits, the maturity of which it was not permitted to behold."

LEYL*A* KH*A*NIM (1275=1858), the sister of 'Izzet Molla, and aunt of the famous Fu'*a*d Pasha, was a poetess of considerable merit. Her *Diwan*, which contains many fine passages, consists for the most part of *tarikhs* on events that occurred during the first half of the present century.

Ziya Beg (1296=1879 *ca.*), son of an Albania father, was one of the most distinguished men of letters of modern Turkey. He was a member of what is known as the «Young Turkey» party, Having temporarily fallen under the displeasure of Sultan 'Abdu-'l-'Aziz, whose secretary he was, he retired to London, where he became connected with the papers, *Mukhbir*, « Informer,» and *Hurriyyet*, « Liberty,» published by his party in the English capital. When Sultan 'Abdu-'l-Hamid II. opened the Ottoman Parliament, Ziya Beg, now Ziya Pasha, was among those whom the people chose as their representatives. He has written a good deal of poetry and compiled an excellent Turkish, Persian, and Arabian Anthology, called *Kharabat*, «The Tavern,» from which many of the poems translated in the present work have been selected. Ziya was more a courtier than a statesman, and his poems were held in high esteem by Sultan 'Abdu-'l-'Aziz. He was a friend and associate of Kemal Beg, the poet, and of the celebrated writer 'Ali Su'avi Efendi.

NOTES

1. These dates are the year of the poet's death; the first, according to the Muhammedan, the second, to the Christian era.

2. The *Diwan* of '*A*shiq Pasha is a long mystical poem, modeled after Mevl*ana* Jel*a*lu-'d-D*i*n's famous *Mesnevi*. The extract here translated is given by Lat*ifi* in his *Tezkera*, or Biography of Poets. '*A*shiq's poem is a *mesnevi*, not a *Diwan* at all, in the ordinary sense of the word.

3. *Jinn* — the genii; a race of material, intelligent beings, whose bodies are similar to the essence of fire or smoke. See Lane's «Thousand and One Nights.»

4. Prince Cantemir, in his «History of the Othman Empire,» remarks: «The Turks say that God has created 17,000 worlds, but that this will be the last.» And on page 272 of Mr. Redhouse's translation of the First Book of Jel*a*lu-'d-D*i*n's *Mesnevi* occur these lines: —

> «Though worlds there may be, eighteen thousand globes, and more,
> Not every eye has power to witness all their store.»

5. The *Iskender-Nama* is a romantic *mesnevi*, detailing the mythic and mystic history of Iskender, or Alexander the Great, a hero who, as we have seen in the Introduction, is a great favorite with the Orientals. Besides the story of the Macedonian conqueror, the whole of the science and philosophy of the Muslims is set forth in this immense and extraordinary book. The Persians Nizam*i* and Jam*i*, Khusraw of Dihl*i*, and the Jagat*a*y Turk New*a'i* wrote *mesnevis* on the history of Iskender.— Like several other monarchs of ancient Persia, Iskender is frequently quoted as the type of a great and warlike sovereign.

6. The '*Anq*a is a fabulous bird which figures largely in Oriental poetry and romance. It is sometimes called the *Simurg*, and is very similar to, if not identical with, the better known *Rukh*. It is said to dwell somewhere in the mountains of Q*a*f, which, like a vast ring, inclose the Circumambient Ocean (*Bahru-'l-Muhit*) that surrounds the whole habitable earth, which, according to this cosmography, is flat, not round. These mountains are composed of green chrysolite, the reflection of which causes the greenish (or bluish) tint of the sky. El-Q*a*zw*ini* says that the 'Anq*a* is the greatest of all birds, and carries off an elephant as a hawk does a mouse. This strange creature is further said to be rational, and to possess the power of speech.

The 'Anq*a* plays to a certain extent the same part in the East as the Phœnix and Griffin in the West.—In the line before us Sheykh*i* is, of course, simply calling on his own muse, which, in the spirit of his class, he declares to be sweet as the nightingale, and wondrous as the 'Anq*a*.

7. *Ruhu-'l-Emin*, «the Trusted Spirit,» is the Archangel Gabriel, who is held to be trusted by God with all His revelations to the Prophets.

8. Iskender here complains to his Vez*i*r *A*rist*u* (Aristotle) of having no more worlds to conquer.

9. *Rub'-i Meskun* the «Inhabited Quarter» of the earth, is divided into the Seven Climates, each under one of the Seven Planets, an account of which will be found in El-Mes'*ud*i's «Meadows of Gold and Mines of Gems,» translated from Arabic into English by Dr. Aloys Sprenger.

10. The romances of Khusrev and Sh*i*r*i*n, Leyl*i* and Mejn*u*n, and Y*u*suf and Zuleykh*a* are the three favorite love-stories of the Muslim poets. Khusrev (according to Ottoman, Khusraw, to Persian pronunciation) is the general title of the Kings of the Fourth, or S*a*s*a*n*i*, Persian dynasty; but it is specially applied to Khusrev Perv*i*z. The Greek *Chosroe*, or *Chosroes*, is a corruption of this word.

The glories of Khusrev Perv*i*z, his matchless steed Shebd*i*z, and his charming mistress Sh*i*r*i*n are favorite subjects with the poets of the East. Wishing to perpetuate in stone the lovely features of his mistress, Khusrev ordered Ferh*a*d, the first sculptor of the age, to carve her likeness on the solid rock; but the artist, smitten by the charms of Sh*i*r*i*n, madly endeavored to gain her love. The monarch took advantage of his infatuation, and employed him in many works, encouraging him with the hope of gaining Sh*i*r*i*n; and at length definitely promised that if he cut through a certain mountain and brought a stream through, the lady should be his. Ferh*a*d had all but completed his task, when Khusrev, fearing he should have to part with his beautiful mistress, sent an old woman to the «mountain-hewer» to tell him that Sh*i*r*i*n was dead; on hearing which Ferh*a*d cast himself headlong from the rock. Khusrev, however, met with his due reward; for his son Sh*i*r*u*ya, likewise enamored of the enchanting Sh*i*r*i*n, stabbed him, in the vain hope of gaining that wonderful lady.

Ferh*a*d is often mentioned in Ottoman poetry as the type of a sincere but unfortunate lover. The sculptures and cuneiform inscriptions, deciphered by Sir Henry Rawlinson, on the mountain of B*i*sit*u*n (or Behist*a*n) near Kerm*a*nsh*a*h in Persia, are legendarily reported to be the work of Ferh*a*d.

11. A *moon* is a constantly recurring metaphor for a *beautiful woman* or *youth*.

12. The «curling serpents» are her shining, curling tresses.

13. The «dawn» is her fair face.

14. The Signs of the Zodiac are divided into Fiery, Earthy, Airy, and Watery. Aries, Leo, and Sagittary are Fiery; Taurus, Virgo, and Capricorn are Earthy; Gemini, Libra, and Aquarius are Airy; and Cancer, Scorpio, and Pisces are Watery. There are many other ways of dividing the Signs, such as Masculine and Feminine, etc.
The allusion in the text is, of course, a play upon the moon-like Sh*i*r*i*n bathing in the pond.

15. Orientals express surprise by biting the fore-finger.

16. That is: her locks covered her eyes. Be it said, once for all, that in Ottoman poetry the *hyacinth* continually represents the hair, and the *narcissus*, the eye.

17. The *hair* is also frequently likened to *musk*, being dark and sweet-scented.

18. Here the *moon* means her *face*, as does «her day» in the last line.

19. These three last couplets are of course mystic: the «Loved One» is God. See Introduction, Sec. I.

20. The *Muhammediyya* is a long poem, descriptive of the creation of the universe, the dogmas of Islam, and the life of the Prophet.

21. The following passage, from Sale's Preliminary Discourse to his translation of the Qur'*a*n, will serve as a commentary to this poem; I have spelled the Arabic words in accordance with Turkish pronunciation: «They [the commentators] say it [Paradise] is situated above the Seven Heavens [or in the Seventh Heaven], and next under the Throne of God; and, to express the amenity of the place, tell us, that the earth of it is of the finest wheat flour, or of the purest musk; or, as others will have it, of saffron; that its stones are pearls and jacinths, the walls of its buildings enriched with gold and silver, and that the trunks of all its trees are of gold; among which the most remarkable is the tree called *Tuba*, or the 'Tree of Happiness.' Concerning this tree they fable that it stands in the palace of Muhammed, though a branch of it will reach to the house of every true believer; that it will be loaden with pomegranates, grapes, dates, and other fruits of surprising bigness, and of tastes unknown to mortals. So that if a man desire to eat of any particular kind of fruit, it will immediately be presented to him, or if he choose flesh, birds ready dressed will be set before him, according to his wish. They add, that the boughs of this tree will spontaneously bend down to the hand of the person who would gather of its fruits, and that it will supply the blessed not only with food, but also with silken garments, and beasts to ride on, ready saddled and bridled, and adorned with rich trappings, which will burst forth from its fruits; and that this tree is so large that a

person mounted on the fleetest horse would not be able to gallop from one end of its shade to the other in a hundred years.

«As plenty of water is one of the greatest additions to the pleasantness of any place, the Qur'*a*n often speaks of the rivers of Paradise as a principal ornament thereof: some of these rivers, they say, flow with water, some with milk, some with wine, and others with honey; all taking their rise from the root of the tree T*u*ba; two of which rivers, namely, El-Kevser and the *River of Life*, we have already mentioned. And, lest these should not be sufficient, we are told, this garden is also watered by a great number of lesser springs and fountains, whose pebbles are rubies and emeralds, their earth of camphire, their beds of musk, and their sides of saffron; the most remarkable among them being Selseb*i*l and Tesn*i*m.

«But all these glories will be eclipsed by the resplendent and ravishing girls of Paradise, called from their large black eyes, H*u*ru-'l-'uy*u*n, the enjoyment of whose company will be a principal felicity of the faithful.»

This gorgeous picture—which in all its details is regarded as true by the illiterate, and, by reason of its splendor and beauty, is accepted in poetry as the idea of Paradise—rests solely on one or two simple passages of the Qur'*a*n, of which the following is perhaps the most explicit:—

'And the foremost foremost!*
These are they who are brought nigh,
In gardens of pleasure!
A crowd of those of yore,
And a few of those of the latter day!
And gold-weft couches, reclining on them face to face.
Around them shall go eternal youths, with goblets and ewers and a cup of flowing wine; no headache shall they feel therefrom, nor shall their wits be dimmed!
And fruit such as they deem the best;
And flesh of fowl as they desire;
And bright and large-eyed maids like hidden pearls;
As a reward for that which they have done!
They shall hear no folly there and no sin;
Only the speech, 'Peace, Peace!'
And the fellows of the right—what right lucky fellows!
Amid thornless lote-trees.
And talh [banana] trees with piles of flowers;
And outspread shade,
And water out-poured;
And fruit in abundance, neither failing nor forbidden;
And beds upraised!
Verily we have produced them [the celestial damsels] a production.
And made them virgins, darlings of equal age [with their spouses] for the fellows of the right!
A crowd of those of yore, and a crowd of those of the latter day!'†

*On the Last Day mankind will be divided into three companies: (1) Those who have been foremost in professing the faith upon earth, who shall be foremost then—among these will be many of the olden time, but few of the latter day; (2) The "fellows of the right," the rest of the blest; (3) The "fellows of the left," the lost.

†Qur'*a*n, lvi., 10–39, Professor Palmer's translation.

It is almost needless to state that the great majority of cultured Muslims regard this and similar passages as figurative. (See Syed Ameer Ali, chap. xvi.)

22. This repetition of the rhyming word is in imitation of the original.

23. Their ruby-lips are like red wine. Whenever in Ottoman poetry a lady's *rubies* are mentioned, her *lips* are meant. The *lips* are likened to *wine*, not only on account of their color and sweetness, but also because of their intoxicating power.

24. «Therein are maids of modest glances,
As though they were rubies and pearls.»—Qur'an, lv., 57–58.

25. Alluding to the famous sentence, said to have been addressed by God to Muhammed: *Lev laka lema khuliqatu-'l-eflaku*, «Had it not been for thee, verily the heavens had not been created.»

26. «For the blest are prepared,» said Muhammed, «such things as eye hath not seen, nor hath ear heard, nor hath it entered into the heart of man to conceive.» Compare Isaiah, lxiv., 4; 1 Corinthians, ii., 9; and Qur'an, xxxii., 17.

27. *Habibu-'llah*, «the Beloved of God,» is the special designation of Muhammed; as *Safiyyu-'llah*, «the Pure Friend of God,» is that of Adam; *Nejiyyu-'llah*, «the Saved of God,» that of Noah; *Khalilu-'llah*, «the Intimate Friend of God,» that of Abraham; *Kelimu-'llah*, «the Addressed of God,» that of Moses; and *Ruhu-'llah*, «the Spirit of God,» that of Jesus.

28. In a diagram in my copy of the *Muhammediyya* the Tuba Tree is represented as an enormous hanging plant, springing from under the *'Arsh*, or Throne of God (which is above the highest Mansion of Paradise), and descending thence through all the Seven Mansions, which are arranged one over the other, like seven stories. These Seven Mansions of Paradise are in order as follows, commencing at the lowest: 1st, *Daru-'s-Selam*, «the Mansion of Peace,» formed of ruby; 2d, *Jennetu-'l-Meva*, «the Garden of the Abode,» of green chrysolite; 3d, *Jennetu-'l-Khuld*, «the Garden of Eternity,» of coral; 4th, *Jennetu-'n-Na'im*, «the Garden of Delight,» of white silver; 5th, *Jennetu-'l-Firdevs*, «the Garden of Paradise,» of red gold; 6th, *Jennetu-'l-Qarar*, «the Garden of Permanence,» of white pearls; 7th, *Jennetu-'l-'Aden*, «the Garden of Eden,» of great pearls. Above these, but under the *'Arsh*, which crowns everything, are the *'Illiyyun*, «the Sublime Heights,» often reckoned as an Eighth Mansion. Different writers arrange the Mansions differently, but the above is the order shown in my diagram. Of course, all these Seven, or Eight, Mansions of Paradise are above the Nine Spheres, concerning which see Note 84.

29. *Ebu-Qasim*, «the Father of Qasim,» is one of the styles of Muhammed. Qasim was the name of that Prophet's only son.

30. No one figures more frequently in Ottoman poetry than the Cup-bearer, who is supposed to be young and fair, but cruel and hard-hearted, and pitiless toward his or her hapless lovers.

31. (These figures have been accidentally omitted in the text; they should appear at the end of the second line of Sultan Murad's *Ruba*'i.) The *rebab*, which I translate by «rebeck,» is a kind of viol with only one chord. A picture and description of this instrument are given in Lane's «Modern Egyptians,» Ed. 1860, p. 364. Two sketches of the *cheng*, or «Persian harp» (the instrument mentioned as the harp in these poems), may be seen in the same author's «Thousand and One Nights,» Ed. 1842, vol. I., p. 228.

32. The *cypress* is an emblem of the *slender figure* of a beautiful woman or youth, whose *graceful movements* are likened to the *waving* of that tree. The *pine*, the *juniper*, the *box-tree*, the *palm*, and the *ban*, or Oriental willow, are all used with the same sense, but much less frequently. With some of these it is rather a twig than the whole tree that is alluded to. They may be regarded as the types of *the beauty of motion*. These comparisons show how absurd is the notion that the Turks admire excessive fatness in women.

33. Her bewitching and all-subduing tresses, blown across her beautiful face, are like the invincible Ottoman heroes scouring the fair province of R*u*m-Eyli (Rumelia).

34. *Reng u B*u, «Tint and Scent,» is a favorite expression for embellished beauty. «Her quarter» is the ward of the town where she lives; *K*u means «street» in Persian but «ward of a town» in Turkish.

35. Compare «Twelfth Night,» Act I., scene 5: —

> «With adorations, fertile tears,
> With groans that thunder love, with sighs of flame.»

The practice of introducing the *takhallus*, or, poetic *nom de plume*, toward the end of a *gazel* has been noticed in the Introduction, Sec. II.

36. The *Ka'ba* is the Sacred Temple at Mekka toward which all Muslims turn in their devotions; the *mihrab* is the niche in a mosque wall showing the direction of the Holy City. «Worship» is a much better translation than «prayer» for *salat*, the five-times-a-day repeated devotional exercise of the Muslims. It is simply an act of adoration, not of prayer in the sense of entreaty at all, as any one may see by reading the formula given in Lane's «Modern Egyptians,» pp. 76–78. A short petition, it is true, *may* be offered immediately before the close of the ceremony; but, far from being obligatory, this is not even recommended, it being thought more respectful to leave the issues of all things entirely in the hands of God. The word for «prayer» is *du'a*.

37. These words, which in the original are in Arabic, occur several times as an injunction in the Qur'an, though not exactly in the order used by the Sultan in this *gazel*. Whenever Arabic clauses occur in these poems they are represented in the translations by italics.

38. *Rijal-i Gayb*, «the Unseen Ones,» are a set of forty mysterious beings who wander over the surface of the earth, ready to impart spiritual aid to those who seek it. For an account of them see pp. 82, 83 of an interesting work called «The Dervishes,» by the late Mr. John P. Brown, of Constantinople (Trubner and Co.).

39. The «Saints» here mentioned are the *Velis*, or «Friends of God,» concerning whose miracles and supernatural powers many wonderful stories are related.

40. The Prophet is sometimes called Ahmed Mukhtar instead of Muhammed Mustafa, both names having the same meaning.

41. See Introduction, Sec. I., for the true signification of this and similar expressions.

42. *Tutya*, «zinc,» «oxide of zinc,» «sulphate of zinc,» is used as a remedy for the eyes; pearls are powdered with it, hence a poet often compares it to the dust on which his mistress has trodden, mingled with his own pearly tears.

43. *Ambergris*, like musk, is a favorite simile for the *hair*, being likewise dark and sweet-scented.

44. Her moon-like brow, perfumed by her musky hair, is seen beside her rose-cheeks and hyacinth-tresses.

45. Her curling snake-like locks are fallen across her day-fair face: just as the snake gains strength for his deadly work by sleeping in the daytime, so do her locks seem all the more beautiful against her white skin, and thereby increase their power to wound her lover.

46. This is a pretty example of the Oriental rhetorical figure *Husn-i ta'lil*, which may be translated, «Eloquent Indication of the Cause:» it consists in attributing the cause of a well known fact to some poetical and fanciful idea. Flowers, as is well known, tied to slips of wood, are carried through the bazars for sale; but here the poet says that it is on account of having stolen their tint and scent from his mistress's cheek, that they are bound and paraded through the public places, as is done with criminals.

47. A lady's *chin* is frequently likened to an *apple*; the meaning of the line is: «some one has been amorously biting thee.» Throughout this *gazel* (which is more curious than beautiful) the poet upbraids his mistress for entertaining his rivals.

48. A *peach* is the poetical expression in Turkish for a *kiss*; so «they've eaten peaches in thine orchard» means: «they have been kissing thee.»

49. Bitten by the passionate rival.

50. Kevser is the name of a river in Paradise (see Note 21); here it is used for ***kindly speech***, the ripples being the words; so the line means: «speak to us.»

51. The ***down*** upon the cheek of the beloved is frequently alluded to by Asiatic poets. There is here, in the original, a favorite equivoque, the word ***khatt*** meaning alike «down» and «writing.» Zeyneb's idea is: «when thou movest thy face, the down (***khatt***) upon thy cheek traces in the air lines of writing (***khatt***), so fragrant that they form, as it were, a written command to the breeze to go, and, through the sweetness with which they have impregnated it, conquer the native land of musk.»

52. From (Cathay *Khata*) and Eastern Tatary, the home of the musk-deer, the finest musk is procured.

53. Somewhere in the western portion of the Circumambient Ocean (Note 6) lies the *Bahr-i Zulumat*, «The Sea of Darknesses,» and in this sea is situated the *Dar-i Zulumat*, or «Land of Darknesses.» There flows the «Fountain of Life,» whereof if any drink he lives forever; but so many and terrible are the dangers that confront the traveler in the Dark Regions, that only one man has ever succeeded in overcoming them and partaking of the Water of Life. This is Khizr.* Nothing certain is known of this mysterious personage, though many legends are current concerning him. Iskender (Alexander the Great), with all his army, penetrated into the Dark Land in quest of the Life-giving stream. He sent forward Khizr, who acted as his guide, to explore. Finding his way in the surrounding gloom by means of the light emitted by a great jewel that he held in his hand, Khizr penetrated to the very centre of these mysterious regions. There he saw a narrow stream, like a thread of silver, issuing from the ground. That was the Water of Life. He knelt down, drank a deep draught, then rose, looked to the ground, and lo! the Stream had disappeared. Iskender wandered backward and forward for a time in the Land of Darkness, but could find no trace either of Khizr or the Fountain of Life, and, at length giving up the hopeless search, returned to his own country. Khizr is by some thought to be identical with Elijah, by others with St. George; others again believe him to have been the vezír of *Zu-'l-Qarneyn*, an equally vague and uncertain hero, who is said to have been a universal conqueror and to have lived at the time of the patriarch Abraham. We are told that Khizr often comes to assist or direct poor Muslims in difficulty, when his appearance is that of a venerable man clad in green vestments. No myth is a greater favorite than this of the Fountain of Life; the Ottoman poets continually refer to it, generally mentioning at the same time *Darkness* and *Khizr* or *Iskender*.

*In the translations, for the sake of metre, I have generally spelled this name Khizar, but Khizr is the correct spelling and pronunciation.

The lips of the beloved are frequently compared to it, as in these lines by Husn*i*: —*

My loved one's lips a bright carnelion called I;
But vain words these, did all my comrades count:
«For that,» said they, «a worthless stone of Yemen;
But this, in sooth, the margin round Life's Fount.»

54. Lat*i*f*i*, after quoting this poem of Zeyneb, gives in his *Tezkera* the following *gazel* of his own composition, as a *Nazira* (Introduction, Sec. II.) to the verses of the poetess; it is translated here to serve as a specimen of the *Nazira*: —

Huri, again our feast as shining Paradise array!
With thy sweet lip the beaker fill brim-high with Kevser's spray.
O *Sufi*! if thy cell be dark and gloomy as thy heart,
Come, then, and with the wine-cup's lamp it light with radiance gay.
Heap up, like aloes-wood,† the flame of love within thy breast;
From thine own breath to all earth's senses odors sweet convey.
O Zephyr! shouldst thou pass the home of her we love so well,
Full many blessings bear to her from us who her obey.
Come, O Lat*i*f*i*, and ere yet the Sphere roll up thy scroll,
(Mad be not,) make thy songs a book, and brook thou no delay.‡

55. The down on the cheek, which, as we have already seen (51), is frequently mentioned, is often spoken of as *green* (*khatt-i sebz*). The word *green* in this expression is not used in its sense of *color*, but in its meaning of *fresh, tender;* as the young corn when newly come up is beautifully *green* and *delicate*. However, for the sake of their literary conceits, the poets, while using the word *sebz* in this sense, still retain in view its original meaning of green color. Such is the case in the present instance, when Prince Jem desires his mistress to lay her green (*i. e.*, soft) down (*i. e.*, her cheek) upon his breast, scorched by the fire of love, because *it is right that fresh greens be spread upon roasted meat*. Such a simile as this, though revolting to European taste, is neither repellent nor ridiculous in the eyes of the bolder Asiatics; and we shall by-and-by see some others like it.

56. The *basil* is his *disheveled hair*, or perhaps his *beard;* the *gardeners* are his *eyes;* and the *water* they nightly sprinkle over the basil is his *tears*. The basil, like the hyacinth, is a common metaphor for the *hair*.

57. *Kevn u Mekan*, «Existence and Space,» the whole Universe.

58. *Durr-i shehwar*, «a regal pearl,» the finest of the twelve classes into which, according to their lustre and purity, pearls are divided. The word *durr*, one of the general terms for «pearl,» is also the special name of the second quality. See Note 146.

*The original will be found in Mr. Redhouse's «Turkish Poetry,» p. 32.
†Aloes-wood is celebrated for the fragrance it emits when burned.
‡These two lines are full of untranslatable equivoques.

59. The occasions when the *qasidas* were composed, from which this and the two following extracts are taken, are mentioned in the Biographical Notice of Nejat*i*, page 211.

60. Key-Khusrev (Cyrus) is one of the greatest monarchs of the Keyan*i* dynasty of Persia. For his adventures see Atkinson's *Shah-Nama*.

61. Alluding to the dark heart of the tulip. The comparison of the centre of the tulip to a burn or sear is of constant occurrence.

62. According to the Oriental tradition, Jesus did not die, but was translated to heaven.

63. Jemsh*i*d was the fourth King of the P*i*shd*a*d*i* dynasty, the first line of Persian Kings whose adventures are recorded in the *Shah-Nama*. He was eminent in learning and wisdom. Coats of mail and swords, and garments of silk were first made in his time. He reached the summit of power and glory, compelling the very demons to construct for him a gorgeous palace: —

> He taught the unholy Demon-train to mingle
> Water and clay, with which, formed into bricks,
> The walls were built, and then high turrets, towers,
> And balconies, and roofs to keep out rain,
> And cold, and sunshine. Every art was known
> To Jemsh*i*d, without rival in the world.*

After a time, however, pride got the better of this King, and his arrogance and presumption so displeased God that He raised up an Arabian usurper named Zuh*a*q, who drove the Persian sovereign from his throne. After years of wandering in poverty and misery, he fell into the hands of his enemy, who put him to a cruel death. Jemsh*i*d is represented as a joyous monarch, fond of wine, music, and other pleasures; his splendor and subsequent fall are favorite themes with the Eastern poets.

64. *Rum* is «Rome»; *Rumi*, «Roman.» The names «Greek» and «Greece» are unknown in the East: *Yunan* represents «Ionia.» The Roman conquest of Greece, Asia Minor, and Syria completely wiped from the Asiatic mind all recollection of the former movers in these lands: Alexander the Great is known only as *Iskender-i Rumi*, «Alexander the Roman.» From that day to this the dwellers in these regions have been indiscriminately called «Romans» by the Orientals; and their emperor — Byzantine or Ottoman — is *Qaysar-i Rum*, «Cesar of Rome»: no other Qaysar is recognized in the East. Therefore the Ottoman Empire is, and has been for centuries, styled the *Roman Empire*, or simply *Rome*, by Persians, Eastern Turks, Afgans, and Indians; an Ottoman Turk is called by these a Roman, and the Ottoman language, the Roman language. See Note 259.

* Atkinson's *Shah-Nama*, p. 8.

65. Khusrev, as has been noticed (Note 10), though sometimes applied specially to Khusrev Perviz, is the general title for the Kings of the Sasani dynasty, just as Cesar is the peculiar style of the Emperors of Rome; Pharaoh, of the ancient Kings of Egypt; Nejashi, of those of Abyssinia; and so forth. It is used here in this general sense, simply to signify a powerful sovereign.

66. These verses are addressed by Nejati to a painted handkerchief which he is about to send as a present to his mistress. The custom of sending presents of painted handkerchiefs, which are much esteemed by the Turks, has given rise to the otherwise groundless fable, current in Europe, of the Sultan throwing a handkerchief toward her among his *odaliqs* whom he desires to honor with his favors.

67. To rub up, as artists do their colors. The meaning of the second line of the last verse is that the poet sheds tears of blood (Notes 77–80) so profusely that a thousand handkerchiefs would be stained crimson by them in a single moment.

68. This is from Mesihi's petition-*qasida* which he addressed to the Nishanji Pasha. See Biographical Notices, page 213.

69. This ode of Mesihi is perhaps more widely known in Europe than any other Turkish poem. Sir William Jones first published the original along with prose renderings in English and Latin, and a paraphrase in English verse. His Latin version was reproduced by Toderini in his *Letteratura Turchesca;* and his English prose rendering by Davids in his «Turkish Grammar.» A German paraphrase appears in Von Hammer's work, and a French one in Servan de Sugny's; in fact, I doubt if there be any European treatise on Ottoman literature in which this poem does not figure. It does not appear, however, to have attained such a celebrity in its native land, at least it is not mentioned by either Latifi or Qinali-Zada, nor does Ziya Beg reproduce it in his *Kharabat.*—The present translation has already appeared in the Appendix to Mr. W. A. Clouston's «Arabian Poetry for English Readers.»

70. The season (*hengam*) of spring is said to cover the gardens with *hengamas:* a *hengama* is a circle of beholders drawn round a juggler or any other strange sight; here it means the clusters of flowers, or perhaps the parties of friends who walk about in the gardens in spring. In the next line the almond-tree is represented as throwing down its white blossoms, like the silver coins scattered at weddings: perhaps it is supposed to throw them to the imaginary jugglers.

71. Ahmed, as we have seen (Note 40), is another form of Muhammed. The «parterre» here referred to is the world (of Islam), the garden, or mead, being its poetic symbol. The «Light of Ahmed» (*Nur-i Ahmed*) means, primarily, «the Glory of Muhammed»; but it seems also to be the name of some flower, and, lastly, probably refers here to some Turkish victory recently gained, or peace concluded.

72. The expression «gipsy-party» is a paraphrase here. The original word *tavila* means, in this instance, «a row of horses from a stable, picketed out at grass in the open.» Therefore the line

Zhaleler aldi hewa-yi tavila-la gulsheni

signifies: «the dew-drops have taken possession of the garden, with the wish to picket their horses there,» *i. e.*, hold a pic-nic party in it.

73. This again may allude to some battle in which many illustrious Turks fell. Sir W. Jones' original, which is in many places corrupt, has in this line *shemsin*, «of the sun,» instead of *shimshek* «lightning.»

74. Literally: «had its head in its heart,» referring to the unopened rosebud.

75. «May the worthy,» *i. e.*, may those who appreciate these verses, etc.—A youth with new moustaches is called «four-eyebrowed.» The «four-eyebrowed beauties» are the verses of four hemistichs each.

76. It is perhaps needless to remind the reader of the well-known Eastern myth concerning the love of the *bulbul*, or Nightingale, for the Rose, and his consequent joy in springtide and despair in autumn. Mesîhi himself is the *bulbul* here. The nightingale is sometimes called the Bird of Dawn, or of Night.

77. «To drink one's own blood» means to suffer intense sorrow; similarly, «to shed tears of blood» is to weep in bitter anguish.

78. Jupiter, in astrology, is the most auspicious of all the planets. He is called *Sa'd-i Ekber*, «the Greater Fortune;» Venus is *Sa'd-i Asgar*, «the Lesser Fortune;» Saturn, on the other hand, is *Nahs-i Ekber*, «the Greater Infortune;» while Mars is *Nahs-i Asgar*, «the Lesser Infortune.» The Sun, the Moon, and Mercury are indifferent, but their positions exercise a great influence in horoscopes.

79. See Note 53. Iskender was the name of Mihri's beloved (see Biographical Notices page 215), hence the aptness of the allusion.

80. This *gazel*, like most of the works of Sultan Selîm I., is written in Persian: in it he refers to his many conquests. This is the only poem in the present collection the original of which is not in Ottoman Turkish.

81. *Istambol* is the Turkish name for Constantinople, whence the European corruption, *Stamboul*. *Iran* is Persia.

82. The Turks used to call the Persians *Qizil-Bash*, «Gold-Heads,» on account of the gold, or gilt, helmets worn by the guards of the Shah. *Qizil* means «red» in Ottoman, but « gold» in Persian (*Azerbayjani*) Turkish: Fuzuli sometimes uses it in this latter sense.

83. Alluding to the Memluk, or Slave-Sultans of Egypt, overthrown by Selîm's courage or resolution.

84. In Note 28 the Nine Spheres are referred to as being between the earth and the lowest of the Mansions of Paradise. According to the Ptolemaic astronomy of the Muslims, these Spheres are as follows, commencing from below and going upward: 1st, the Sphere of the Heaven of the Moon; 2d, of Mercury; 3d, of Venus; 4th, of the Sun; 5th, of Mars; 6th, of Jupiter; 7th, of Saturn; 8th, of the Fixed Stars, the Firmament, the Starry Vault; 9th, the Empyrean, the *Primum Mobile*, the Heaven of Heavens, «beyond which God holds His state in unapproachable, inconceivable grandeur, majesty, and splendor.» When personified in poetry, the Moon usually represents a fair girl or youth ; Mercury, a penman; Venus, a beautiful female musician; the Sun, a sovereign; Mars, a warrior; Jupiter, a judge; and Saturn, an old man.

85. 'Ir*a*q and Hij*a*z are the names of well-known musical modes as well as of provinces, hence the *jeu de mot.*

86. The *kuhl*, «kohol,» «stibium,» of Isfah*a*n is the most celebrated. Sel*i*m means to say that he defeated the lords of Isfah*a*n.

87. The *Amu* is the river Oxus.

88. Literally, «elephant-mated:» the Bishop in chess is called the «elephant» in the East. That piece is here mentioned on account of India being celebrated in connection with elephants. «Queenly troops» are troops formidable, as is the Queen in Chess. See Note 220.

89. That is: «God gave me the dominion of the world because I loved Him.» Sa'du-'d-D*i*n, the Historian of the Empire, the author of the *Taju-'t-Tevar*ikh, «The Tiara of Histories» calls Sel*i*m I. a Dervish in heart.

90. Ibl*i*s is the Muslim name for Satan. The word is probably the same as *Diabolus.*

91. The moth's love for the taper is a constant theme with Asian poets. The moth is a truer lover than even the nightingale; for, whereas the latter tells its love and its woes to all the world, the former, without a sigh, perishes in its beloved flame.

92. The Eastern poets always speak of *wounds* as *flowers.*

93. Oriental writers frequently call a pretty woman or youth *nigar*, «a picture»; just as we might say, «a perfect picture of a girl.» In the fourth line occurs the phrase *ab u dana*, «water and grain,» all that a bird requires to live upon; here, of course, it is an equivoque referring to the *watered* and *grained* steel.

94. *Ergawan*, «the Judas-tree,» *Cercis Siliquastrum*, is often mentioned in Oriental poetry, always in connection with its beautiful red flowers. It is common in Persian gardens, where it attains the height of the laburnum.

95. Joseph is the type of youthful beauty. In this poem of Lami'i, the Sun is compared to him by reason of its lustre. The Sun enters *Libra* in September; Joseph sold corn to the Egyptians by *weight:* hence their «passing to the Balance.» The loves of Joseph and Zuleykh*a* (Potiphar's wife) are as famous in the East as those of Khusrev and Sh*i*r*i*n, or Leyl*i* and Mejn*u*n. Zuleykh*a* spent great riches in purchasing and rearing Joseph; here «the year's Zuleykha» is autumn, and the gold coins she scatters are the yellow leaves.

The following is an abridgment of the romance of Joseph and Zuleykh*a*. Joseph, the youngest and best beloved son of Jacob, was so lovely even in his infancy that his aunt, who nursed him, owing to the death of his mother, attempted, though vainly, to retain possession of him by fraud.

The King of Magreb (Marocco) had a daughter called Zuleykh*a*, the most beautiful of her sex, as Joseph was the fairest of his. One night this Princess saw Joseph in a vision, and, though she knew not who he was, fell deeply in love with him, and her passion so preyed upon her that she lost her health and all pleasure in her old pursuits. On two other occasions the beautiful object of her love appeared to her in visions, on the second of which, in reply to her question as to his name and country, he told her that he was Grand Vez*i*r of Egypt. Ambassadors from many kings came to her father, asking her in marriage for their masters, but Zuleykh*a* would have none of them, and induced her father to send a messenger to the Grand Vez*i*r of Egypt, requesting him to accept her as his wife. The Egyptian noble at once agreed, and Zuleykh*a* was sent with a splendid retinue to the capital of the Pharaohs; but great was her dismay on seeing in the Vez*i*r an aged man, very different from the lovely youth of her visions.

In the meantime, Joseph's brothers, envious of the great love borne by their father toward the fair boy, persuaded Jacob to allow his darling son to accompany them to the fields, and there cast him into a deep pit, purposing to let him perish of hunger. A caravan happened shortly afterward to pass that way, when one of the merchants, feeling thirsty, came to draw water from the well into which Joseph had been cast. The latter, when the bucket was let down, got into it, and was drawn up; the merchant being greatly delighted at finding so valuable a prize. He took his fair captive with him to the Egyptian capital, and exposed him for sale in the slave-market there. The fame of the wondrous beauty of the young Hebrew was noised all over the city, and princes and nobles bid against each other to obtain possession of him. The sad Zuleykh*a* in her splendid palace heard of the lovely slave, and determined to go and see for herself this peerless beauty. She did so, and at once recognized in him the youth she had seen in her dreams, and for whose sake she had left her father's land and come to the banks of the Nile. She implored the Vez*i*r to buy the boy and bring him up as his own son; for, as the translator of Jam*i*'s poem says, «Zuleykh*a*'s nominal husband belonged to 'that unhappy class which a practice of immemorial antiquity in the East excluded from the pleasures of love and from the hope of posterity.'" The noble did so, *Zuleykha* giving many of her jewels and treasures to aid in the purchase. Under the same roof with the object of her love, the Magrebi Princess imagined that her woes were over, but she was greatly mistaken. Joseph was as virtuous as he was beautiful, and all *Zuleykha*'s wiles and entreaties were in vain, for the descendant of the Prophets would not even raise his eyes to hers. The love of the Grand Vezir's lady for her slave, and his coldness toward her, became the talk of the city; and the ladies of the capital severely blamed *Zuleykha* for her conduct. In order to reprove them, the Princess invited them all to a grand banquet, in the course of which she asked if they would like to see Joseph; they all replied that there was nothing they desired so much. She then gave to each an orange and a knife, telling them not to cut the fruit till Joseph appeared. Then she summoned the youth, on beholding whose perfect loveliness all the ladies, bewildered, cut their hands instead of the oranges. They at once declared that *Zuleykha* was free from all blame, for it was impossible to resist such charms. Angered at last by Joseph's stubbornness, *Zuleykha* determined that she should not be the only one to suffer; so she falsely accused him to the Vezir of having tried to seduce her. The minister, enraged at this return for his many kindnesses, cast his slave into prison; but *Zuleykha*'s love still burned fiercely as ever, though she was the cause of Joseph's present misfortune, and her only pleasure lay in gazing on the roof of the dungeon in which he was inclosed. Joseph soon made friends with his fellow-captives, among whom were two officers of the King's household. One night they each had a singular dream, which they related to their Hebrew friend: he told the one that his vision signified impending execution; the other that his indicated approaching release and restoration to favor, and requested the latter to mention his own hard case before the King. Things fell out as Joseph had predicted; but the fortunate officer forgot all about his friend until the King has a strange dream of seven fat kine followed by seven lean, and seven full ears of corn followed by seven thin. No one was found able to interpret this vision, till the officer, bethinking himself of Joseph, ran to the prison and inquired of him the signification. The Hebrew answered that it meant seven years of plenty followed by seven years of dearth. Hastening back to the King, the officer related what he had heard; the monarch, delighted, requested Joseph to appear before him, but this the latter declined to do until his innocence was established. So *Zuleykha* and the ladies who had been present at her banquet were summoned to the royal presence, where they all acknowledged that *Zuleykha* herself was the guilty one. Joseph was then brought before the King, who made him Grand Vezir and practical ruler of his dominions. The

Old Grand Vez*i*r died soon afterward, and Zuleykh*a* lost all her worldly wealth. With hair turned grey through bitter sorrow, and eyes blinded from constant weeping, she dwelt, a poor beggar, in a hut of reeds by the roadside. Pondering there on her sad lot, she thought how ill her god had treated her, and she resolved to embrace the One True Faith. So she rose and broke her idol; and a little afterward she stood in Joseph's way as he rode past, and begged for alms. The Vez*i*r did not recognize her, but struck by her sad voice, he ordered her to be brought to his palace. There she told her tale, and how she had embraced Isl*a*m; she entreated Joseph to pray to Allah that she might receive back her sight and her beauty. He did so, and she became again fair as when she left her native land. Her husband being dead, there was nothing now to prevent her union with Joseph; so they were wedded with all pomp, and lived in happiness till death sundered them.

96. The yellow leaves.

97. Brides in Turkey sometimes deck their faces with gilt spangles: the line alludes to the vine-leaves beginning to wither.

98. The stems of the vine are supposed to be in the stream.

99. The «hands» of the plane-tree are its *palmated* leaves.

100. Hinna, *Lawsonia inermis*, the well-known red dye with which Oriental women stain their hands. Here again Lami'*i* refers to the leaves withering.

101. Shooting-stars are supposed to be flaming bolts, hurled, by the angels that guard the confines of the lowest heaven, at those demons who creep up to overhear the divine secrets discussed in Paradise. The meteors are, of course, the falling leaves.

102. That is, blossoms. The «poor,» in the second last line, are the bare trees.

103. The tossing of the rosebud in the wind is here likened to the acrobatic performances of the «tumbler» pigeon.

104. Like dancers with tambourines, and knives tossed about.

105. The original word here is *jorjuna*, meaning wild orgies. The allusion is to the motion of branches in the wind.

106. This is the concluding strophe of an Elegy on Sultan Sel*i*m I.; the original will be found in Mr. Redhouse's «Turkish Poetry,» p. 28.

107. *Asef*, the Asaph of the Psalms, is reputed in the East to have been the *vezir* of Suleym*a*n (Solomon); he is the type of ministerial wisdom.—A *mushir* is a «field-marshal.» Sel*i*m was his own vez*i*r and mush*i*r, minister and general.

108. This couplet is very highly esteemed in Turkey; it is quoted in all the anthologies. In a brief reign of less than nine years, Sel*i*m I. doubled the extent of the Ottoman dominions. I have attempted

to preserve here the equivoque between '*asr*, «epoch,» and '*asr*, «afternoon.»

109. The entire strophe shows many instances of the Oriental figure called *tejnis*, which I render by «equivoque»; but as this and the three following lines contain even more examples than the others, I give them here in Turkish (printing the *tejnis* in italics) to serve as a specimen of this favorite, and often very ingenious, literary conceit; I have made an effort to retain some of them in the translation:—

Rezm ishinda ve *bezm* '*ishinda*,
Gurmedi pír-i cherkh ana nazír.
Chiqsa *eywan-í bezma*, mihr-i munír!
Girsa *meydan-í rezma*, shír-i dilír!

110. This poem was composed by Gazal*í*, on the occasion of the execution of his patron, the Defterd*a*r Iskender Chelebi.

111. The «perfection» of a star is its ascension, its «defect» is its setting. Iskender held high place near the Sultan.

112. The intrigues of his rival, Ibr*a*h*í*m Pasha, were the cause of Iskender's execution. The «lofty decree for his high exaltation» is the Divine order for him to be raised to heaven.

113. Like a bird.

114. Concerning the supposed connection between Isl*a*m and fatalism, Mr. Redhouse says: «*Qader*, 'Providence,' is the Isl*a*mic word which Europeans so unjustly translate by the terms 'fate' and 'destiny.' Isl*a*m utterly abhors those old pagan ideas, and reposes on God's *providence* alone; which some will say is the same thing. The terms *qaza* and *qismet*, quasi-synonyms of *qadr* and *qader*, mean, the former, God's *decree*, the latter *one's allotted portion*. Both may correctly be translated by our term *dispensation*. True that astrologers, dervishes, and poets talk about *the Sphere* (Felek) as ruling or influencing sublunary events. To Isl*a*m, this is either rank paganism and blasphemy, or a special application of the admitted truism that here below God acts through secondary causes.»*

In these poems *Fate* and *the Sphere* are frequently mentioned, sometimes even prayed to; the Sphere especially being often spoken of as bringing good or evil in its revolutions. But such expressions are no more to be regarded as true declarations of the poet's belief than are his repeated calls for wine to be looked upon as indicating a desire for the actual juice of the grape.—The word used in the present poem is not the Arabic *qader*, but the Persian *ruzkar*, which literally means «day-maker»; it therefore includes the ideas of *time*, *fortune*, *events*, *accidents*, etc.—everything which goes to make up days as they affect man. These last two lines of Gazal*í* savor more of Hind*u*ism than of Isl*a*m.

* *El-Esma'u-'l-Husna*, "The Most Comely Names," p. 51. Tr*u*bner and Co. Reprinted from the "Journal" of the Royal Asiatic Society, 1880.

115. The parrot is called the *sugar-eater*. Being a beautiful creature, and possessed of the wondrous power of speech (when taught), a fair woman with a sweet voice is not unfrequently compared to it.

116. *Nur-i Muhammed*, «the Light,» or «Essence of Muhammed,» was the first thing God created in eternity, though its incarnation was late. It is legendarily reported that the body of the Prophet cast no shadow.

117. Referring to the Egyptian ladies who cut their hands through their bewilderment on seeing Joseph's beauty. See Note 95.

118. In the Qur'*an*, liv., 1., we read: «And the moon is split asunder.» This is traditionally referred to a miracle; the unbelievers having asked Muhammed for a sign, the moon appeared cloven in twain.

119. The legend runs that when Jesus was translated from the world, he was found to have nothing earthly about him, save a needle stuck in his garment. But in consequence thereof he got only half-way to Paradise, and now lives in the Fourth Heaven, that of the Sun, where he will abide till he comes again in glory.

120. Alluding to generation.

121. The «golden birds» are the stars; the «quicksilver-resplendent deep» is the sky. This is a very mystic *gazel;* the couplet in question means: «What if I send my intellect to fathom the mysteries of the Universe.»

122. The Eastern poets seem to confuse the colors *blue* and *green*, or rather, to look upon the former as a variety of the latter; as we might call crimson and pink both red. Lami'*i*'s poems offer two instances of this; in the last line of No. I. he compares a tree with some of its leaves withered to the starry sky; and in the eighth line from the end of No. III. he likens the green mead, covered with drops of dew, to the star-filled heavens. So Khiy*ali* here speaks of the Nine Spheres (the sky) as being emerald-hued.

123. Von Hammer says that Prince Bayez*i*d composed these lines a few days before his death.

124. Bells are worn by the beasts in a caravan. The meaning is: «The animals are being harnessed for the journey, and I shall soon be off.»

125. Suleym*a*n, or Solomon, the King of Israel, is looked upon as the *beau ideal* of an Eastern monarch. The Oriental writers speak with enthusiasm of his justice and wisdom, his might and magnificence; he is held to have been a prophet; he was perfect in all sciences, and understood the language of birds and beasts. The winds were subject to his command, and used to bear his carpet, on which stood his throne and his troops, wheresoever he willed. Jinns, demons,

and fairies were all under his control, and constrained to do his bidding. The secret of his wonderful power was his Ring (Solomon's Seal), on which was graven *The Most Great Name;* by virtue of this magic Signet he was lord of creation. The evil jinns, whom he thus subdued, he compelled to adopt the Faith of Islam—«*There is no god but God,*»—and in case of refusal, he thrust the obstinate misbelievers into copper vessels, which he secured by the impress of his Seal, and cast them into the Circumambient Ocean. These were occasionally washed on shore in after ages. Every one will recollect the story of the Fisherman, in the «Thousand and One Nights,» who found one while pursuing his vocation.

The legend alluded to by Fuzuli is as follows: A demon, called Sakhr, managed to get possession of the Ring by appearing in the shape of Suleyman to one of that monarch's concubines, Emina by name, to whom the King used to intrust the Signet when he washed. Having received the Ring from her, Sakhr seated himself upon the throne, and did what seemed to him good. But so infamous was his conduct, that, on the fortieth day, the Grand Vezir Asef, and some doctors of the Law, determined (perhaps in the hope of admonishing him) to read the Scriptures, in his presence. No sooner did the Word of God fall upon the demon's ear than he resumed his native form, and fled in haste to the seashore, where the Signet dropped from him. By the providence of God, the Ring was swallowed by a fish. When Suleyman had been deprived of his throne, the light of prophecy departed from him, and no one recognized him. So for forty days he wandered about the country, begging for alms. On the fortieth he entered the service of a fisherman, who gave him as his daily wages two fishes. The fish which had swallowed the Signet was taken by the fisherman and given to Suleyman, who thus recovered his Ring, and with it his kingdom. Sakhr was caught, imprisoned in one of the copper vessels already mentioned, sealed with the Ring, and cast into the Sea of Tiberias, where he must remain till the Resurrection Day.

The identity of name between the great Turkish Sultan (Suleyman I.) and the sage Hebrew King is a very lucky coincidence for the Ottoman poets, as it affords them endless opportunities for comparing and purposely confusing these two mighty sovereigns, each the greatest of his nation. Thus it is not unlikely that Fuzuli alludes in these lines to the defeat of some rebellious beg or pasha who had risen against Sultan Suleyman's authority.

126. «The heart turning blood» means suffering profound vexation.

127. It is believed in the East that rubies are common stones on which the sun has shone for ages.

128. *Mihr-i rukhsarin.* *Mihr* means alike «sun» and «love.»

129. The eye is compared to a metallic mirror, such as is commonly used in the East.

130. A pretty *mouth* is sometimes likened to Suleyman's Ring (125), not only on account of its form, but also by reason of its bewitching power. At other times the *mouth* is a *casket;* the *teeth* being *pearls,* and the *gums, rubies* or *coral.*—See the first gazel of Muhibbi.

131. When God created man, He commanded the angels to bow before him; for the human nature is higher than the angelic, inasmuch as man has his eternal destiny in his own hands, and the choice of doing good or evil; for Islam is not, as is generally believed by Europeans, fatalistic. See Qur'an, ii., 32, etc.; also Note 114.

132. In this beautiful couplet the moon and sun both represent the poet's mistress; he is the taper.

133. There is a poetic and very ancient Eastern notion that pearls are formed in oysters by drops of rain or dew falling into them.

134. The word *dud* means both «smoke» and «sigh;» the *sigh* is supposed to be the *smoke* of the heart, consumed by the *fire* of sorrow.

135. The district where my love dwells is, through her presence, Paradise; but there is grief enough there for me, by reason of her unkindness and my rivals' persecution.

136. Ziya Beg has written a sort of parody on this *museddes* of Fuzuli, which appears in his *Kharabat.*

137. A poet sometimes likens the *tongue* of his mistress to the small pistachio-nut.—From *qand,* the Eastern word used here, comes our «candy.»

138. A lady's *crescents* are her eyebrows.

139. Her face is the moon; her hair, the clouds.

140. This is the explanation of these two lines: A cypress grows by the water, spring, or fountain—(poetically) sets its foot in it: *Bash guz-ustuna,* «on (my) head and eye» («I shall willingly do thy pleasure»), is a common phrase. Conquerors set their feet on the neck of the vanquished: Thus a cypress-like beauty may set her foot on the head, in the (streaming) eye the (fount) of her vanquished lover; but if she put it in his eye, the lashes may pierce her tender foot.

141. Her hair hung over her cheeks.

142. Eastern women sometimes tatoo their feet, hands, or face. See «Modern Egyptians,» page 39.

143. That is: «How have thy white feet become red?»

144. Her curls twisting over her face are compared to a scorpion's claws; therefore her face, encircled by her hair, is the Moon in the Sign Scorpio, a conjunction regarded as menacing by astrologers.

145. Her *dog-rose and tulip* are her white face and red cheeks.

146. The pearls of 'Aden and the Persian Gulf are highly esteemed. *Khosh-ab*, «fair lustres,» are the second class of pearls, called also *nejmi*, «starry,» and '*uyun*, «eyes,» «founts.» See Note 58.

147. The *bubbles* are drops of perspiration. Moisture on the face is frequently praised by Eastern poets, and compared to dew.

148. The comb is supposed amorously to bite the ringlets.

149. In Arabic, *shems*, «the sun,» is feminine, and *qamer*, «the moon,» masculine; therefore, in Muslim poetry, the greater luminary is represented as a female, and the lesser as a male, as is the case in old Teutonic lore.

150. *Silvery*, when applied to the human frame, means *delicate*.

151. This line contains a very ingenious example of the *mihr* equivoque (121). «The fillet, being in thy hair, does not inclose thy *mihr* «sun (-like face),» but the chain, hanging round thy cheeks, does; therefore, I am not like the former, but the latter, because I, too, inclose thy *mihr*, «love»; *i.e.*, «love for thee is within my breast.»

152. *Surma*, a preparation of antimony used for painting the edges of the eyelids.

153. The comparison of the *eyebrow* to a *bow*, and the *glance* to the *arrow* or *shaft*, is a favorite. Eastern ladies employ powdered antimony to form streaks on the eyelids, and a paste of indigo to paint the eyebrows with. Perhaps it used to be customary to make bows of poplar branches. Fuzuli likens the lady's indigo-stained eyebrows to bows of *green* poplar; this may be an instance of the confusion of the colors *green* and *blue*, mentioned in Note 122.

154. The tale of Leyli and Mejnun is perhaps the favorite love-story of the East. As the names of the hero and heroine are of very frequent occurrence in Turkish Poetry, I give here an outline of the romance. Qays, the son of an Arab chief of Yemen, falls in love with a maiden of another clan — a damsel bright as the moon, graceful as the cypress, with locks dark as the night, whence her name Leyli — *i.e.*, «Nocturnal.» His passion is returned; but with the departure of his beloved's tribe to the distant uplands of Nejd, his woes begin. In the wild hope of reaching her new abode, Qays rushes out into the desert, where, with matted locks and bosom bare to the scorching sun, he wanders on, making the rocks to echo with his cries of «Leyli!» In vain his friends bring him back — he always escapes, and flies again to the waste; so, seeing that his reason is shattered, they change his name to *Mejnun* — *i.e.*, «Bewitched.» In the course of his wanderings he enters the land of a chief called Nevfel, who finds the wretched lover and, hearing his story, conceives a warm friendship for him, and resolves to aid him. So Nevfel and his warriors go to Leyli's father, and demand the maiden for Mejnun: but the father refuses. Then a battle takes place, in which Nevfel and his men are victorious; but when Leyli's father comes to

offer submission, he threatens to slay the maiden before their eyes if they persist in their demand. They therefore retire, and Leyl*i* is constrainedly married to one of her father's friends. After a time a stranger seeks out Mejn*u*n in the desert, and tells him that Leyl*i* is desirous of seeing him. At once the true lover speeds to the appointed place; but when Leyl*i* learns he is there, her sense of duty triumphs over the passion of her life, and she resolves to forego the dangerous meeting; and Mejn*u*n, disappointed, returns to the wilderness, where the wild beasts become his friends. In the course of time Leyl*i*'s husband dies, and Mejn*u*n hastens to his loved one's side. Overpowered by emotion, both are for a space silent; at length Leyl*i* addresses Mejn*u*n in tender accents, but when he finds voice to reply, it is evident that the reaction has extinguished the last spark of reason. Mejn*u*n is now a hopeless maniac, and he rushes from the arms of Leyl*i* and seeks the desert once more. Leyl*i* never recovers the shock occasioned her by this discovery. She pines away, and, ere she dies, requests her mother to convey to Mejn*u*n the tidings of her death, and to assure him of her constant, unquenchable love. When he hears of her death, Mejn*u*n seeks her tomb, and, exhausted with his journey and his sorrow, and the privations he had so long endured, lays himself down upon the turf that covers her remains, and dies. Zeyd, an attendant who had always befriended Mejn*u*n, comes to watch by the sepulchre where the lovers sleep; there one night he sees the vision which forms the subject of the last extract from Fuz*u*l*i*'s works.

155. There is an untranslatable equivoque in this line and the next; *merdum* means «the pupil of the eye» ; *merd im*, «I am a man (a hero).» *Merdum*, or *merdumek*, means, properly, «manikin,» and refers to the small image of ourselves that we see reflected in the pupil. It is these (*i. e.*, themselves) that Fuz*u*l*i* says in damsels drink blood — but the blood of their lovers this time.

156. There is a proverb to this effect.

157. *Kimiya*, «the Philosopher's Stone,» that imaginary wondrous substance which transmutes all baser metals into gold. The European appellation of *stone* seems to be a fanciful one, as it does not appear from the writings of the alchemists that the great arcanum was of a lapideous nature.

158. This line means: «I looked to find sincerity (truthfulness) in the mirror, but even there I only saw a persecuted swain (my own reflection).»

159. *Subh-i Sadiq*, «the True Dawn,» opposed to *Subh-i Kazib*, «the False Dawn,» *i.e.*, the Zodiacal Light, a transient brightness in the horizon about an hour before the rise of the true dawn. This phenomenon is frequently mentioned in Eastern literature, where it is sometimes called «the Wolf's Tail.» See two interesting papers by

Mr. Redhouse in the *Journal of the Royal Asiatic Society*, Vols. X. and XII. (New Series).

160. The *gilman*, or «native youths of Paradise»; the *huris*, its fairy maidens.

161. The whole of this long and beautiful poem of Fazlí has been published in the original, along with a German translation, by Von Hammer. That learned Orientalist considered it one of the finest productions of the Ottoman muse; it has the merit of originality, so far as its plot is concerned, not being, like most Turkish *Mesnevis*, copied from a Persian model. The story is an elaboration of the myth of the Nightingale's love for the Rose. A king called Spring has a beautiful daughter, Rose, whom he appoints Governor of Parterre, one of his cities. She, vain of her own loveliness, sends her courier, Zephyr, to search the world and see if she have any peer in beauty. While pursuing his quest he meets with Nightingale, a Prince disguised as a beggar, who is a very sweet singer. Him he tells of his errand and of his mistress's beauty, on hearing the description of which the Prince falls deeply in love with Rose. They proceed together to the latter's city, but the Princess refuses to receive Nightingale, who therefore wanders about the city singing his woes. Thorn, a *lala*, or governor, of Rose, hearing how a miserable beggar is going about the town telling all men that he is the Princess's lover, attacks Nightingale, wounds him with his sword, and drives him out of the city. He then goes and tells King Spring, who sends some guards to seize the Prince and imprison him in an iron cage. Rose, grieved at her true lover's misfortune, goes to his prison and consoles him by telling him of her love. In the meantime a great conqueror, called King Summer, has arisen in the East; he declares war against King Spring, and sends his army, commanded by his general, Sun, to take the city of Parterre. The invaders are completely successful, consuming by their flaming artillery all who venture to bar their road; and King Spring seeks safety in flight. After grievously oppressing the people, King Summer and his legions take their departure. King Autumn, in the North, hearing that the fair city is desolate, determines to take possession of it. At first his rule is pleasing, for he showers much gold (withered leaves) on all hands, but afterward it grows harsh and severe. In the West is a great, terrible Monarch, King Winter; he holds council with his generals, and determines to expel King Autumn from Parterre. So his general, Snow, steals quietly into the city one night, and when the inhabitants waken in the morning they find the town in the possession of his forces. Very cruel is King Winter; so severe are his laws that no one dares leave his house. When King Spring had been driven from his city, he had taken refuge in the South with a kinsman, King New-Year (Note 214); this monarch marshals his army, and, accompanied by his deposed friend, sets out to reinstate him in his kingdom. King Winter is driven from the land, and the rightful monarch restored to the throne. All the people are delighted, and,

amid general rejoicings, Rose and Nightingale are married.—This story, like all others of its kind, is an allegory: the city of Parterre represents the body; Rose, the soul; Nightingale, the heart; King Spring, the understanding; King Summer, anger, which drives away the understanding; King Autumn, lust, which paves the way for King Winter, disease; King New-Year is the grace of God. The story in detail is a very pretty one, and the language in which it is told appropriate and graceful.

162. *Rum*, Asia Minor. See Note 64.

163. The lily's leaf, on account of its shape, is often compared to a sword. See Mesihi's *Murebba'*, stanza 4.

164. Alluding to the idea that the thorn transfixes the Nightingale when that bird tries to get near its beloved Rose: the same notion is referred to in the story told in Note 161, where Thorn wounds Nightingale with his sword.

165. The *uskuf* was a pointed felt cap worn by the Janissaries and dervishes. The earlier Sultans used it covered with gold embroidery, as their regal head-dress. Under Muhammed II. it was appropriated to the officers of the Janissaries, and later, with certain modifications, to the Agas of the Seraglio. The cap called *altin-uskuf*, or *sirmali-uskuf*, was the same decorated with a gilt band (*yuklun*), which hung down across it in front. The *uskuf* has entirely disappeared since the destruction of the Janissaries, in 1826. See M. Barbier de Meynard's *Dictionnaire Turc-Français*.

166. A mole on the face is considered as a great beauty in the East, just as it used to be in England, when ladies represented it by a black patch. It is frequently compared to a grain of musk, which is of a dark color.

167. The Oriental letter *Nun* «N,» is represented by a curve.

168. Joseph, as already said (Note 95), is the type of youthful beauty; the «well» is an allusion to the pit into which he was lowered by his brethren.

169. That is, red—blood. See Note 77.

170. This *qasida*, by the greatest of Ottoman poets, in praise of Sultan Suleyman I., is here translated in its entirety.

171. The Sun is described as a tambourinist, referring to its form, round, like a tambourine; it is usually a sovereign (Note 84); for its sex when personified see Note 149.

172. Saturn is often spoken of as the Elephant-driver of the Heavens.

173. See Note 125. Referring, of course, both to Solomon and the Sultan.

174. *Keyani* connected with the Key*ani*, or Median, dynasty of Persia; here meaning simply, «Imperial.»—*Khusrevani*, connected with the Khusrevs, or Kings, of the *Sasani* (Sassanian) House, is used in the same way.

175. The rich merchant, Autumn, scatters gold (yellow leaves) profusely on each hand; yet even he stands in need of the Sultan's bounty.

176. Key-Qub*ad* (Dejoces), the founder of the Key*ani* dynasty. For his adventures see Atkinson's *Shah-Nama*.

177. Qahram*a*n is a legendary hero who was solicited by the Kings of the Fairies to aid them in repelling the Demons, who were constantly making war upon their subjects. He complied, and met with many strange adventures, which are related in the *Qahraman-Nama*.

178. This extravagant idea of the Sphere revolving through being struck by the Sultan's mall-bat is paralleled by the following passage in H*a*fiz:—

> «My King's-dragoon, my sweet one, what doll shows half thy graces!
> Urged by thy whip, the steed-like Sphere its rapid circle traces.»*

This is *Husn-i Ta'lil* (Note 46).

179. *Shamiyan*, «Sham*i*s,» means alike «Syrians» and «darknesses of evening.» Thus the night-black locks are compared to Syrian, or evening, dancers, who have tucked up their skirts for a dance to Hij*a*z in Arabia, or to the musical mode so called (Note 85).

180. *Sujud* is that position in canonical worship in which the forehead touches the ground; *qiyam*, that in which one stands upright. See Lane's «Modern Egyptians,» pp. 76, 77. This is another example of the figure *Husn-i Ta'lil* (46); the rose and jasmine bend, of course, when the wind blows, but here they are said to do so in adoration of the cheek so much fairer than they; and the cypress, naturally erect, is said to stand up to worship the figure more elegant than itself.

181. «*BE!*» *and it is*. Qur'*a*n, ii., 3, etc. *KUN!* «BE!» was God's fiat to creation. The hall, «*BE! and it is*,» simply means the Universe.

182. Irem, the terrestrial paradise, planted ages ago by King Shedd*a*d, and now sunk somewhere in the deserts of Arabia. The mead here means the world of Isl*a*m; the nightingales in the next line are poets. During Suleym*a*n's reign Ottoman Poetry reached its highest point.

183. Doubtless some allusion lurks in this couplet; perhaps B*aqi* prays that the Sultan may live to be an old man, till «the world-illuming sun,» his face, display «a silver candelabrum,» a white beard.

184. The slaty night-sky studded with stars is sometimes compared to steel inlaid with gold.

* Bicknell's *Hafiz of Shiraz*, page 42.

185. This assonant is in imitation of the original.

186. *Baqi* here compares the elegant figure of his mistress to his own graceful poetry; her thin waist resembles one of the subtle allusions in his verses — *i. e.*, it is so fine, one can hardly see it!

187. The Lote-tree of Paradise, that stands on the right hand of the Throne of God, and beyond which not even the angels may pass. For the T*u*ba-tree see Note 28. Moore mentions these two heavenly trees in «Lalla Rookh» (*Lala-Rukh*, «Tulip-Cheek»): —

> «Farewell, ye odors of earth that die,
> Passing away like a lover's sigh; —
> My feast is now of the Tuba-tree,
> Whose scent is the breath of Eternity.
>
> Farewell, ye vanishing flowers that shone
> In my fairy wreath, so bright and brief;
> O what are the fairest that e'er have blown,
> To the Lote-tree springing by Allah's throne,
> Whose flowers have a soul in every leaf!»

188. By the usual figure (Note 92), he likens the wound on his breast to a flower — the rosebud; the shaft (her glance), that caused it, is compared to a leaf curled up in the bud.

189. The wonderful cures and resuscitations wrought by Jesus, who is the type of a skillful and benign physician, are as celebrated among Muslims as among Christians. His healing power is said to have been in the breath.

190. A beautiful girl is called *kafir*, «infidel,» because of her cruelty.

191. The legend runs: After the Creation God assembled the souls of all who were to dwell upon the earth, and to each separately put the question: *A-Lestu bi-Rabbikum?* «Am I not your Lord?» to which each made reply: *Bela*, «Yea.» He had previously put the same question to the earth, the sky, and the mountains; but none of these dared take the responsibility of answering «Yea.»* The remembrance of this primeval vow is said by the S*u*f*i*s and dervishes to exercise an all-engrossing power over the souls of the initiated.

192. The *eye* is the *hope;* the word in the next line, translated *air*, means also *longing*. In this couplet, by mentioning the four elements, B*a*q*i* introduces that figure of speech called by Oriental rhetoricians *Mutazadd*, «contrariety.» In Mr. Bicknell's translation of H*a*fiz occurs this example: —

> «My heart and soul oft fly to love as earth in air away;
> At times with water, as a duck, I passion's fire allay.»

Eb*u*-'l-Fer*a*j-i R*u*m*i* has the following, quoted by Mr. Bicknell: —

> «Air art Thou, entering my frame as breath;
> Fire art Thou, burning hearts with love till death;
> Water art Thou, by which all creatures grow;
> Earth also art Thou, to which all must go.»

* Qur'an, vii., 171.

Mr. Whinfield's translation of the quatrains of 'Omer Khayyam yields yet another instance: —

«Man's seed is water from the void sea-spray;
And on his heart grief's fire doth ever prey;
And blown is he like wind about the world;
And last his crumbling earth is swept away.»

193. This couplet contains several allusions to the Game of Chess. The word *rukh* means both «cheek» and «castle» («Rook»); *at* the «steed» is the «Knight»; thus King, Queen, Castle, Knight, and Pawn are all mentioned.

194. The streams, turbid with heavy rains, are said to offer gold (their yellow water) to the trees that grow upon their banks, as though they were wishing to bribe these.

195. A pretty girl is often styled a *Torment*, a *Torment of the Soul*, or a *Torment of the World*.

196. According to Von Hammer, this Elegy is the most beautiful poem in the whole range of Ottoman literature. The first strophe is addressed to the reader.

197. The Persians throw aside the lees after drinking a cup of wine.

198. A pebble thrown into a beaker is the signal for a party to break up. See Note 215.

199. *Rakhush*, «Lightning» (the word translated here by «charger»), was the name of Rustem's famous steed. Rustem is the national hero of Persia, the Hercules or 'Antar of Iran; a great portion of the *Shah-Nama* is taken up with his wondrous adventures and glorious victories over his country's enemies, both human and demon.

200. Dara is Darius, the last monarch of the Keyani dynasty.

201. Alluding to the bent, or curved, appearance of the vault of heaven.

202. A beautiful example of the *Husn-i Ta'lil* (Note 46); the tears that fill the eyes when one attempts to look upon the sun are here ascribed to sorrow for the loss of the Sultan, whose glorious visage the splendor of that luminary recalls to mind.

203. The *huma* is a fabulous bird often mentioned in Eastern poetry. It is of the happiest augury; every head that it overshadows will one day wear a crown. Another of its good traits is that it lives entirely upon bones, never hurting any living creature.

204. Their rills.

205. The petal of a rose is in shape somewhat like the human ear.

206. The strophes, consisting of seven rhyming couplets each. The meaning of the second last of these in this stanza is: «Should our eyes shed so many tears that the whole earth was turned by them

into an ocean, still even in so vast a sea there would be no chance of the production of a pearl that could vie with thee.»

207. It will be remembered that Sultan Suleyman I. died in his camp before Szigeth in Hungary.

208. The Sun.

209. *Tears* are sometimes compared to *babes*, being sprung from man; perhaps from *merdumek*, «the manikin» of the eye (Note 155). Here those babes are to die and be buried; *i.e.*, the unsympathizing man is to have cause to saturate the ground with his bitter tears.

210. *Gazi ve Shehid*, «Muslim conqueror and martyr;» both are alike pleasing to God; whoever dies in battle, or in the field, against the infidels is crowned with martyrdom; while the conqueror will be rewarded for his labors in the Next World. Prince Cantemir says: «The Turks are persuaded that he (Suleyman) was a great favorite of heaven, because he not only lost his life at the siege of Szigeth, and so became *Shehid* (martyr), but was also *Gazi*, two cities being taken under the command of his relics, and annexed to the Ottoman Empire.»

211. This strophe is in honor of Sultan Selim II., Suleyman's son and successor. The third line of this verse is incorrect, it ought to be:—

The old Vezir hath passed away from th'Egypt of the world;

the allusion is to Zuleykha's first husband (95), the Grand Vezir of Egypt (*'Aziz-i Misr*): Suleyman is of course meant, Selim being Joseph. In the next couplet the dawning represents Suleyman and the Sun, Selim; and so on throughout the stanza.

212. Behram (Varanes V.), fourteenth monarch of the Sasani dynasty of Persia, is chiefly remarkable for his love of the chase. He was particularly fond of hunting the *gur*, or wild-ass, on which account he is often called Behram-i Gur, «Behram of the Wild-Ass.» This passion eventually cost him his life, for while pursuing one of these creatures, his horse plunged with him into a deep morass, and he was seen no more. *Gur* means «tomb,» in Persian, as well as «wild-ass,» thus giving an opportunity for an excellent equivoque, of which the poets are not slow to avail themselves; thus Baqi says here: «This chase (life) hath at length caused the Behram of the age (Sultan Suleyman) to reach the *gur* (the tomb and the wild-ass).»

Erdeshir is the Persian name that is corrupted into Artaxerxes and Ahasuerus. The Ahasuerus of the Book of Esther was not, however, a Sasani, but a Keyani monarch: perhaps Erdeshir-i Diraz-Dest (Artaxerxes Longimanus), sixth sovereign of that race; but this is by no means certain. Behram here represents Suleyman; Erdeshir, Selim.

213. The Peacock plays a conspicuous part in the story of Eden and Adam and Eve; before the Fall he was the most beautiful bird

in Paradise, his plumage shone like pearl and emerald, and his voice was so melodious that he was appointed to sing the praises of God daily in the streets of heaven.

214. *Nev-Ruz*, «the New Day,» the first day of the new year with the ancient Persians, is the «New Year's Day» of the Muslim poets. It is the day when the Sun enters Aries.

215. Death, as succeeding life, is sometimes compared to the end of a banquet, when the guests are gone and the lights put out.

216. According to Brown's «Dervishes,» the Qalenderi Order of Dervishes was founded by Yusuf-i Endelusi (Yusuf of Andalusia, in Spain), a contemporary of Haji Bektash. They are under the obligation of perpetually traveling about, and are compelled to live wholly upon alms. A wandering dervish of any order is, by extension, called a Qalender. The members of the real Qalenderi Order shave their beards and eyebrows.

217. Iflatun (Plato) is a type of wisdom.

218. Or: «Flood the world with thy splendor, and still remain without ostentation.» When the Sun sinks it seems to rub its face in the dust.

219. This poem with the following, its reply, forms, perhaps, the only instance of a war-correspondence conducted in *gazels*. The Grand Vezir Hafiz Pasha, having failed to recover Bagdad from the Persians, sent this *gazel*, begging for reinforcements, to his master, Murad IV., at Stamboul.

220. Here again we have the equivoques on *rukh*, meaning at once the «Rook» at Chess, and the «Cheek,» thus *rukh-be-rukh* is both «Rook to Rook» and «Face to Face»; and on *at* for the «Knight» and the «Horse» (193). The allusions to Chess in these lines, as well as those near the beginning of the Padishah's rejoinder, remind us of the famous letter of Nicepherus to Harunu-'r-Reshid, which called forth from that Khalifa his yet more famous reply. The *Queen* presents a difficulty in these Turkish poems: to make an Oriental talk of a queen, not only as taking part in a battle (for the chess-board represents a battle-field, but as being the strongest combatant, is absurd. The piece which we in the West misname the «Queen» is in the East called *Ferz* or *Ferzin*, a Persian word meaning «counselor» or «minister»—a much more appropriate title, in fact the correct one, for Chess is an Oriental game. Some derive our Queen from the Eastern *Ferz*, through the following corruptions and translations: Chess, it is contended, was introduced by the Arabs into Spain and France; the French, on learning the game, adopted some of the Oriental terms and translated others; of the former was the *Ferz*, written in old French books *Fierce;* this in time became *Vierge*, thence *Dame*, *Queen*. Till the fifteenth century this piece was, both in Asia and Europe, one of the weakest on the board, being

allowed to move diagonally only, and but one square at a time. It is clear, however, that long before these two poems were written, the *Ferz* had attained, if not the entire power it now possesses, at least a greatly extended range, for Selim I. (who died in 1520) speaks of it as though it were a very strong piece.

221. The Rafizis are the Shi'is, the adherents of the heretical sect of Islam that holds in Persia.

222. Ebu-Hanifa, founder of that one of the four great sects of orthodox Islam to which the Turks belong, lies buried in Bagdad.

223. A *Lugaz*, as stated in the Introduction (Sec. II), is an «enigma,» in which the essence of a thing (not the letters of its name, as is the case in a *Mu'amma*) forms the subject of the riddle. Enderuni Khazineli Jihadi Beg, one of Sultan Murad's courtiers, gave the following solution to this puzzle:—

> My King, a lamp's the castle; the oil therein, the main;
> The wick is yonder fish too that there its home hath ta'en;
> The flame's the shining jewel it holdeth in its mouth,
> That burns the fish as long as it therein doth remain.
> Thou promisedst, O Monarch, the solver to reward:
> A fief Jihadi seeketh and sergeantship to gain.

224. These verses of 'Azizi, which posses no beauty, are inserted merely to serve as an example of that style of poem known as *shehr-engiz*, «city-disturbing.» As mentioned in the Second Section of the Introduction, the subject of these compositions is the description of certain persons who, through their beauty, are supposed to disturb the town. The ladies in whose honor these verses were written were, no doubt, the Phrynes and Laises of seventeenth-century Stamboul. Some, at least, of the names appear to be sobriquets. The only literary merit which the lines possess consists in equivoques on the names of the courtezans described; these I have indicated by translating the names and printing in italics the supposed *bon-mots*. The verses here translated are selected from a number cited in the fifth volume of the *Mines de l'Orient*.

225. *Merjan Du'asi*, «Coral Prayer»; I do not know what this is; I never saw the expression anywhere else, nor is it given in the dictionaries. Von Hammer says in a note: «*Ein berühmtes Gebeth von Rubinengräber*,» and that is all I have been able to learn.

226. Literally: *qatad*, «the tragacanth» or «goatsthorn.»

227. This poem is called a *Munajat*, a «Prayer»; a number of such are usually found in a *Diwan* after the verses in praise of God and the Prophet.

228. Manuscript copies of the *Shah-Nama* are usually decorated with miniatures, representing the progress of the history.

229. «Lights Twain» are the Sun and Moon: the world is like a mirror, where the influences of the planets are reflected.

230. «We have indeed created man in the best of symmetry.» (Qur'*a*n xcv., 4.)

231. Literally: «Founded on the product of vileness is Thy Glory:» sin is vile; man is vile; Thou forgivest; thence Thy Glory.

232. Hel*a*g*u*, the grandson of Jeng*i*z Kh*a*n, leveled the beautiful city of Bagd*a*d with the ground, and ruthlessly massacred its inhabitants.

233. The *fes* is the red cap of the Turks; it is commonly, but erroneously, written and pronounced *fez* in Europe: the *s* is sharp like *ss* in our word «fosse.»

234. That is, the Bridge of S*i*r*a*t, «narrower than a hair, sharper than a razor,» that leads to Paradise, spanning the Abyss of Hell. Across this, they say, must all pass to the Abode of Bliss.

235. Hayder, «the Lion,» is a surname of 'Al*i*, the Prophet's son-in-law; Duldul was the name of his celebrated mule.

236. Referring to the rapid, vibrating motion peculiar to Eastern dancing.

237. A beautiful girl is sometimes styled «an Idol.»

238. The needle formerly used in Turkey and other Eastern countries for blinding state prisoners is here referred to. The meaning of this distich is: «My verses are so obscure and involved that to the uneducated they are enemies to clear perception (*i. e.*, they are incomprehensible), just as the blinding-needle is the enemy to clear sight, as know the blinded.»

239. Referring to the shape of the head-dress, modeled after the tiara of the ancient Kings of Persia, introduced by Sel*i*m I., and worn, with certain modifications, by all his successors till changed by Muhammed IV. This head-dress, which was worn by the Sultan alone, if turned upside down, would somewhat resemble in shape the alms-bowl carried by beggars in Turkey. The form of the royal tiara may be seen in the portraits of Sel*i*m I., Suleym*a*n I., and Mur*a*d IV.

240. Her hair-slim waist is so slight that it is said by hyperbole to exist not; if it exists not, of course it cannot be embraced; thus the truthfulness of the rival's boast is itself as slender as a hair.

241. Nimrod, by his cruel persecution of Abraham, and arrogant insolence in building the Tower of Babel, to wage war with God, drew upon himself the Divine wrath. To punish his pride the Lord chose the meanest of His creatures, the gnat, as the instrument of His vengeance. A vast army of these insects was sent against the tyrant's men, whom they compelled to flee, for they consumed their flesh, and picked their eyes out of their heads. Nimrod himself fled to a thick-walled tower, but a gnat entered with him and worked its way through

his nostril into his brain, which it commenced to devour. The pain it caused was so great that Nimrod could find no relief save by dashing his head against the wall, or getting some one to strike his forehead with a hammer. But the gnat grew continually larger till, on the fortieth day after its entrance, Nimrod's head burst open, and the insect, which had attained the size of a pigeon, flew out.

242. Sami here compares the eight *beyts*, or distichs, of his *gazel*, blooming with flowers of rhetoric, to the Eight Mansions of Paradise. (Note 28.)

243. What we call to «smoke» tobacco is expressed in Turkish, as it was formerly in England, by to «drink» tobacco. The *nargila*, or bowl of the water-pipe (commonly called *hookah* in English) represents the beaker; the *lula*, or little red clay bowl, of the long *chibuq* is called a *sumbul*, or hyacinth; this must refer to the curling smoke-wreaths ascending from the *lula*.

244. Edirna is the Turkish name of Adrianople; apparently the lady dwelt in Istambol (Constantinople), for the meaning of these lines is: «The inhabitants of Adrianople, when turning to the Ka'ba at Mekka (in worship, bow toward Constantinople, which, like the Sacred City, lies to the south.»

245. In Persia wine was formerly chiefly sold by Magians; hence the word Magian is used in poetry to signify a vintner or tavern-keeper; but mystically, a learned and holy teacher.

246. *Daru-'s-Selam*, «The home of Peace,» is the sobriquet of Bagdad and Damascus; here the latter is meant, *Sham* being «Syria;» *Sham* means a «mole» in Arabic, which gives an untranslatable equivoque in the line. *Der-i Sa'adet*, «The Gate of Felicity,» is the style of Constantinople.

247. The original of this *Gazel*, written most ingeniously in the shape of a sort of wheel, forms the Frontispiece of the present volume. It appeared in the «Journal» of the Royal Asiatic Society (vol. xviii., 1861), accompanied by a prose translation, and an interesting account of the poet and his family, from the pen of Mr. Redhouse. It is to this article that I am indebted for the particulars in my notice of the author.

248. The reed of which the flute is made has to be pierced before it gives forth sound.

249. «As the sun draws up the dew-drops so doth thy bright face draw forth my tears.»

250. Queen Humay was a Persian sovereign of the Keyani dynasty; her reign is detailed in the *Shah-Nama*.

251. «If the caviller questioned the beauty of thy face like the sun, the sight of thy lover hovering like a mote in its beams ought to convince him.»

252. *Husn u 'Ishq*, «Beauty and Love,» is an allegorical romance of the nature of Fazlî's *Gul u Bulbul*. Love, the hero, becomes enamored of Beauty, the heroine; the elders of the tribe, however, demand as her dowry the Philosopher's Stone, which can only be found in the City called Heart. The road thither is known to abound with fearful perils, and to be haunted by *guls* and demons. Love, nothing daunted, sets forth accompanied by a friend, Zeal; and their adventures form the subject of the greater part of the poem. They pass through a dreary wilderness, where they encounter all manner of evil spirits, then through a waste of snow, where utter darkness reigns, then across a sea of fire, and so on through many terrors till Love at length reaches the City of the Heart, where he finds Beauty awaiting him. The first extract is the lullaby which Love's nurse sings over his cradle; the second, a song called forth by the recollection of past happiness, that the hero sings on reaching a beautiful country after crossirg the sea of fire.

253. It is common in Eastern gardens to plant cypresses near the edge of a stream.

254. The headings of chapters, etc., in Oriental MSS. are usually written in red ink; so a page shows the colors black and red on white paper.

255. *Rengin*, «colored,» is the Easten equivalent to our «flowery,» applied to poetry.

256. In the *Zenan-Nama*, «Book of Women,» Fazil Beg passes in review the women of the principal nations of Asia, Europe, and North Africa, praising what he conceives to be their good qualities both of mind and body, and criticising what he fancies to be their defects. The author displays considerable ingenuity, not only in the equivoques which abound in his work, but in his satirical allusions to the peculiarities of the different races; he, however, occasionally commits himself to remarks that would be offensive to European taste.

257. This is in feeble imitation of an equivoque in the original; the black heart of the tulip is likened to a burn.

258. *Pak-damen*, «pure of skirt,» is a favorite expression for «virtuous.»

259. *Rum*, as already said (64), this word is «Roman,» not «Greek;» I retain the word «Greek» in the translation, not because it is correct, but because it is the term in common use in Europe. Concerning the mongrel race, dignified in the West with the name of «Greek,» but called *Rum*, *Rumi*, or *Urum* in the Levant and throughout Asia and North Africa, Mr. Redhouse says: «Their local name, now, as ever since the Christian era, is *Rum*, ‹Roman,› not ‹Greek.› This remark applies to all the so-called ‹Greek› population of Turkey, in Europe as in Asia. From the time of the Roman conquest

they, natives and intruders, all learned to call themselves Romans. There is really very little, if any, properly Greek-descended population in Turkey, or out of it. The race, never numerous, was killed out or dispersed and lost long ago, though a remnant of the old Greek language survives locally as a colloquial patois round the coasts and here and there in the interior. This has latterly been dressed up anew to serve as a written tongue in commerce and literature. The common name of *Rum*, the use of the Roman-Frankish Greek patois, and the liturgy of the Eastern Church, are the links that unite a very heterogeneous lower Roman mass of three or four millions, when all told, in the Hellenic Kingdom, in Turkey, and scattered elsewhere, which Europe has been led to call ‹ Greeks ! › »* In another place writes the same distinguished scholar: « After the conversion of Constantine to Christianity, and the transference of the seat of Empire to New Rome, Constantinople, the Greek language, already bastardized by the conflux of a hundred different races into the capital and provinces, acquired a new importance as the language of the Eastern Church. But as massacres were constant and fresh hordes from all quarters were frequently pouring in, the language of the church books soon became unintelligible to the masses, who all styled themselves Romans, and the result was the modern jargon called by those mixed natives themselves the Roman language, the *Romaic*, but which has been fondly styled ‹ Greek, › by the rest of Europe.»†

260. This is simply an address to the friend at whose request Fazil says he wrote the book; it is couched in these terms because he is about to describe Christians.

261. They are of easy virtue.

262. This also is in imitation of an equivoque in the original.

263. *Qush dili*, « bird language,» is the Turkish term for the imitative language of children. All this passage refers to the imperfect way in which the « Greeks » speak Turkish.

264. For: The wine, O noble lord, wilt thou not sip? in imitation of the original, which has *Hasretin bade isersin, selebi?* for *Hazretin, bade ichersin, chelebi?* They cannot pronounce some of the Turkish letters. The three following lines are in correct Turkish.

265. Easterns drink to the *love*, not the *health*, of another.

266. She walks so lightly.

267. *Kokona* is the Romaic for a « lady; » *qoqu ne* (Turkish), « what a perfume ! » occurs in the next line, thus giving an untranslatable equivoque.

* « On the Significations of the Term ‹ *The Turks* › (reprinted from the Transactions of the Royal Society of Literature, Vol. xi., Part iii., New Series), page 9.

† « A Theory of the Chief Human Races » (reprinted from the Transactions of the Royal Society of Literature, Vol. xii., Part ii., 1880), page 14.

268. A *peri* is a fairy.

269. 'Imran is the name given in the Qur'an to the father of the Virgin Mary.

270. Alluding to the eggs dyed red with logwood, and eaten hard-boiled by the Eastern Christians at Easter.

271. «Genus» and «genius» are in imitation of an equivoque in the original: *jinsin*, «thy genus,» and *jinn sin* «thou art a jinn,» genie, genius.

272. The last strophe of this poem in honor of Qapudan (Admiral) Huseyn Pasha, one of the Ottoman officers who served against Napoleon in Egypt, is a chronogram; but as it simply consists of a series of quite untranslatable verbal quibbles, I have not attempted to reproduce it.

273. Nirem, or Neriman, and Sam are two old Persian heroes who performed many marvelous exploits in the days of the Pishdadi Kings; the latter was grandfather of the celebrated Rustem. Their adventures are told in the *Shah-Nama*.

274. The *'Arsh* is the highest heaven (84). The line means: «Hang up thy sword in the sky as a constellation.»

275. *Ummu-'l-Bilad* or *Umm-i Dunya*, «Mother of Cities,» or «Mother of the World,» a title of Cairo.

276. Nef'*i*, the most famous poet of the time of Sultan Murad IV., one of whose *gazels* is translated on page 134. He wrote a *qasida* the opening couplet of which is used by Wasif as the refrain for this poem.

277. Jem is a shorter form of Jemshid (63).

278. An «Egyptian horse» was an Arab blood-horse, such as was then esteemed and used by the chivalrous Memluks of Egypt, for war purposes and tournaments. They are now called *'Areb*, *Nejdi*, or *'Anczi*.

279. A *sharqi*, as stated in the Introduction, is a song for singing.

280. The «Scio Rose» is a choice variety of rose. Wasif would seem to have had a favorite *odaliq* who came from that island, in whose honor this and several others of his verses were written; as he frequently speaks of his «Scio Rose.»

281. «Say, 'O my servants! who have wronged their own souls!' do not despair of the mercy of God; verily God forgiveth sins, all of them; verily He is forgiving, merciful.» (Qur'an, xxxix., 54.) I doubt if this poem can be correctly called a *gazel;* it is in form similar to a strophe of a *Terji'-Bend*.

282. The *Mihnet Keshan* is a long poem of about 7,000 couplets. The name may be read «The Sufferer,» «The Sufferers,» or «The Suffering

of (at) Keshan.» The town of Keshan was the scene of the author's banishment.

283. The seed, or grain of the heart, the heart's core — said to be the principle of life, or the sign of original sin.

284. *Ban* is a Sclavonic title meaning «governor» or «ruler.» The wardens of the eastern marches of Hungary were thus styled. Many Sclavonic, Hungarian, Romaic, and Frankish words have been adopted into the Ottoman language.

285. This *Qit'a* is a *Tarikh* «Chronogram» on the death of 'Andel*i*b Kh*a*nim, «Lady Nightingale,» an adopted sister of Sultan Mahmud II. In the original the *menqut* or «dotted» letters, occurring in the last line, give on addition the date 1252 (1836), the year of the lady's death. I have preserved the conceit by using Roman letters which have a numerical value, such as C, D, I, etc., to make up the same amount — 1252.

286. «O thou comforted soul! return unto thy Lord, well pleased and well pleased with!» (Qur'*a*n, lxxxix, 28.)

287. For a description of the variety of composition styled *Takhmis*, see Introduction, Sec. II. Baq*i*'s *gazel* is here printed in italics.

288. For this war-song, which was composed on the occasion of the last Russian attack upon Turkey, I am indebted to Mr. H. A. Homes, of New York, the translator of Gaz*a*l*i*'s *Kimiya-yi Sa'adet*.

289. The banner of the Janissaries displayed the *Zu-'l-Fiqar*, the double-pointed sword of the Khal*i*fa 'Al*i*.

290. *Teyatro-Khana*, perhaps the first mention of a «theatre» in Oriental poetry.

291. Key means any King of the Keyan*i* Dynasty.

THE LOVE-SONG

OF

KING SULEIMAN

INTRODUCTION

THIS most beautiful of Oriental love-songs is typical of Arabic and Ottoman lyric poetry. As explained in the Introduction to this volume, symbolism is made use of for various ends, especially that of the garden and landscape.

The idyllic charm of this Hebrew version of the dramatic poem has been considerably dimmed by forced interpretations. As it stands it may be accepted as a setting of the old yet ever fresh story of the universal heart, common in every age the world over.

By some scholars the simple Shulamite maiden is supposed to have refused her royal suitor on account of his oppressive pomp and state. Others hold that the King paid court to her anew in the guise of a shepherd youth, and having won her favor, revealed his rank and claimed her as his own.

The matter is of no great importance when the theme is so charming, and the poetry of such exquisite Oriental feeling. Among the several renderings of the « Song," conjectural at best, we present the one which seems most satisfactory, making such occasional modifications in arrangement and expression as simplify the dialogue and sustain the poetical level.

THE LOVE-SONG OF KING SULEIMAN

The Shulamite Maiden Recounts Her Lover's Wooing

The voice of my beloved!
Behold, he cometh leaping upon the mountains,
Skipping upon the hills.

My beloved is like a roe or a young hart:
Behold, he standeth behind our wall,
He looketh forth at the windows,
He showeth himself through the lattice.

My beloved spake, and said unto me:
Rise up, my love!
Rise up, my fair one!
And come away;
For, lo, the winter is past,
The rain is over and gone.

The flowers appear on the earth,
The time of the singing of birds is come,
The voice of the turtle-dove is heard in our land;
The fig tree putteth forth her green figs,
The vines with the tender grape give a goodly smell;
Arise, my love, my fair one,
And come away!

O my dove!
Who art in the clefts of the rock,
In the secret places of the stairs,
Let me see thy countenance,
Let me hear thy voice,
For sweet is thy voice
And comely thy countenance!

(She gives voice to her delight in a spontaneous song)

My beloved is mine,
And I am his!
He feedeth his flock among the lilies.
Until the day break,
And the shadows flee away,
Turn, my beloved,
And be thou like a roe
Or a young hart upon the mountain.

The King Visits Her in State

Who is this that cometh out of the wilderness
  Like pillars of smoke,
Perfumed with myrrh and frankincense,
With all powders of the merchant?
Behold his bed, which is Solomon's;
Threescore valiant men are about it,
  The valiant of Israel.
They all hold swords, being expert in war;
Every man hath his sword upon his thigh
  Because of fear in the night.
King Solomon made himself a chariot
  Of the wood of Lebanon.
He made the pillars thereof of silver,
  The bottom thereof of gold,
The covering of it of purple,
The midst thereof being paved with love,
For the daughters of Jerusalem.
Go forth, O ye daughters of Zion,
Behold king Solomon with the crown
Wherewith his mother crowned him
In the day of his espousals,
And in the day of the gladness of his heart.

She Tells Him Her Dream

By night on my bed I sought him
Whom my soul loveth;
I sought him, but I found him not,
I will rise now, and go about the city in the streets
And in the broad ways I will seek him
Whom my soul loveth;
I sought him, but I found him not.
The watchmen that go about the city found me;
To whom I said:
Saw ye him whom my soul loveth?
It was but a little that I passed from them,
But I found him whom my soul loveth;
I held him, and would not let him go,
Until I had brought him into my mother's house,
And into the chamber of her that conceived me.

And I said:
I charge you, O ye daughters of Jerusalem,
By the roes, and by the hinds of the field,
That ye stir not up, nor awake my love,
Till he please.

The King's Love-Making

Behold, thou art fair, my love;
Behold, thou art fair;
Thou hast doves' eyes within thy locks;
Thy hair is as a flock of goats, that appear from Mount Gilead.
Thy teeth are like a flock of sheep smoothly shorn,
Which came up from the washing;
Whereof every one bear twins,
And none is barren among them.

Thy lips are like a thread of scarlet.
Thy speech is comely;
Thy temples are like a piece of a pomegranate within thy locks.
Thy neck is like the tower of David
Builded for an armory,
Whereon there hang a thousand bucklers,
All shields of mighty men.

Thy two breasts are like two young roes that are twins,
Which feed among the lilies,
Until the day break,
And the shadows flee away,
I will get me to the mountain of myrrh,
And to the hill of frankincense.
Thou art all fair, my love;
There is no spot in thee.
Come with me from Lebanon,
My spouse, with me from Lebanon;
Look from the top of Amana,
From the top of Shenir and Hermon,
From the lions' dens,
From the mountains of the leopards.

Thou hast ravished my heart,
My sister, my spouse;
Thou hast ravished my heart
With one of thine eyes,
With one chain of thy neck.
How fair is thy love,
My sister, my spouse!
How much better is thy love than wine!
And the smell of thine ointments than all spices!
Thy lips, O my spouse, drop as the honeycomb;
Honey and milk are under thy tongue;
The smell of thy garments is like the smell of Lebanon.
A garden inclosed
Is my sister, my spouse;
A spring shut up,
A fountain sealed.

Thy plants are an orchard of pomegranates, with pleasant
fruits;
Camphire, with spikenard.
Spikenard and saffron;
Calamus and cinnamon,
With all trees of frankincense;
Myrrh and Aloes, with all the chief spices:
A fountain of gardens,
A well of living waters,
And streams from Lebanon.

(She exclaims)

Awake, O north wind!
Come, O thou wind from the south!
Blow upon my garden,
That the spices thereof may flow out.
Let my beloved come into his garden,
And eat his pleasant fruits.

(The King continues)

I am come into my garden,
My sister, my spouse;
I have gathered my myrrh with my spice;
I have eaten my honeycomb with my honey;
I have drunk my wine with my milk;
Eat, O friends,
Drink, yea drink abundantly, O beloved!

The Shulamite Maiden Tells Her Companions of Her Love

I Sleep, but my heart waketh:
It is the voice of my beloved that knocketh, saying,
Open to me, my sister,
My love, my dove, my undefiled,—
For my head is filled with dew,
And my locks with the drops of the night.
I have put off my coat; how shall I put it on?
I have washed my feet; how shall I defile them?

My beloved put in his hand by the hole of the door,
And my bowels were moved for him.
I rose up to open to my beloved;
And my hands dropped with myrrh,
My fingers with sweet smelling myrrh,
Upon the handles of the lock.

I opened to my beloved;
But my beloved had withdrawn himself,
And was gone:
My soul failed when he spake;
I sought him, but I could not find him;
I called him, but he gave me no answer.
The watchmen that went about the city found me,
They smote me, they wounded me;
The keepers of the walls took away my veil from me.
I charge you, O daughters of Jerusalem,
If ye find my beloved,
That ye tell him, that I am sick of love.

(They ask her)

What is thy beloved more than another beloved,
O thou fairest among women?
What is thy beloved more than another beloved,
That thou dost so charge us?

(She replies)

My beloved is white and ruddy,
The chiefest among ten thousand.
His head is as the most fine gold;
His locks are bushy, and black as a raven;
His eyes are as the eyes of doves by the rivers of waters,
Washed with milk, and fitly set:
His cheeks are as a bed of spices,
As sweet flowers:
His lips like lilies,
Dropping sweet smelling myrrh:

His hands are as gold rings set with the beryl;
His belly is as bright ivory overlaid with sapphires;
  His legs are as pillars of marble,
  Set upon sockets of fine gold;
  His countenance is as Lebanon,
  Excellent as the cedars.
  His mouth is most sweet:
  Yea, he is altogether lovely.
    This is my beloved,
    This is my friend,
  O daughters of Jerusalem.

(They ask)

Whither is thy beloved gone,
O thou fairest among women?
Whither is thy beloved turned aside?
That we may seek him with thee.

(She replies)

My beloved is gone down into his garden,
  To the beds of spices,
To feed in the gardens, and to gather lilies.
  I am my beloved's,
  And my beloved is mine;
  He feedeth among the lilies.

The King Pictures His Beloved

    Thou art beautiful,
    O my love, as Tirzah,
Comely as Jerusalem,
Terrible as an army with banners.
Turn away thine eyes from me,
For they have overcome me:

Thy hair is as a flock of goats that appear from Gilead.
Thy teeth are as a flock of sheep
Which go up from the washing,
Whereof every one beareth twins,
And there is not one barren among them.

As a piece of a pomegranate are thy temples within thy
locks.
There are threescore queens,
And fourscore concubines,
And virgins without number.

My dove, my undefiled, is but one;
She is the only one of her mother,
She is the choice one of her that bare her.
The daughters saw her, and blessed her;
Yea, the queens and the concubines,
And they praised her.

Who is she that looketh forth as the morning,
Fair as the moon, clear as the sun,
Terrible as an army with banners?

I went down into the garden of nuts
To see the fruits of the valley,
To see whether the vine flourished,
And the pomegranates budded.
Or ever I was aware,
My soul made me like the chariots of Ammi-nadib.
Return, return, O Shulamite;
Return, that we may look upon thee.

How beautiful are thy sandaled feet, O prince's daughter!
The joints of thy thighs are like jewels,
The work of the hands of a cunning workman.
Thy navel is like a round goblet,
Which wanteth not liquor:
Thy belly is like an heap of wheat set about with lilies.
Thy two breasts are like two young roes that are twins.
Thy neck is as a tower of ivory;
Thine eyes like the fishpools in Heshbon,
By the gate of Bath-rabbim:

Thy nose is as the tower, of Lebanon which looketh toward
        Damascus.
Thine head upon thee is like Carmel,
And the hair of thine head like purple;
The king is held captive in thy entangling hair!

How fair and how pleasant art thou,
O love, for delights!
This thy stature is like to a palm tree.
Thy breasts to clusters of grapes.

I said, I will go up to the palm tree,
I will take hold of the boughs thereof:
Now also thy breasts shall be as clusters of the vine,
And the smell of thy nose like apples;
And the roof of the mouth like the best wine for my be-
        loved,
That goeth down sweetly,
Causing the lips of those that are asleep to speak.

The Shulamite Yearns for her Lover

I am my beloved's, and his desire is toward me.
O that thou wert as my brother,
That sucked the breasts of my mother!
When I should find thee without,
        I would kiss thee;
        Yea, I should not be despised.
        I would lead thee,
And bring thee into my mother's house,
        Who would instruct me:
I would cause thee to drink of spiced wine
Of the juice of my pomegranate.
His left hand should be under my head,
And his right hand should embrace me.
I charge you, O daughters of Jerusalem,
        That ye stir not up,
        Nor awake my love,
        Until he please.

The Betrothal Procession

Who is this that cometh up from the wilderness
Leaning upon her beloved?

HE

Under the apple tree I awakened thee;
There thy mother brought thee forth;
There she that bare thee brought thee forth.

SHE

Set me as a seal upon thy heart,
As a seal upon thine arm;
For Love is strong as death;
Jealousy is cruel as the grave:
The coals thereof are coals of fire,
Which hath a most vehement flame.
Many waters cannot quench Love;
Neither can the floods drown Love:
If a man would give all in his house for Love
It would utterly be contemned.

HE

I have compared thee, O my love,
To a company of horses in Pharaoh's chariots,
Thy cheeks are comely with rows of jewels,
Thy neck with chains of gold.
We will make thee borders of gold
With studs of glittering silver.

The Marriage Day

Solomon had a vineyard at Baal-hamon;
He let out the vineyard unto keepers;
Everyone for the fruit thereof was to bring a thousand pieces of silver.

, SHE

My vineyard, which is mine, is before me;
Thou, O Suleiman, must have a thousand,
And those that keep its fruit, two hundred.
Make haste, my beloved,
Be thou like to a roe or a young hart
Upon the mountain of spices.

HE

Behold, thou art fair, my love!
Thou hast dove's eyes!
Behold, thou art fair, my beloved!
Yea, ever art thou pleasant,
And our bridal bed is green;
The beams of our house are cedar;
Our rafters are of fir.

SHE

While the King sitteth at his table,
My spikenard sendeth forth its fragrance;
A bunch of myrrh is my well-beloved to me;
He shall lie all night betwixt my breasts.

HE

Behold, thou art fair, my love!

SHE

Kiss me with the kisses of thy mouth,
For thy love is better than wine;
Thy name is as scented ointment poured forth,
Therefore do the Virgins love thee.
Draw me, I will run after thee;
The King hath brought me into his chambers.
We will be glad, and rejoice;
We will cherish love more than wine!

HE

Behold, thou art fair, my love!

SHE

I am black, but comely,
O ye daughters of Jerusalem,
As the tents of Kedar,
As the curtains of Suleiman.
Look not down upon me
Because I am black,
Because the sun hath looked upon me
My mother's children were angry with me;
They made me the keeper of the vineyards,
But mine own vineyard have I not kept.

HE

Come, my beloved, let us go forth into the field,
Let us lodge in the villages:
Let us get up early to the vineyards,
Let us see if the vine flourish,
Whether the tender grape appear,
Whether the pomegranates bud forth,
There will I give thee my loves,
The mandrakes give forth fragrance,
At our gates are all the luscious fruits
New and old, which I have kept for thee,
O my beloved!

SHE

I am my beloved's
And his desire is toward me!

HE

Behold, thou art fair, my love!
Behold, thou art fair!

PERSIAN AND ARABIAN POEMS

FIRDAUSI

The great epic of Persia is the Shahnamah, or Book of Kings. It was completed by the poet Abul Kasim Mansur, who took up the work begun by Dakiki. So excellent was Mansur's verse that the Sultan re-named him Firdausi, the Paradisaic. He died A. D. 1020.

The story of Rustem, the national hero, has often been told in verse. The fight with Sohrab is described, and the following verses tell of

THE DEATH OF SOHRAB

AGAIN they met. A glow of youthful grace
Diffused its radiance o'er the stripling's face,
And when he saw, in renovated guise,
The foe so lately mastered; with surprise
He cried—"What! rescued from my power, again
Dost thou confront me on the battle plain?
Or dost thou wearied draw thy vital breath,
And seek, from warrior bold, the shaft of death?
Truth has no charms for thee, old man; even now,
Some further cheat may lurk upon thy brow;
Twice have I shown thee mercy, twice thy age
Hath been thy safety—twice it soothed my rage."
Then mild the Champion: "Youth is proud and vain.
The idle boast a warrior would disdain;
This aged arm perhaps may yet control
The wanton fury that inflames thy soul!"

Again, dismounting, each the other viewed
With sullen glance, and swift the fight renewed;
Clenched front to front, again they tug and bend,
Twist their broad limbs as every nerve would rend;
With rage convulsive Rustem grasps him round;
Bends his strong back, and hurls him to the ground;

Him, who had deemed the triumph all his own;
But dubious of his power to keep him down,
Like lightning quick he gives the deadly thrust,
And spurns the stripling weltering in the dust,
—Thus as his blood that shining steel imbrues,
Thine too shall flow, when Destiny pursues;
For when she marks the victim of her power,
A thousand daggers speed the dying hour.
Writhing with pain Sohrab in murmurs sighed—
And thus to Rustem—"Vaunt not in thy pride;
Upon myself this sorrow have I brought,
Thou but the instrument of fate—which wrought
My downfall; thou art guiltless—guiltless quite;
Oh! had I seen my father in the fight,
My glorious father! Life will soon be o'er,
And his great deeds enchant my soul no more!
Of him my mother gave the mark and sign,
For him I sought, and what an end is mine!
My only wish on earth, my constant sigh,
Him to behold, and with that wish I die.
But hope not to elude his piercing sight,
In vain for thee the deepest glooms of night,
Couldst thou through Ocean's depths for refuge fly,
Or midst the star-beams track the upper sky!
Rustem, with vengeance armed, will reach thee there,
His soul the prey of anguish and despair."

An Icy horror chills the Champion's heart,
His brain whirls round with agonizing smart;
O'er his wan cheek no gushing sorrows flow,
Senseless he sinks beneath the weight of woe;
Relieved at length, with frenzied look, he cries:
"Prove thou art mine, confirm my doubting eyes!
For I am Rustem!" Piercing was the groan,
Which burst from his torn heart—as wild and lone,
He gazed upon him. Dire amazement shook
The dying youth, and mournful thus he spoke:
"If thou art Rustem, cruel as thy part,
No warmth paternal seems to fill thy heart;

Else hadst thou known me when, with strong desire,
I fondly claimed thee for my valiant sire;
Now from my body strip the shining mail,
Untie these bands ere life and feeling fail,
And on my arm the direful proof behold!
Thy sacred bracelet of refulgent gold!
When the loud brazen drums were heard afar,
And, echoing round, proclaimed the pending war,
Whilst parting tears my mother's eyes o'erflowed,
This mystic gift her bursting heart bestowed:
'Take this,' she said, 'thy father's token wear,
And promised glory will reward thy care.'
The hour is come, but frought with bitterest woe,
We meet in blood to wail the fatal blow."

The loosened mail unfolds the bracelet bright,
Uhappy gift! to Rustem's wildered sight;
Prostrate he falls — "By my unnatural hand,
My son, my son is slain — and from the land
Uprooted." — Frantic, in the dust, his hair
He rends in agony and deep despair;
The western sun had disappeared in gloom,
And still the Champion wept his cruel doom;
His wondering legions marked the long delay,
And, seeing Rakush riderless astray,
The rumor quick to Persia's Monarch spread,
And there described the mighty Rustem dead.
Kaus, alarmed, the fatal tidings hears;
His bosom quivers with increasing fears.
"Speed, speed, and see what has befallen to-day
To cause these groans and tears — what fatal fray!
If he be lost, if breathless on the ground,
And this young warrior with the conquest crowned —
Then must I, humbled from my kingdom torn,
Wander like Jemshid through the world forlorn."

The army roused rushed o'er the dusty plain,
Urged by the Monarch to revenge the slain;
Wild consternation saddened every face.
Tus, winged with horror, sought the fatal place,

And there beheld the agonizing sight,—
The murderous end of that unnatural fight,
Sohrab, still breathing, hears the shrill alarms,
His gentle speech suspends the clang of arms:
"My light of life now fluttering sinks in shade,
Let vengeance sleep, and peaceful vows be made.
Beseech the King to spare this Tartar host,
For they are guiltless, all to them is lost;
I led them on, their souls with glory fired,
While mad ambition all my thoughts inspired.
In search of thee, the world before my eyes,
War was my choice, and thou the sacred prize;
With thee, my sire! in virtuous league combined,
No tyrant King should persecute mankind.
That hope is past—the storm has ceased to rave—
My ripening honors wither in the grave;
Then let no vengeance on my comrades fall;
Mine was the guilt, and mine the sorrow, all;
How often have I sought thee—oft my mind
Portrayed thee to my sight—o'erjoyed to find
My mother's token; disappointment came,
When thou deniedst thy lineage and thy name;
Oh! still o'er thee my soul impassioned hung,
Still to my Father fond affection clung!
But fate, remorseless, all my hopes withstood,
And stained thy reeking hands in kindred blood."

His faltering breath protracted speech denied;
Still from his eyelids flowed a gushing tide;
Through Rustem's soul redoubled horror ran,
Heart-rending thoughts subdued the mighty man.
And now, at last, with joy illumined eye,
The Zabul bands their glorious Chief descry;
But when they saw his pale and haggard look,
Knew from what mournful cause he gazed and shook,
With downcast mien they moaned and wept aloud;
While Rustem thus addressed the weeping crowd:
"Here ends the war! let gentle peace succeed,
Enough of death, I—I have done the deed!"

Then to his brother, groaning deep, he said—
"Oh, what a curse upon a parent's head!
But go—and to the Tartar say—No more
Let war between us steep the earth with gore."

Then to his dying son the Champion turned,
Remorse more deep within his bosom burned;
A burst of frenzy fired his throbbing brain;
He clenched his sword, but found his fury vain.
The Persian chiefs the desperate act repressed,
And tried to calm the tumult in his breast;
Thus Gudarz spoke—"Alas! wert thou to give
Thyself a thousand wounds, and cease to live,
What would it be to him thou sorrowest o'er?
It would not save one pang—then weep no more;
For if removed by death, O say, to whom
Has ever been vouchsafed a different doom?
All are the prey of death—the crowned, the low,
And man, through life, the victim still of woe."
Then Rustem: "Fly! and to the king relate
The pressing horrors which involve my fate;
And if the memory of my deeds e'er swayed
His mind, Oh, supplicate his generous aid;
A sovereign balm he has, whose wondrous power
All wounds can heal, and fleeting life restore;
Swift from his tent the potent medicine bring."

But mark the malice of the brainless king!
Hard as the flinty rock, he stern denies
The healthful draught, and gloomy thus replies:
"Can I forgive this foul and slanderous tongue?
The sharp disdain on me contemptuous flung?
Scorned 'midst my army by a shameless boy,
Who sought my throne, my sceptre, to destroy!
Nothing but mischief from his heart can flow;
Is it, then, wise to cherish such a foe?
The fool who warms his enemy to life,
Only prepares for scenes of future strife."

Gudarz, returning, told the hopeless tale —
And thinking Rustem's presence might prevail;
The Champion rose, but ere he reached the throne,
Sohrab had breathed the last expiring groan.

Now keener anguish rack'd the father's mind,
Reft of his son, a murderer of his kind;
His guilty sword distained with filial gore,
He beat his burning breast, his hair he tore:
The breathless corpse before his shuddering view,
A shower of ashes o'er his head he threw;
"In my old age," he cried, "what have I done?
Why have I slain my son, my innocent son?
Why o'er his splendid dawning did I roll
The clouds of death,— and plunge my burthened soul
In agony? My son! from heroes sprung!
Better these hands were from my body wrung;
And solitude and darkness, deep and drear,
Fold me from sight than hated linger here.
But when his mother hears, with horror wild,
That I have shed the life-blood of her child,
So nobly brave, so dearly loved in vain,
How can her heart that rending shock sustain?"

Now on a bier the Persian warriors place
The breathless Youth, and shade his pallid face;
And turning from that fatal field away,
Move toward the Champion's home in long array.
Then Rustem, sick of martial pomp and show,
Himself the spring of all this scene of woe,
Doomed to the flames the pageantry he loved,
Shield, spear, and mace, so oft in battle proved;
Now lost to all, encompassed by despair;
His bright pavilion, crackling, blazed in air.
The sparkling throne the ascending column fed;
In smoking fragments fell the golden bed;
The raging fire red glimmering died away,
And all the Warrior's pride in dust and ashes lay.

KHAKANI

Efsal-ed-din Hakaiki was a lyric poet of great merit and fame, who was honored with the name Khakani by his sovereign the Prince of Shirvan. He died in the year 1186.

THE UNKNOWN BEAUTY

O waving cypress! cheek of rose!
O jasmine-breathing bosom! say,
Tell me each charm that round her glows;
Who are ye that my heart betray;
Tyrant unkind! to whom I bow,
O life destroyer! — who art thou?

I saw thy form of waving grace!
I heard thy soft and gentle sighs;
I gazed on that enchanting face,
And looked in thy narcissus eyes;
Oh! by the hopes thy smiles allow,
Bright soul-inspirer! — who art thou?

Where'er she walks, amidst the shades,
Where perfumed hyacinths unclose,
Danger her ev'ry glance pervades —
Her bow is bent on friends and foes.
Thy rich cheek shames the rose — thy brow
Is like the young moon — who art thou?

The poet-slave has dared to drain
Draughts of thy beauty, till his soul,
Confused and lost in pleasing pain,
Is fled beyond his own control.
What bliss can life accord me now
But once to know thee! — who art thou?

SA'DI

The writer of the *Gulistan* and the *Bustan*, the "Rose Garden" and the "Fruit Garden," was born in 1184, and lived, it is said, over a hundred years. His verse is characterized by proverbial wisdom, and has been a classic for seven centuries.

THE SINNER AND THE MONK

In Jesus' time there lived a youth so black and dissolute,
That Satan from him shrank, appalled in every attribute;
He in a sea of pleasures foul uninterrupted swam,
And gluttonized on dainty vices, sipping many a dram.
Whoever met him in the highway turned as from a pest,
Or, pointing lifted finger at him, cracked some horrid jest.
I have been told that Jesus once was passing by the hut
Where dwelt a monk, who asked him in, and just the door
had shut,
When suddenly that slave of sin appeared across the way.
Far off he paused, fell down, and sobbingly began to pray.
As blinded butterflies will from the light affrighted shrink,
So from those righteous men in awe his timid glances sink;
And like a storm of rain the tears pour gushing from his
eyes.
"Alas, and woe is me, for thirty squandered years," he cries.
"In drunkenness I have expended all my life's pure coin;
And now, to make my fit award, Hell's worst damnations join.
O would that death had snatched me when a sinless child
I lay.
That ne'er had I been forced this dreadful penalty to pay.
Yet if thou let'st no sinner drown who sinks on mercy's
strand,
O then in pity, Lord! reach forth and firmly seize my hand."

The pride-puffed monk, self-righteous, lifts his eyebrows with a sneer,
And haughtily exclaims, «Vile wretch! in vain hast thou come here.
Art thou not plunged in sin, and tossed in lust's devouring sea?
What will thy filthy rags avail with Jesus and with me?
O God! the granting of a single wish is all I pray;
Grant me to stand far distant from this man in the judgment day.»
From Heaven's throne a revelation instantaneous broke,
And God's own thunder words thus through the mouth of Jesus spoke:
«The two whom praying there I see shall equally be heard;
They pray diverse,—I give to each according to his word.
That poor one thirty years has rolled in sin's most slimy deeps,
But now, with stricken heart and streaming tears, for pardon weeps.
Upon the threshold of my grace he throws him in despair,
And, faintly hoping pity, pours his supplications there.
Therefore, forgiven and freed from all the guilt in which he lies
My mercy chooses him a citizen of Paradise.
This monk desires that he may not that sinner stand beside,
Therefore he goes to Hell, and so his wish is gratified.»

The one's heart in his bosom sank, the other's proudly swelled;
In God's pure court all egotistic claims as naught are held.
Whose robe is white, but black as night his heart beneath it lies
Is a live key at which the gate of Hell wide open flies!
Truly not self-conceit and legal works with God prevail;
But humbleness and tenderness weigh down Salvation's scale.

THE MOTH AND THE FLAME

As once, at midnight deep, I lay with sleepless eyes,
These words between the moth and light did me surprise.
The moth kisses the flame, and says, with tender sigh:
"Dear radiance! I rejoice from love for thee to die.
My love, thou diest not, yet anxious groans and strong
Break loudly from thy heart, through all the darkness long!"
The bright flame says, "O moth! whom love to me attracts,
Know that I also burn with love for this sweet wax.
Must I not groan, as more my lover melting sinks,
And from his life my fatal fire still deeper drinks?"
As thus she spake, the hot tears coursed her yellow cheek,
And with each tear crackled a separation shriek.
Then from her mouth these further words of pleading fall:
"Poor moth! boasting of love, say not thou lov'st at all.
Ah! how thou moan'st when the fierce heat one wing has seared;
I stand till my whole form in flame has disappeared."
And so she talked till morning shone the room about;
When lo! a maiden came to put the candle out;
It flickered up,—the wick a smoking relic lay.
'Tis thus, O gentle hearts! that true love dies away.

NIZAMI

PERSIAN romance has its favorite singer in Nizami, who died at a great age in 1203. His exquisite poem, «Laili and Majnun,» is among the greatest of its class.

THE WORLD BEYOND

ALEXANDER the Great desired to reach the sources of the Nile. After a long march he came to a steep mountain, in color resembling «green glass,» from which flows down the river Nile. Of the people sent up thither not one came back. At last a man is despatched, accompanied by his son, with orders that, arrived at the summit, he should write what he had seen, and throw down the billet to his son, who is to wait for him below. The son returns without his father, but with the following message:

He gave to the King the paper, and the King read written thereon:
«From the toilsomeness of the way,
My soul fainted within me from terror,
For I seemed to be treading the road to Hell.
The path was contracted to a hair's-breadth,
And whoever trod it washed his hands of life.
For in this path, which was slender as a hair,
There appeared no means of again coming down.
When I arrived at the rocky mound of the summit,
I was in an utter strait from the straitness of the way.
All that I beheld on the side which I had seen tore my heart to pieces,
And my judgment was annihilated by its perilous aspect.
But on the other side the way was without a blemish,
Delight upon delight, garden upon garden,
Full of fruit, and verdure, and water, and roses;

The whole region resounding with the melody of birds,
The air soft, and the landscape so charming,
That you might say, God had granted its every wish.
On this side all was life and beauty,
On the other side all was disturbance and ruin;
Here was Paradise, there the semblance of Hell —
Who would come to Hell and desert Paradise?
Think of that desert through which we wended,
Look whence we came, and at what we have arrived!
Who would have the heart from this lovely spot
Again to set a foot in that intricate track?
Here I remain, King, and bid thee adieu;
And mayst thou be happy as I am happy!"

THE EYE OF CHARITY

One evening Jesus lingered in the market-place,
Teaching the people parables of truth and grace,
When in the square remote a crowd was seen to rise,
And stop with loathing gestures and abhorring cries.

The Master and his meek disciples went to see
What cause for this commotion and disgust could be,
And found a poor dead dog beside the gutter laid;
Revolting sight! at which each face its hate betrayed.

One held his nose, one shut his eyes, one turned away;
And all among themselves began aloud to say,—
"Detested creature! he pollutes the earth and air!"
"His eyes are blear!" "His ears are foul!" "His ribs are bare!"

"In his torn hide there's not a decent shoe-string left!"
"No doubt the execrable cur was hung for theft!"
Then Jesus spake, and dropped on him this saving wreath,—
"Even pearls are dark before the whiteness of his teeth!"

The pelting crowd grew silent and ashamed, like one
Rebuked by sight of wisdom higher than his own;
And one exclaimed, "No creature so accursed can be,
But some good thing in him a loving eye will see."

RUMI

JELALEDDIN was born at Balkh in 1207, but in childhood was taken to Asia Minor, where he succeeded his father as head of a college in Iconium. Asia Minor was then and is still called by the Mohammedans Rum (or Roum), as having been part of the Roman Empire. Jelaleddin, from his residence there, obtained the surname Rumi, "the Roman." He was converted to mysticism by a wandering Sufi. Rumi is worshiped as a saint. His great masterpiece is the "Mesnavi," a collection of ethical and moral precepts, anecdotes, comments on verses of the Koran, and sayings of the prophets. Rumi died in 1273.

THE MERCHANT AND THE PARROT

THERE was once a merchant, who had a parrot,
A parrot fair to view, confined in a cage;
And when the merchant prepared for a journey,
He resolved to bend his way toward Hindustan.
Every servant and maiden in his generosity
He asked, what present he should bring them home;
And each one named what he severally wished,
And to each one the good master promised his desire.
Then he said to the parrot, "And what gift wishest thou,
That I should bring to thee from Hindustan?"
The parrot replied, "When thou seest the parrots there,
Oh, bid them know of my condition.
Tell them, 'A parrot, who longs for your company,
Through Heaven's decree is confined in my cage.
He sends you his salutation, and demands his right,
And seeks from you help and counsel.'
He says, 'Is it right that I in my longings
Should pine and die in this prison through separation?
Is it right that I should be here fast in this cage,
While you dance at will on the grass and the trees?

Is this the fidelity of friends,
I here in a prison, and you in a grove?
Oh, remember, I pray you, that bower of ours,
And our morning-draughts in the olden time;
Oh, remember all our ancient friendships,
And all the festive days of our intercourse!'»
The merchant received its message,
The salutation which he was to bear to its fellows;
And when he came to the borders of Hindustan,
He beheld a number of parrots in the desert.
He stayed his horse, and he lifted his voice,
And he repeated his message, and deposited his trust;
And one of those parrots suddenly fluttered,
And fell to the ground, and presently died.
Bitterly did the merchant repent his words;
«I have slain,» he cried, «a living creature.
Perchance this parrot and my little bird were close of kin,
Their bodies perchance were two and their souls one.
Why did I this? why gave I the message?
I have consumed a helpless victim by my foolish words!
My tongue is as flint, and my lips as steel;
And the words that burst from them are sparks of fire.
Strike not together in thy folly the flint and steel,
Whether for the sake of kind words or vain boasting;
The world around is as a cotton-field by night;
In the midst of cotton, how shall the spark do no harm?»

The merchant at length completed his traffic,
And he returned right glad to his home once more.
To every servant he brought a present,
To every maiden he gave a token;
And the parrot said: «Where is my present?
Tell all that thou hast said and seen!»
He answered, «I repeated thy complaints
To that company of parrots, thy old companions,
And one of those birds, when it inhaled the breath of thy sorrow,
Broke its heart, and fluttered, and died.»
And when the parrot heard what its fellow had done,
It too fluttered, and fell down, and died.

When the merchant beheld it thus fall,
Up he sprang, and dashed his cap to the ground.
"Oh, alas!" he cried, "my sweet and pleasant parrot,
Companion of my bosom and sharer of my secrets!
Oh, alas! alas! and again alas!
That so bright a moon is hidden under a cloud!"
After this he threw its body out of the cage;
And lo! the little bird flew to a lofty bough.
The merchant stood amazed at what it had done;
Utterly bewildered he pondered its mystery.
It answered, "Yon parrot taught me by its action:
'Escape,' it told me, 'from speech and articulate voice,
Since it was thy voice that brought thee into prison;'
And to prove its own words itself did die."
It then gave the merchant some words of wise counsel,
And at last bade him a long farewell.
"Farewell, my master, thou hast done me a kindness,
Thou hast freed me from the bond of this tyranny.
Farewell, my master, I fly toward home;
Thou shalt one day be free like me!"

HAFIZ

Khwaja Shams-ad-din Muhammad, known as Hafiz, « the man with the memory, » was born and died in the fourteenth century. It is to Hafiz we turn when searching for the sweetest and most typical of Persian odes and lyrics.

BE THINE OWN TRUE FRIEND

Is there ought sweeter than the delights of the garden
 and companionship of the Spring?
 But where is the cup-bearer?
 Say what is the cause of his lingering?
Every pleasant moment that cometh to your hand,
 score up as an invaluable prize!
 Let no one hesitate,
 for who knoweth the conclusion of the matter?
The tie of life is but a hair! Use thine intelligence;
 be thyself thine own comrade in sorrow,
 and what then is the sorrow
 which Fate can deal thee?
The medium of the Fountain of Life
 and the Gardens of Irem —
 what is it but the enjoyment of a running stream
 and a delicious wine?
The temperate men and the intemperate are both of one tribe:
 what choice is there between them,
 that we should surrender
 our souls to dubious reasonings?
What reveal the silent heavens
 of that which is behind the veil?
 O litigant,
 why dispute with the keeper of the Veil?
If to him who is bound up in error or sin
 there is no room for warning or amendment,
 what meaning is there in the words « Canceling,
 and the mercy of the Forgiving One? »
The devotee longs for draughts from the river Kuther,
 and Hafiz from a goblet of wine.
 Between these, the will of the Creator —
 what would that be?

In the hour of dawn the bird of the garden thus spoke
to a freshly blown rose:
"Be less disdainful, for in this garden
hath bloomed many a one like thee."
The rose smiled, and said,
"We have never grieved at hearing the truth;
but no lover would speak so harshly to his beloved!"
To all eternity, the odor of love will never reach
the brain of that man who hath never swept with his brow
the dust from the sill of the wine-house.
Dost thou desire to drink the ruby-tinted wine
from that gold-begemmed goblet,
how many a pearl must thou first pierce
with the point of thine eyelashes!
Yesterday, when in the Rose Garden of Irem
the morning breeze with its gentle breath
began to disturb the hair of the spikenard,
I exclaimed, "O throne of Jemshid,
Where is thy magic world-reflecting mirror?"
And it replied, "Alas! That watchful Fortune should be slumbering!"
The words of love are not those that come to the tongue:
O cup-bearer,
cut short this asking and answering.
The tears of Hafiz have cast patience and wisdom into the sea:
how could it be otherwise?
The burning pangs of love how could he conceal?

A SEASON TO BE MERRY

The Fast is over, the Festival is come,
and hearts are lifted up, and the wine is sparkling in the wine-house,
and wine we must drink!
The turn of the heavy dealer in abstinence is past,
the season of joy is arrived,
and of joyous revelers!

Why should reproach be heaped upon him,
who like me quaffeth wine?
This is neither sin or fault in the jovial lover!
The drinker of wine,
in whom is no false show and no dissimulation
is better than he who is a trader in semblances.
We are neither dissembling revelers
nor the comrades of hypocrites:
He who is the knower of all secrets knoweth this.
We discharge all our Divine obligations
and do evil to no man;
and whatever we are told is not right,
we say not that it is right.
What mattereth it,
that thou and I should quaff a few goblets of wine?
Wine is the blood of the vine;
it is not thy blood!
This is not a fault which throweth all into confusion;
and were it a fault,
where is the man to be found who is free from faults?
Hafiz, leave thou the «How» and the «Wherefore,»
and drink for a moment thy wine:
His wisdom hath withholden from us
what is the force of the words «How» and «Wherefore.»

I LOVE MY LOVE

I have made a compact with the mistress of my soul,
that so long as I have a soul within my body
I will hold as mine own soul the well-wishers of her village.
In the privacy of my breast I see light from that taper of Chighil;
splendor to mine eye and brightness to my heart
from that moon of Khoten.
Since in accordance with my wishes and yearnings
I have gained the privacy of my breast,
why need I care for the slander of evil speakers
in the midst of the crowd?

If a hundred armies of lovely ones should be lying in ambush
to assault my heart,
I have, by the mercy and to the praise of heaven,
an idol which will shatter armies into pieces.
Would to heaven, my rival, that this night
thou wouldest close thine eye for a while,
that I might whisper a hundred words to her silent ruby lips!
No inclination have I for tulip, or white rose,
or the leaf of the narcissus,
so long as by Heaven's grace
I walk proudly in the rose garden of her favor.
O mine ancient wise one,
lay not thy prohibition on the wine-house;
for abandoning the wine-cup,
I should break a pledge to mine own heart.
My beverage is easy of digestion,
and my love is beautiful as a picture;
no one hath a love—such a love as I have!
I have a Cypress in my dwelling,
under the shade of whose tall statue
I can dispense with the cypress of the grove,
and the box-tree of the meadow.
I can boast that the seal of her ruby lip
is potent as was that of Solomon:
in possession of the Great Name,
why should I dread the Evil One!
After long abstinence,
Hafiz is become a notorious reveler;
but why grieve,
so long as there is in the world an Emin-ad-Din Hassan!
Spring is come again,
and the joy-exciting and vow-breaking rose;
In the delight of gazing on the cheek of the rose,
tear up the root of sorrow from thy heart!
The soft east wind is arrived;
the rosebud in its passion
hath burst forth and torn its own garment.

Learn, O my heart, the way of sincerity
from the clear water;
in uprightness seek freedom
from the cypress of the meadow.
The bride of the rosebud,
with her jewels and sweet smile,
hath stolen away with her black eye
my heart and my religion.
The warbling of the enamored nightingale,
and the piping of the bird of the thousand notes.
come to enjoy the meeting with the rose
from her house of mourning [*i. e.*, her pod].
See how the gentle breeze hath entwined with his hand
the ringlets of the rose!
Look how the plaited locks of the hyacinth
bend over the face of the jessamine!
The story of the revolving sphere
seek to learn from the cup, O Hafiz!
as the voice of the minstrel
and the judgment of the wise advise thee!

MY HEART HATH ITS WINGS

The bird of my heart is a sacred bird,
whose nest is the throne of God:
sick of its cage of the body,
it is satiated with the things of the world.
If once the bird of the spirit
wingeth its flight from this pit of mire,
it findeth its resting place once more
only at the door of that palace;
And when the bird of my heart flieth upward,
its place is the sidrah-tree;
for know that our falcon reposeth only
on the pinnacle of the throne.
The shadow of good fortune falleth upon the world,
whenever our bird spreadeth
its pinions and feathers over the earth.
In both worlds its station
is only in the loftiest sphere;

its body is from the quarry,
but its soul is confined to no dwelling.
Only the highest heaven
is the sacred bower of our bird;
its drinking-place
is in the rose arbors of the Garden of Paradise.
O Hafiz, thou perplexed one,
when thou breathest a word about Unity,
inscribe Unity with thy reed
on the page of man and spirit.

LOVE'S LANGUISHMENT

From the garden of union with thee,
(even) the garden of Rizvan (Paradise) gain lustre of joy;
From the torment of separation from thee,
(even) hell's flame hath torment.

In the beauty of thy cheek and stature,
shelter have taken Paradise and the tuba (tree).
For them, it (the shelter) is good;
and a good place of returning (from this world).

All night (even) as my eye (seeth,
so) the stream of Paradise
Seeth in sleep
the image of thy intoxicated eye (of mercy).

In every season,
spring giveth description of thy beauty;
In every book,
Paradise maketh mention of thy grace.

This heart consumed,
and my soul attained not to the heart's desire;
If it has attained to its desire,
it would not have poured forth blood (of grief).

Oh, many the salt-rights of thy lip and mouth,
Which they have against rent livers and roast hearts.

Think not that in thy circle (only)
lovers are intoxicated (with love for thee):
Of the state of zahids distraught (with love)
no news hast thou.

By the circle of thy (ruddy) lip in thy face,
resplendent as the sun,
I knew that the jewel (lustre) of the ruby
was produced by the sun, world-illuminating.

Open the veil.
This modesty how long wilt thou practice?
With this veil,
what hast thou bound save modesty?

The rose beheld thy face,
and fell into the fire (of love),
Perceived thy fragrance,
and through shame, became (soft and fragrant like) rose water.

In love for thy face,
Hafiz is immersed in the sea of calamity.
Behold he dieth!
Come once! Help!

Hafiz! that life should pass in folly, permit not;
Strive; and understand the value of dear life.

LOVE'S ECSTASY

(When) the rose is in the bosom,
wine in the hand,
And the beloved to my desire,—
on such a day, the world's Sultan is my slave.

Say, into this assembly bring ye no candle for to-night.
In our assembly the moon of the Friend's face is full.

In our order (of profligates)
the wine-cup is lawful;
But O Cypress, rose of body!
without thy face (presence), unlawful.

In our assembly (of lovers),
      mix not its (perfume);
For our soul every moment receiveth perfume
      from the fragrance of the tip of thy tress.

My ear is all (intent) on the voice of the reed
      and the melody of the harp (the instrument of the
         Murshid);
My eye is all (intent) on thy ruby lip,
      and on the circulation of the cup
(The manifestations of glories of God in the night season).

Say ye naught of the sweetness of candy and sugar
      (the delights of the world);
For my desire is for thy sweet lip
      (the sweet stream of Divine grace,
      the source of endless delight).

From the time when the treasure of grief
      for thee was dweller in my ruined heart,
The corner of the tavern is ever my abode.

Of shame why speakest thou?
      For from shame is my name (renown);
Of name (renown) why askest thou?
      For from name (renown) is my shame.

Wine-drinker, distraught of head,
      profligate, and glance-player, I am:
In this city, who is that one
      who is not like this?

To the Muhtasib, utter not my crime;
      for he also
Is ever like me
      in desire of the drinkers of wine.

Hafiz! sit not a moment without wine
      and the beloved.
'Tis the season of the rose, and of the jessamine,
      and of the 'Id of (Siyam)!

LOVE'S LIGHT ECLIPSED

Without the beloved's face, the rose — is not pleasant.
Without wine, spring — is not pleasant.

The border of the sward and the air of the garden
Without the (beloved of) tulip cheek — is not pleasant.

With the beloved, sugar of lip, rose of body,
(To be) without kiss and embrace — is not pleasant.

The dancing of the cypress, and the rapture of the rose,
Without the song of the hazar — is not pleasant.

Every picture that reason's hand depicteth,
Save the picture of the (living beauteous) idol —
is not pleasant.

The garden and the rose and wine (all) is pleasant; but
Without the beloved's society, — is not pleasant.

Hafiz! the soul is (but) a despicable coin;
For scattering (on the true beloved) it — is not pleasant.

LOVE — WAS

That friend by whom our house the (happy) dwelling of
the Pari — was,
Head to foot, free from defect, a Pari — was.

Acceptable to the (All) Wise of mine (is) that moon.
For his,
With beauty of manner, the way of one endowed
with vision — was.

(My) heart said, "I hope of her, in this city I will sojourn;"
Helpless, it knew not that its friend a traveler — was.

Out from my grasp the malignant star plucked her:
Yes: what can I do? The calamity of the revolution of the moon it — was.
Not only from my heart's mystery fell the screen;
Since the sky (time) was, screen-rendering its habit —was.

Sweet was the marge of the water, and the rose and the verdure. But
Alas, that moving treasure a wayfarer — was.

Happy were those times which passed with the friend;
All without result and without knowledge the rest — was.

The bulbul (the true lover) slew himself through jealousy of this, that to the rose (the true beloved)
At morning-time (the last breath of life), with the morning breeze (the angel of death), splendor (of heavenly messages) — was.

O heart! establish an excuse. For thou art a beggar; and here,
In the kingdom of beauty, the head of a crowned one—was.

Every treasure of happiness that God gave to Hafiz,
From the auspiciousness of the evening prayer and of the morning supplication — was.

DJAMI

Nuruddin Abdurrahaman, Persia's last poet of the first rank, was born in 1414, and was called Djami from the place of his birth. His works are seven mystical poems and the famous poetical romance of Joseph and the wife of Potiphar, "Yusuf and Zulaikha," from which the following are taken:—

BEAUTY AND LOVE

Before eternity to time had shrunken,
The Friend [God] deep in his glorious self was sunken.
Around his charms a firm-bound girdle hovered:
No one the lonely path to him discovered.
A mirror held he to each wondrous feature,
But shared the vision's bliss with not a creature.
In cradling Naught's abyss alone he rocked him,
No playmate's face or gambols sportive mocked him.
Then rose He up—swift vanished all resistance—
And gave the boundless universe existence.
Now Beauty, sun-clear, from his right side beameth;
Love, moon-light, quickly from his left side gleameth.
When Beauty's flame lights up the cheek's red roses,
Love fans a fire from which no heart reposes.
Between them glows a league which forms no cinder,
But from all Beauty's food creates Love's tinder.
When Beauty 'midst her snaring ringlets lieth,
Then Love the heart within those fair locks tieth.
A nest is Beauty, Love the brooding linnet:
A mine is Beauty, Love the diamond in it.
From God's two sides they came, twin emanation,
To chase and woo each other through creation.
But in each atom's point, both, clasping, enter,
And constitute all being's blissful centre.

ZULAIKHA

There was a king in the West. His name,
Taimus, was spread wide by the drum of fame.
Of royal power and wealth possessed,
No wish unanswered remained in his breast.
His brow gave lustre to glory's crown,
And his foot gave the thrones of the mighty renown.
With Orion from heaven his host to aid,
Conquest was his when he bared his blade.
His child Zulaikha was passing fair,
None in his heart might with her compare;
Of his royal house the most brilliant star,
A gem from the chest where the treasures are.
Praise cannot equal her beauty, no;
But its faint, faint shadow my pen may show.
Like her own bright hair falling loosely down,
I will touch each charm to her feet from her crown.
May the soft reflection of that bright cheek,
Lend light to my spirit and bid me speak,
And that flashing ruby, her mouth, bestow
The power to tell of the things I know.

Her stature was like to a palm-tree grown
In the garden of grace where no sin is known.
Bedewed by the love of her father the king,
She mocked the cypress that rose by the spring.
Sweet with the odor of musk, a snare
For the heart of the wise was the maiden's hair.
Tangled at night, in the morning through
Her long thick tresses a comb she drew,
And cleft the heart of the musk-deer in twain
As for that rare odor he sighed in vain.
A dark shade fell from her loose hair sweet
As jasmine over the rose of her feet.
A broad silver tablet her forehead displayed
For the heaven-set lessons of beauty made.

Her face was the garden of Iram, where
Roses of every hue are fair.
The dusky moles that enhanced the red
Were like Moorish boys playing in each rose-bed.
Of silver that paid no tithe, her chin
Had a well with the Water of Life therein.
If a sage in his thirst came near to drink,
He would feel the spray ere he reached the brink,
But lost were his soul if he nearer drew,
For it was a well and a whirlpool too.
Her neck was of ivory. Thither drawn,
Came with her tribute to beauty the fawn;
And the rose hung her head at the gleam of the skin
Of shoulders fairer than jessamine.
Her breasts were orbs of a light more pure,
Twin bubbles new risen from fount Kafur:
Two young pomegranates grown on one spray,
Where bold hope never a finger might lay.
The touchstone itself was proved false when it tried
Her arms' fine silver thrice purified;
But the pearl-pure amulets fastened there
Were the hearts of the holy absorbed in prayer.
The loveliest gave her their souls for rue,
And round the charm their own heartstrings drew.
Her arms filled her sleeves with silver from them
Whose brows are bound with the diadem.
To labor and care her soft hand lent aid,
And to wounded hearts healing unction laid.
Like reeds were those taper fingers of hers,
To write on each heart love's characters.
Each nail on those fingers so long and slim
Showed a new moon laid on a full moon's brim,
And her small closed hand made the moon confess
That she never might rival its loveliness.
Two columns fashioned of silver upheld
That beauty which never was paralleled,
And to make the tale of her charms complete,
They were matched by the shape of her exquisite feet.
Feet so light and elastic no maid might show,
So perfectly fashioned from heel to toe.

The hem of her mantle alone might gain
A kiss of that foot, while kings sought it in vain;
And no hand but the fold of her robe embraced
The delicate stem of her dainty waist.

Maidens like cypresses straight and tall,
With Peri faces, obeyed her call;
And by day and by night in her service stood
The Houris' loveliest sisterhood.
No burden as yet had her sweet soul borne;
Never her foot had been pierced by a thorn.
No breath of passion her heart might stir,
And to love and be loved was unknown to her.
Like the languid Narcissus she slept at night,
And hailed like an opening bud the light.

YUSUF SOLD BY HIS BRETHREN

The brothers had lingered not far from the well,
And they burned in their hearts to know what befell;
They saw the merchants arrive, and stood
Waiting for news in the neighborhood.
To Yusuf they called with a secret cry,
But a hollow echo came back in reply.
To the caravan with quick steps, intent
On claiming the boy as their slave, they went,
And with toil and labor they made their way
Within the ring where the merchants lay.
"This is our slave," as they touched him, they cried;
"The collar of service his hand has untied.
The bonds of his duty were loosened, and he
From the yoke of his masters had dared to flee.
Though born in our house we will gladly sell
The idle boy who will never do well.
When a slave is negligent, idle, perverse,
Ever growing from bad to worse,
'Tis better to sell him, though small the price,
Than suffer still from his rooted vice.
We will labor no more to improve the wretch,
But sell him at once for the price he may fetch."
He was sold for a trifle to him whose cord
Had brought him up to the light restored.
Malik — so named was the merchant — gave
A few pieces for Yusuf as household slave.
Then the traders arising their march renewed,
And onward to Egypt their way pursued.

Woe unto those who that treasure sold,
And bartered their souls for some paltry gold!
No life, nor the treasures of Egypt, could buy
One word from his lip or one glance from his eye.
Only Jacob his sire and Zulaikha, the true,
The priceless worth of that treasure knew.
But his worth was unknown to those blinded eyes,
And they took a few pence for the blessed prize.

YUSUF'S FLIGHT

Zulaikha had seen Yusuf in a vision and had fallen in love with him. After refusing many princely suitors, she was married to the Grand Vizier of Egypt. Later she purchased in the slave market the beloved youth of her dreams and brought him to her palace. Finally she declared her love.

She told her love, and her sorrow woke
With a pang renewed at each word she spoke.
But Yusuf looked not upon her: in dread
He lowered his eyes and he bent his head.
As he looked on the ground in a whirl of thought
He saw his own form on the carpet wrought,
Where a bed was figured of silk and brocade,
And himself by the side of Zulaikha laid.
From the pictured carpet he looked in quest
Of a spot where his eye might, untroubled, rest.
He looked on the wall, on the door; the pair
Of rose-lipped lovers was painted there.
He lifted his glance to the Lord of the skies:
That pair from the ceiling still met his eyes.
Then the heart of Yusuf would fain relent,
And a tender look on Zulaikha he bent,
While a thrill of hope through her bosom passed
That the blessed sun would shine forth at last.
The hot tears welled from her heart to her eyes,
And she poured out her voice in a storm of sighs. . . .

"Fair daughter," said he, "of the Peri race —
But no Peri can match thee in form or face —
Tempt me no more to a deed of shame,
Nor break the fair glass of a stainless name.
Drag not my skirt through the dust and mire,
Nor fill my veins with unholy fire.
By the Living God, the great soul of all,
Inner and outward, and great and small,

From whose ocean this world like a bubble rose,
And the sun by the flash of His splendor glows;
By the holy line of my fathers, whence
I have learned the fair beauty of innocence;
From whom I inherit my spirit's light,
And through them is the star of my fortune bright;
If thou wilt but leave me this day in peace,
And my troubled soul from this snare release,
Thou shalt see thy servant each wish obey,
And with faith unshaken thy grace repay.
The lips of thy darling to thine shall be pressed,
And the arms that thou lovest shall lull thee to rest.
Haste not too fast to the goal: delay
Is often more blessed than speed on the way,
And the first paltry capture is ever surpassed
By the nobler game that is netted at last."

Zulaikha answered: "Ah, never think
That the thirsty will wait for the morrow to drink.
My spirit has rushed to my lips, and how
Can I wait for the joy that I long for now?
My heart has no power to watch and wait
For the tender bliss that will come so late.
Thy pleading is weak, and no cause I see
Why thou shouldst not this moment be happy with me."

Then Yusuf answered: "Two things I fear —
The judgment of God and the Grand Vizier.
If the master knew of the shameful deed,
With a hundred sorrows my heart would bleed.
Full well thou knowest my furious lord
Would strike me dead with his lifted sword.
And think of the shame that the sin would lay
On my guilty soul at the Judgment day,
When the awful book is unclosed wherein
Recording angels have scored my sin." . . .

One nook of the chamber was dark with the shade
Of a curtain that glittered with gold brocade.
And Yusuf questioned her: "What or who
Is behind the curtain concealed from view?"

« It is he,» she answered, « to whom, while I live,
My faithful service I still must give:
A golden idol with jeweled eyes—
A salver of musk in his bosom lies.
I bend before him each hour of the day,
And my head at his feet in due worship lay.
Before his presence this screen I drew
To be out of the reach of his darkened view.
If I swerve from religion I would not be
Where the angry eyes of my god may see.»
And Yusuf cried with a bitter cry:
« Not a mite of the gold of thy faith have I.
Thine eye is abashed before those that are dead,
And shrinks from the sight of the lifeless in dread.
And God Almighty shall I not fear,
Who liveth and seeth and ever is near? »

He ceased: from the fond dream of rapture he woke;
From the arms of Zulaikha he struggled and broke.
With hasty feet from her side he sped,
And burst open each door on his way as he fled.
Bolt and bar from the stanchions he drew—
All opened before him as onward he flew.
Of his lifted finger a key was made,
Which every lock at a sign obeyed.
But Zulaikha caught him with steps more fast,
Or ever the farthest chamber he passed.
She clutched his skirt as he fled amain,
And the coat from his shoulder was rent in twain.
Reft of his garment, he slipped from her hand
Like a bud from its sheath when the leaves expand.
She rent her robe in her anguish; low
On the earth, like a shadow, she lay in her woe.

THE WIDOW'S LAMENT

A HAPLESS bird was Zulaikha. She pined
In the narrow cage of the world confined.
Befriended by fortune, in pride and power,
When a rose-bed bloomed in her secret bower;
With her lord beside her to shade and screen
The tender plant when her bud was green —
With all dainty things, if she cared but to speak;
When no lamp was so bright as her youthful cheek:
Yusuf e'en then her whole heart possessed —
The sweet name on her lips, the dear hope in her breast.
Now, when from her side her protector was reft,
When nought of her rank and her treasures was left,
The sole friend of her heart, who ne'er changed his place,
Was the sweet remembrance of Yusuf's face.
She thought of him ever; her sad house seemed
Her dear fatherland when of him she dreamed.
No food could she eat, and she closed not her eyes;
She wept tears of blood and she said with sighs: —
"Beloved Yusuf, where, where art thou?
Why false and faithless to pledge and vow?
Oh, that again those sweet hours I might see,
When one happy home held my love and me!
When no fear of parting could mar delight,
And I gazed on his beauty from morn till night.
When stern fate robbed me of this sweet joy,
I sent to the prison that innocent boy.
Unseen by night to his presence I stole,
And the sight of his cheek was as balm to my soul;
And a glance at the walls where my darling lay
Rubbed the rust of grief from my heart by day.
No joy is now left me, no solace like these;
My heart and frame perish of pain and disease.
All I have left is the image which still,
Where'er I may be, this sad bosom must fill.
The soul of this frame is that image, and I
Bereft of its presence, should languish and die."

Then her breast and her heart she would fiercely tear,
And engrave the form of her darling there.
She would strike her soft knee with her hand till the blue
Of the lotus supplanted the jasmine's hue.
«I am worthy the love of my love,» she would cry,
«For my love is the sun and the lotus am I.
As my love is the lord of the east and the west,
The place of the lotus for me is the best.»

AMRIOLKAIS

This Arabian poet flourished before the time of Mohammed.

A PERILOUS TRYST

With many a spotless virgin, whose tent had not yet been frequented, have I held soft dalliance at perfect leisure.

To visit one of them, I passed the guards of her bower, and a hostile tribe, who would have been eager to proclaim my death.

It was the hour when the Pleiads appear in the firmament like the folds of a silken sash variously decked with gems.

I approached: she stood by the curtain; and as if preparing for sleep, had put off all her vesture but her night-dress.

"By Him who created me," she said, and gave me her lovely hand, "I am unable to refuse thee; for I perceive the blindness of thy passion is not to be removed."

Then I rose with her; and as we walked, she drew over our footsteps the train of her pictured robe.

As soon as we had passed the habitations of her tribe, and come to the bosom of a vale, surrounded by hillocks of spiry sand,

I gently drew her toward me by her curled locks, and she softly inclined to my embrace; her waist was gracefully slender, and its swelling was encircled with ornaments of gold.

Delicate was her shape; fair her skin; her body well-proportioned; her bosom was as smooth as a mirror,

Or like the pure egg of an ostrich, of yellowish tint blended with white, and nourished by a wholesome stream not yet disturbed.

She turned aside and displayed her soft cheek; she gave a timid glance with languishing eyes like those of a roe looking tenderly at her young.

Her neck was like that of a milk-white hind, but when she raised it, exceeded not the justest symmetry; nor was the neck of my beloved so unadorned.

Her long black hair decorated her back, thick and diffused, like bunches of dates clustering on the palm-tree.

Her locks were elegantly turned above her head; and the riband which bound them was lost in her tresses, part braided, part disheveled.

She discovered a waist taper as a well-twisted cord; and a leg white and smooth as the stem of a young palm, or a fresh reed, bending over a rivulet.

The brightness of her face illumined the veil of night, like the evening taper of a recluse hermit.

On a girl like her, a girl of moderate height, between those who wear a frock and those who wear a gown, the most bashful man must look with an enamored eye.

ZOHAIR

ZOHAIR is one of the «Pleiads,» a favorite poet of the earlier period.

AN ARAB CHANT

How nobly did the two descendants of Gaidh, the son of Morra, labor to unite the tribes, which a fatal effusion of blood had long divided!

I have sworn by the sacred edifice [the Kaaba at Mecca], round which the sons of Koraish and Jorham, who built it, make devout processions;

Yes, I have solemnly sworn that I would render due praise to that illustrious pair, who have shown their excellence in all affairs, simple and complicated.

Noble chiefs! you reconciled Abs and Dhobyan after their bloody conflicts; after the deadly perfumes of Minsham had long scattered poison among them.

You said: «We will secure the public good on a firm basis; whatever profession of wealth or exertion of virtue it may demand, we will secure it.»

Thence you raised a strong fabric of peace; from which all partial obstinacy and all criminal supineness were alike removed.

Chiefs, exalted in the high ranks of Maad, father of Arabs! may you be led into the paths of felicity! The man who opens for his country a treasure of glory should himself be glorified.

They drove to the tents of their appeased foes a herd of young camels, noted for the goodness of their breed, and either inherited from their fathers or the scattered prizes of war.

With a hundred camels they closed all wounds; in due season were they given, yet the givers were themselves free from guilt.

The atonement was auspiciously offered by one tribe to the other; yet those who offered it had not shed one cupful of blood.

Convey this lesson from me to the sons of Dhobyan, and say to the confederates: Have you not bound yourselves in this treaty by an indissoluble tie?

Attempt not to conceal from God the designs which your bosoms contain; for that which you strive to hide, God perfectly knows.

He sometimes defers the punishment, but registers the crime in a volume, and reserves it for the day of account; sometimes He accelerates the chastisement, and heavily it falls!

ANTARA

ANTARA, whose warlike career is the theme of the celebrated Arabian romance, composed one of the poems of the Mo'allakat.

A SONG OF WAR

GO ASK the warriors, O daughter of Malec, if thou art ignorant of my valor, ask them that which thou knowest not;

Ask how I act, when I am firmly fixed in the saddle of an elegant horse, swimming in his course, whom my bold antagonists alternately wound;

Yet sometimes he advances alone to the conflict, and sometimes he stands collected in a multitudinous throng of heroes with strong bows;

Ask, and whoever has been witness to the combat will inform thee that I am impetuous in battle, but regardless of spoils.

Many a warrior, clad in a suit of mail, at whose violent assault the boldest men have trembled, who neither had saved himself by swift flight nor by abject submission,

Has this arm laid prone with a rapid blow from a well-straightened javelin, firm between the knots:

Broad were the lips of the wound; and the noise of the rushing blood called forth the wolves, prowling in the night, and pinched with hunger;

With my swift lance did I pierce his coat-of-mail; and no warrior, however brave, is secure from its point.

I left him, like a sacrificed victim, to the lions of the forest, who feasted on him between the crown of his head and his wrists.

The instructions which my valiant uncle gave me I have diligently observed; at the time when the lips are drawn away from the bright teeth.

In the struggle of the fight, into whose deepest gulfs the warriors plunge themselves without complaint or murmur.

When my tribe has placed me as a shield between them and the hostile spears, I have not ignobly declined the danger, although the place where I fixed my foot was too narrow to admit a companion.

ASADI

Asadi or Essedi of Tus was the teacher of Firdausi, and yet survived his illustrious pupil. He was attached to the court of Mahmud. He introduced into Persian poetry the form afterward called in Provençal literature the *tenson* or dispute, of which a specimen is here given.

THE DISPUTE OF DAY AND NIGHT

Day and Night, who each can yield
Joy and solace to the race,
Thus contended for the field,
Claiming both the highest place.
Night spoke frowningly: "'Twas I
Who from all eternity
Ruled the chaos of the world,
When in dire confusion hurled.
The fervent prayer is heard at night;
Devotion flies day's glaring light.
'Twas night, the Mount when Moses left;
At night was Lot avenged by fire;
At night the moon our Prophet cleft,
And saw Heaven's might revealed entire.

"The lovely Moon for thirty days
Spreads radiant glory from afar:
Her charms for ever Night displays,
Crowned like a queen with many a star.
Her seal-bearer is Mars; a band
Of planets wait on her command.
Day can but paint the skies with blue,
Night's starry hosts amaze the view.
Man measures time but by the moon;
Night shrouds what Day reveals too soon.

"Day is with toil and care oppressed,
Night comes and, with her, gentle rest.
Day, busy still, no praise can bring;
All night the saints their anthems sing;
Her shade is cast by Gabriel's wing!
The Moon is pure; the Sun's broad face
Dark and unsightly spots deface.
The Sun shines on with changeless glare,
The Moon is ever new and fair."

Day rose, and smiled in high disdain:
  "Cease all this boasting, void and vain;
The Lord of Heaven and earth and thee
  Gave me a place more proud than thine;
And men with joy my rising see,
  And hail the beams that round me shine.
The holy pilgrim takes by day
To many a sacred shrine his way;
By day the pious fast and pray,
And solemn feasts are held by day.
On the Last Day the world's career is run,
As on the First its being was begun.

"Thou, Night, art friendly, it may be,
For lovers fly for help to thee.
When do the sick thy healing see?
  Thieves by thy aid may scathless prowl;
Sacred to thee the bat and owl;
And, led by thee, pale spectres grimly howl!

"I sprang from Heaven, from dust art thou;
  Light crowns my head with many a gem;
The collier's cap is on thy brow,
  For thee a fitting diadem.
My presence fills the world with joy;
Thou com'st all comfort to annoy.
I am a Moslem — white my vest;
Thou a vile thief, in sable dressed.

« Out, negro face! — dar'st thou compare
Thy cheeks with mine, so purely fair?
Those hosts of stars, thy boast and pride,
How do they rush their sparks to hide,
How to their native darkness run,
When, in his glory, comes the Sun!

« True, Death was first; but tell me who
Thinks Life less worthy of the two?
'Tis by the Moon the Arab counts;
  The lordly Persian tells his year
By the bright Sun, that proudly mounts
  The yielding heavens, so wide and clear.
The Sun is ruddy, strong and hale;
The Moon is sickly, wan and pale.
Methinks 'twas ne'er in story told
That silver had the worth of gold!
The Moon, a slave, is bowed and bent,
She knows her light is only lent;
She hurries on, the way to clear,
Till the great Shah himself appear!

« What canst thou, idle boaster, say,
To prove that Night excels the Day?
If stubborn still, let Him decide
With whom all truth and law abide;
Let Nasur Ahmed, wise as great,
Pronounce and give to each his state.»

INDEX TO NOTES